How to Buy
Your First Home

Valparaiso Public Library
103 Jefferson Street
Valparaiso, IN 46383

by Diana Brodman Summers
Attorney at Law

Second Edition

SPHINX® PUBLISHING
AN IMPRINT OF SOURCEBOOKS, INC.®
NAPERVILLE, ILLINOIS
www.SphinxLegal.com

Second Edition: 2005

Published by: **Sphinx® Publishing, An Imprint of Sourcebooks, Inc.®**

<u>Naperville Office</u>
P.O. Box 4410
Naperville, Illinois 60567-4410
630-961-3900
Fax: 630-961-2168
www.sourcebooks.com
www.SphinxLegal.com

This publication is designed to provide accurate and authoritative information in rega
to the subject matter covered. It is sold with the understanding that the publisher is n
engaged in rendering legal, accounting, or other professional service. If legal advice
other expert assistance is required, the services of a competent professional pers
should be sought.
From a Declaration of Principles Jointly Adopted by a Committee of the
American Bar Association and a Committee of Publishers and Associations

This product is not a substitute for legal advice.

Disclaimer required by Texas statutes.

Library of Congress Cataloging-in-Publication Data
Summers, Diana Brodman.
How to buy your first home / by Diana Brodman Summers.-- 2nd ed.
p. cm.
Includes index.
ISBN 1-57248-497-7 (pbk. : alk. paper)
1. House buying--United States. 2. Residential real
estate--Purchasing--United States. 3. Mortgage loans--United States. I.
Title.

HD259.S86 2005
643'.12'0973--dc22   2005027282

Printed and bound in the United States of America.
BG — 10 9 8 7 6 5 4 3 2 1

ACKNOWLEDGMENTS

I want to thank Sourcebooks for the opportunity to pass on my years of experience at real estate to others. The real estate market has been a lifelong hobby for me. There is nothing more intriguing for me than reading real estate ads for those expensive castles or following the tales of preservationists and rehabbers.

I also want to thank my husband, Jim, who has shown an infinite amount of patience with my passion for real estate. He willingly passes me the real estate section from the Sunday paper and tags along when I just have to see the latest open house. Even on our honeymoon, Jim agreed to go through an open house with me, despite the fact that we were 2,000 miles away from home.

Contents

Section 1: FREQUENTLY ASKED QUESTIONS

Section 2: PRELIMINARIES

Section 3: SEARCHING FOR YOUR HOME

Problems with Real Estate Agents
  Changing Agents
Whose Interest is Protected by the Real Estate Agent
How Real Estate Agents get Paid
Multiple Listing Services (MLS)
Comparables
Viewing a House Up for Sale
  Notes and Checklists
  Home Warranty
  Home Inspection
What Not to Say to Real Estate Agents and Sellers
Games Played to Make the Sale
  Inflating the Worth of the House
  Another Offer
When Do You Legitimately Need to Act Fast

  Emotions in House Hunting
    Under a Deadline
    House is Beautifully Decorated
    It is a Real Steal
    Using the Seller's Emotions
  Buyer's Remorse
    When Buyer's Remorse is Legitimate
    Legal Consequences of Allowing Buyer's Remorse to Run
    Amuck

Section 4: FINANCES

  Prequalifying
  Preapproval
  Mortgage Lender Types
    Portfolio Lenders
    Mortgage Bankers
    Direct Lenders
    Mortgage Brokers
    What Does This Mean for You
  Mortgage Types
    Adjustable Rate Mortgage (ARM)

The Loan
  Approval
  Advantages
  Disadvantages

Section 5: THE BUYING PROCESS

Closing Costs
Problems

Section 6: THE FUTURE

Introduction

I was very pleased to be asked to help others take that important step to buy their first home. I have bought and sold nine or ten homes. Some houses were bought just to fix up and resell at a profit, and others were my dream house of the moment. I have stayed in my dream houses for as short as three months to the current nineteen years. To everyone who buys this book I hope you will benefit from my experiences and mistakes without the pain of going through them yourself.

A home can be the most important thing in a person's life. It represents stability and safety. It holds our dreams and hopes for the future. Even when friends desert us, and family passes to their just reward, we still have our home to provide us with a sanctuary from the problems of life. People grow attached to their homes; the structure becomes their roots, the mental picture that your mind shows you when someone says the word "home."

My parents, like many of yours, bought only one home in their lifetime. That home became the center of every important family activity, even after all the children left to find homes of their own. This was the place we all returned to at holidays, in crises, and when we wanted to become a kid again. This universal feeling is why to this day buying a home is called "The American Dream."

Once you have made that decision to go with "The American Dream," the hardest thing is the waiting to make it come true for you. There is nothing worse than really wanting to own your own home, but thinking that right now you can't even afford to look. For those who are frustrated because home ownership seems years in the future, there are activities that you can start doing today to prepare for this biggest purchase of your life. In fact, the more time you have to prepare for a home purchase the more likely that the purchase will go smoothly and you will get the exact home you want.

The three top things you need to get your own home are:
- patience;
- Internet access; and,
- a willingness to work hard to make your dream come true.

Notice that *a lot of money* is NOT on this list. While money is part of any purchase, it is more important that you have the patience and willingness to research for the right home to meet your budget. In this case, the more information you have, the easier it will be to select a home that you can afford. Remember that you can always sell the house you bought on a budget when your salary increases.

The latest edition of this book has expanded almost every chapter to include the most up-to-date information. We have included information on buying a condominium and building a home. In addition we have provided step-by-step procedures to help the first home buyer clear up credit errors, information for buying a home with a partner, a *Frequently Asked Questions* (FAQ) section, and lots more.

PURPOSE OF THIS BOOK

The purpose of this book is to provide the first-time home buyer with a few tools to make that experience less traumatic. These tools include an overview of the fundamentals of purchasing a home, generic worksheets to use in finding the right home, and Internet websites where the reader can get more extensive information. It would be an impossible task for one book to list all available information on home buying for every part of the country. Therefore, this book is designed to present a general overview of the buying process and acquaint the first-time home buyer with the fundamentals of the purchasing process.

HOW TO USE THIS BOOK

This book is divided into five sections that correspond to the stages a person goes through in finding the right home. Each section has chapters on individual topics. At the end of the book is a Glossary with definitions of real estate terms, Worksheets to help you along the way, and an Appendices of useful information.

You may want to start with a quick overview of the Glossary. (I'll bet that you will be surprised with the number of real estate terms you already know.) Then read the entire book, including those sections that are beyond your stage in a house search. Write in the margins, underline important items, highlight—make this book your own. When you come across a chapter that references a worksheet, make several copies of the worksheet located at the back of the book. Change the terms on the worksheet to fit your needs. Once you have read through the book, use it as a reference tool for your dream house search—now, and later.

Real Estate Laws

In order to use this book, you need to know a few things about real estate law. The primary thing is that laws vary. Laws and regulations on real estate can be different from state to state, county to county, and even city to city. For example, a long-time, well-known law regarding how real estate agents operate in California, may be the exact opposite in Illinois or Texas.

Even cities and towns have their own real estate regulations. In some states, a *transfer tax fee* is charged by both the state and the city where a home is sold. Some cities require water certificates, the prepayment of an estimated water bill, or other water and sewer fees as part of the real estate transaction. (In the area that I live, there are state, county, and city laws that govern all real estate transactions and fees that need to be paid to all three entities.)

If you are concerned with the effects of local or state laws on your estate transaction, do some additional research on the Internet. Local realtors who have their own websites can be a source for local laws, as is your state's and county's website.

This book explains the fundamentals of buying a first home in a generic manner. Because real estate laws and regulations differ by location, your state, county, or city may have a specific law that completely disagrees with the book. However the fundamentals of buying that first home remain the same in every part of the country.

Section One:
Frequently Asked Questions

Top 20 Questions of First-Time Home Buyers

1. What are the responsibilities of home ownership?

The main responsibility is paying the mortgage payment on time. Home ownership also requires that you maintain the outside of your home and the landscaping around it in order to maintain the value of your home and your neighborhood. You will also be responsible to repair things that break in your home. Some of those things can be very expensive, like a furnace. Then there are those monthly utility bills for water, electricity, and gas (or oil).

Not all home ownership responsibilities come with a price tag. As a home owner, you will also be responsible for those intangible things like aiding in keeping your neighborhood safe, voting on local referendums, and being a good neighbor to those around you. (see Chapter 16.)

2. Can a person with bad credit buy a home?

Yes. Start by obtaining a credit report to see just how bad your credit is. The next step is to correct any errors. Then, try to pay off any judgements against you. You should also start repairing your credit. The good news is that even those with bad credit or prior bankruptcies may be able to qualify for a mortgage. This mortgage may be at a higher interest rate or may include other expenses, but these mortgages can be found. (see Chapter 2.)

3. Can a person who has worked at the same job for less than two years buy a home?

Yes. The length of time you have worked at one job may not be very important. The lender looks at your credit history and history of employment. Even those who have had several jobs can qualify for a mortgage depending on their current employment and their credit history. (see Chapters 2 and 3.)

4. Can a single mother buy a home?

Anyone who can financially afford a mortgage can purchase a home. Mortgage lenders are required by law to not discriminate by refusing to offer a mortgage to a qualified potential buyer on the basis of sex, race, marital status, and other items. (see Chapters 2 and 8.)

5. How can I avoid buying a house that turns out to be lemon?

The best protection for a buyer is to get an inspection report from a professional house inspector. This report should list the home's defects and problems. (see Chapter 14.) As for the neighborhood, you should follow the plan in Chapter 4 to determine if the neighborhood will increase in value.

6. How much money do I need to buy a home?

That depends on the price of the house, the amount of the down payment, the interest rate on the mortgage, taxes on the home, and insurance costs. There are also closing costs that can be from 3%–4% of the home's price. (see Chapter 8.)

7. What is the normal down payment required to buy a home?

Previously, a buyer needed at least a 20% down payment to buy a home. However, there are many mortgages that require less of a down payment. In addition, there are many federal mortgage programs available to assist you. (see Chapters 8 and 9.)

8. How can I find a mortgage lender?

It is common for your real estate agent to suggest lenders in your community that may have mortgages that fit your situation. You may also want to consider financial institutions where you have checking or savings accounts, your credit union, or places where your parents or other family members have their mortgage. You can also find lenders on the Internet. (see Chapter 8.)

9. What are the most important questions to ask about a mortgage?

What type of mortgage is this? What is the interest rate? Can I lock-in the interest rate? Is there a fee to lock-in this rate? How long will the lock last? How much will my points be? What are my closing costs? What is my monthly mortgage payment? (see Chapter 8.)

10. What are points?

Points are costs paid to the lender in order to get mortgage financing. One point is usually one percent of the mortgage loan. (see Chapter 8.)

11. Why do I want to lock-in a mortgage interest rate?

In an economy where interest rates are rising, you want to get as low of an interest rate as possible. Once you get a low rate, ask the lender to guarantee that you can get that rate for a period of time—that is a lock-in. (see Chapter 8.)

12. What is a prepayment penalty?

Some mortgages will charge a fee if you pay the mortgage off before the end date. Since we are a society that moves around a lot, get a mortgage that does not charge you for paying off the mortgage before the 30-year or 15-year term ends. (see Chapter 16.)

13. How long does it usually take to process a mortgage loan application?

This depends on lots of things. The lender will need to get the property appraised. There needs to be a title search to determine if the title is free of liens. Your credit history will also be reviewed, again. Of course, if the lender is in a busy period that may also slow down the process, and that will depend on the area of the country. It is probably safe to allow at least 45 to 60 days for the process to be completed. Try to get dates from your loan officer, your real estate agent, or your attorney. (see Chapters 8, 9, and 10.)

14. Is it true that a person should try to pay off their mortgage as quickly as possible?

Many financial experts point out that this is *not* true. Credit cards and loans have a higher interest rate than the mortgage. These should be paid off before you attack that mortgage loan. Also, having a mortgage makes good tax sense as the mortgage interest is tax deductible. (see Chapter 16.)

15. What does a mortgage payment cover?

Mortgage payments have four parts: the principal (the amount of the loan), the interest (the percentage you pay to get the loan), taxes (these are real estate taxes assessed by your community), and insurance (insurance can be traditional home insurance, and mortgage insurance). During the life of a mortgage loan, you will pay more in interest charges than in the principal. Sometimes a new home buyer is shocked by how much they will pay in interest over the 30-year or 15-year term of the loan. *Remember: most people do not pay off that loan, they just move and get another one.* (see Chapter 8.)

16. How much should I offer for a home?

Your real estate agent can help you with this one. Follow the suggestions in this book for increasing your knowledge about home prices in a specific area. Look at real estate ads, read the local paper, and ask your real estate agent to show you what similar houses in the area have sold for. (see Chapters 4, 6, 7, and 13.)

17. What is the most important thing to put in a contract when making an offer on a home?

For maximum protection, the buyer should put in several contingency clauses. The top three contingency clauses are: 1) that the buyer be able to obtain a mortgage; 2) that the home pass a professional inspection and appraisal; and, 3) that the title is free of liens. (see Chapter 13.)

18. What happens if my contract offer is rejected?

Many times the seller rejects an offer and makes a counter offer for a higher selling price, larger down payment, or some other issue. Some people enjoy haggling. You will need to review the pluses of the house, the neighborhood, and your ability to pay more in mortgage payments. Do not let anyone push you into making a higher offer if you are not comfortable with the payment. (see Chapters 6 and 13.)

19. What will happen at closing?

Closing is a complex situation for every home buyer. You will be asked to sign documents for the mortgage, insurance, taxes, and tons of other things. Your attorney and your real estate agent will help you have a basic understanding of what you are signing. This is a very stressful situation where documents from several different people must come together at the same time. Each document is required to be correct. Expect delays and bring your patience. (see Chapter 15.)

20. What happens if I lose my job and can't pay the mortgage?

Technically, your lender can foreclose on the home. That is, the mortgage lender takes the home back and sells it for the amount remaining on the loan. There may be ways to avoid foreclosure. You may even be able to refinance your home using government assistance to lower your payments. (see Chapter 17.)

Section Two:
Preliminaries

chapter one

Buying versus Renting

Your friends have asked, your parents have asked, maybe even that person in the mirror has asked—why do you want to buy a home? While the need to own a piece of property seems to be one of those basic things like the need to eat, this chapter will present practical reasons to put down roots.

WORDS

Now would be a good time to review the glossary so that you are familiar with some of the real estate terms used in the preliminary chapters. (See pages 175–215.) Most of the terms are things you have heard before.

Three words we use a lot are *closing, mortgage,* and *foreclosure.* Closing is the activity in which the house is sold. We could also say "at the sale of the house," but most real estate people call this event a closing. (Chapter 15 is about the closing.)

CLICK ON THIS:

My personal award for the top three Internet sites that provide a variety of information that will help you in buying your first home:

- **FIRST PLACE:**
  www.homeloanlearningcenter.com
- **SECOND PLACE:**
  www.ginniemae.gov
  www.fanniemae.com
- **THIRD PLACE is a three-way tie:**
  www.fha.com
  www.interest.com
  www.msn.com
  (house and home selection)

Mortgage is a type of loan that a bank or other financial institution provides the buyer so that the house can be bought. The buyer makes monthly payments on the mortgage, and after a certain number of years, the mortgage is paid off.

Foreclosure is when the bank or financial institution (*lender*) takes the house from the buyer because the buyer defaulted (did not pay) on the loan. The lender will file a lawsuit against the buyer if loan payments are not made as promised. A court order, also known as a *judgment*, must be entered against you to finalize the foreclosure. This lawsuit must be filed in the area (*jurisdiction*) where the property is located. (Chapter 17 discusses foreclosures in a more complete manner.)

FIRST TIME HOME BUYERS

If you think that buying a home is limited to a married couple with 2.3 kids, you are out-of-step with the times. The largest growing segment of home buyers are single women, followed by single men, and non-married partners. In a 2004 *Profile of Home Buyers and Sellers* survey, the National Association of Realtors reported that single buyers account for 33% of the home buying public. Of this 33%, 22% of the home buyers are single women. In addition, of single women, the number of single partners (both same-sex and opposite-sex partners) buying homes has also significantly increased in the past five years.

In many areas of the country, the numbers of ethnic or immigrant home buyers has also increased. The term immigrant is used in real estate to identify people who are not considered natives of the United States or who may be recent arrivals to this country. In some parts of the country where immigrant home buyers constitute a large number of home sales, realty agents and home builders are reaching out to this segment of the home buying population. Brochures are published in languages other than English; many Internet sites set up by builders and real estate agents allow the reader to select *en Español.* In addition, multilingual and bilingual agents and brokers are in high demand within the real estate industry.

FINANCIAL REASONS

The primary reason to own your own home—money. The money saved in taxes; the money accumulated as equity; and, the money made when selling the house.

Equity

When people talk about home ownership, they always mention the word *equity*. Technically, equity is the value of your home above the liens (mortgage and loans) against the property. A *lien* is any loan or mortgage where the house is put up as *collateral*. Basically, the lien documents say "if you do not pay this back, I will take your house."

CLICK ON THIS:

For a Buy vs. Rent calculator, go to: www.ginniemae.gov

For a calculator to see how much you can save in taxes by buying instead of renting, go to: www.freddiemac.com

Example #1:

A couple purchases an $80,000 house. They put $15,000 down and take a mortgage for $65,000. At the point of sale, this couple has $15,000 equity in the home.

Example #2:

Look at that same couple in ten years. The mortgage has been paid down to $50,000 (or is the amount of the lien on the home). The house, itself, has increased in value because of the economy and the improvements that the couple made to the home. Ten years later, the home is worth $150,000. Our couple now has $100,000 of equity in their home. (That $15,000 down payment has increased more than if it were invested in some hot stock.)

So that you do not get the idea that this large increase is always the way it turns out, let's give our example couple some problems.

Example #3:

At that same 10-year mark with the home worth $150,000, our couple drops 50% of their income due to one person losing his job. In order to just make their monthly creditor payments, our couple gets a loan for $50,000 against the value of the house. (This is a lien.) This means that with the mortgage of $50,000 and the new loan of $50,000 the total liens against the house are $100,000. Our couple now only has $50,000 equity in their home. (However, this is still better than most investment plans.)

Equity is the value of the house minus any liens against it. *House value* is determined by upkeep of the home, upgrades made to the home, the neighborhood, and the economy.

Liens against your home are not always mortgages. Sometimes when applying for a loan, the lender will require that you put up your home as *collateral*. Whenever your home becomes collateral, there is a lien against your home. Lenders with liens against a home can force the homeowner into court to settle the debt. In some states, this settlement can mean that the home is sold. The IRS and other governmental bodies can also put a lien against your home for back taxes, unpaid fines, and for court judgments. In addition, a lien can be placed against your property by an "unpaid" private contractor. (In some states this is known as a *mechanic's lien*.)

Tax Advantages

Home owners are allowed to deduct mortgage interest and property taxes from their annual federal income tax filing. Some states also allow these deductions. In the first years of a mortgage, this is a large amount of money because that is when most interest is paid. If you paid *points* when you signed for the mortgage loan, the points cost may be able to be deducted in that year's income tax.

Passing to Heirs

For many of us, owning a home and building equity in it allows us to pass something of value to our children. Most of us do not have vast estates or great wealth and, unless we win the lottery, we never will have a lot to pass to the next generation. In fact, the only thing of real value most people have is the home they live in.

For the majority of people, their home is a provider of equity while they are alive, a place of security for their family, and is the only wealth that they can provide their family at death. The family home becomes the center of gatherings, the place where memories are made, and tangible evidence that we have taken the time and worked hard to provide for the future of our family.

An Investment

In thinking about buying a home you will undoubtedly run across articles about purchasing real estate merely as an investment. Buying a home is much more than just a place to get a return on your dollar.

Real estate, unlike stocks, is usually not a quick return investment. In many areas of the country, you will need to hold on to a home for a minimum of two years in order to get back what you paid for the home plus all the nasty transaction costs that go with purchasing a home. Transaction costs are the highest cost in a real estate purchase. For example, if you sell $500,000 in stocks, the brokerage fee is around $400. If you sell a $500,000 house, the transactions costs and fees to sell can be around $40,000.

Real estate is also not the most *liquid investment* a person can make. Liquidity is measured on how quickly an investment can be turned into cash. In recent years with rapid refinancing, home equity loans, and lines of credit backed by your home's value, the liquidity of a home is improving. However, a home purchase should not be considered as only an investment.

> **ATTORNEY TIP:**
>
> In actuality, you would probably get a larger and a quicker return on your dollar if you prudently invested in mutual funds. If this is your first home purchase, it is not the time to experiment with your money.

Buying vs. Renting

The usual way of thinking about buying a home is that it is less expensive to rent than to buy. For some people, this is still true. However, as rents increase and property values increase, buying a home is becoming a real money-saver.

The best way to compare buying versus renting for your particular situation is to go on the Internet and click on **www.ginniemae.gov**. This site has a section called "Buy vs. Rent." It contains several tools to compare the advantages and disadvantages of owning versus renting. It also includes a calculator to compare your current rent to the purchase price of a home, an up-to-date buy vs. rent comparison, year-by-year savings comparison, and several other charts which compare the costs of buying and renting.

In general, buying a home gives you two financial positives and one large personal positive.

Financial positives:

1. You are accumulating wealth. This wealth is in the form of *financial equity*. Financial equity is measured in the amount of ownership, the amount of down payment, the total amount that the owner has paid in principal on the mortgage loan, plus how much the home has appreciated in value.

2. You will be paying less taxes. Both mortgage interest paid and real estate taxes paid are tax deductible. These significant deductions give the owner a lower, after-tax payment when calculating the annual IRS filing.

Personal positive:

You have the security of owning your own home. The home owner can decorate as he or she pleases; is not subject to a landlord's rules; and, does not have to wait for the landlord to fix the property.

On the minus side, in order to buy a home, a person may have to put down a sizeable down payment. There are additional costs such as taxes, insurance, and utilities for home owners. A home owner also has the responsibility for fixing and maintaining the property, which is usually included in the cost of rent. If you have an active lifestyle, you may not have the time to keep up with the property maintenance. Paying a lawn care service to maintain the property is yet another cost. However, even with several minuses, owning a home financially comes out on top.

TRUE COST OF HOME OWNERSHIP

You will read a lot in this book about the costs of home ownership. Know right from the beginning that sometimes you will long for those days when your landlord picked up the bill for these costs. Owning a home means that you will pay for maintenance and repair. Of course you can cut these costs by becoming a do-it-your-selfer. Ownership also means paying property taxes, utility bills, and maybe *Homeowners Association* costs. Some of these costs, such as taxes and Homeowner Association fees, can be estimated before you agree to buy the house and should be in your calculations to determine if you can afford that particular property.

Ask questions about costs before you decide to buy a house. Ask the real estate agent, the sellers, anyone who can help. Also, look at the house with an eye as to what will need repair and/or mainte-nance. For example, if the house has an in-ground pool, there are associated costs with mainte-nance of that pool. If the house is in an area with a homeowners association and/or a "gated com-munity," there will likely be a monthly fee that is paid to that association. If the house has an old furnace, leaky faucets, broken windows, and other obvious problems that may need to be fixed immediately, calculate the costs of repairs *before* you offer to buy the house.

ATTORNEY TIP:

Some company benefits offer the employee assistance in finding a mortgage lender. Other companies allow employees time off, with pay, for their house closing. Be sure to ask your employer what benefits they have regarding an employee purchasing a home.

You cannot eliminate costs that come along with owning a home, but you can anticipate and be prepared for most costs.

INTANGIBLE REASONS

In addition to financial reasons, there are various nonfinancial rationales for owning a home.

Status

Let's be honest, owning a home gives a person a certain amount of prestige or status. It is an ego boost to be able to brag to your high school friends, who may still be living with their parents, that you own a home. In a family, siblings usually compete with each other for who has the nicest or biggest home. Even without siblings, some of us will brag about our house to relatives and friends.

Being a home owner puts a person in a certain bracket even to employers. It equates to an employee who is stable, who will not do things to jeopardize his or her job because of the obligation of paying the mortgage. Some employers believe that home ownership is so important that they provide their employees with benefits in connection with buying a home.

Privacy and Work Schedules

For those of us who have lived in an apartment while being blessed with work schedules or shifts that are opposite to the regular 9 to 5, we know how difficult it can be to sleep when everyone else is up. During our sleep-time, the upstairs neighbors stomp around in their army boots or practice their bowling techniques. Conversely, during the downstairs neighbor's sleep time, we are up making noise. Guaranteed, no matter how soundproofed the building is, that one day when we dearly need to get to sleep, the next door neighbor is having a party. If this sounds like your life, you are a prime candidate for owning a home.

A real benefit of owning your own home is coming and going when you want. You do not have to tiptoe around for fear of having neighbors pound on your door. You can actually turn up the radio to a hearing level instead of merely whisper quiet.

Recently, a major department store has played a TV commercial of a man and wife in their own home. She is up doing exercises on a treadmill and he asks her why she is exercising at three in the morning. The wife responds that she is exercising "because I can." This commercial could be for home ownership. If you own your own home, you can exercise at 3 a.m. without disturbing neighbors or having the landlord hassle you with complaints.

Home ownership also allows personal privacy. In many rental communities, privacy is sorely lacking. Neighbors watch the times others come and go. Visitors are screened. Even those well-meaning neighbors can become busybodies due to thin walls and close proximity.

Community

Community is both a financial and intangible reason to own your own home. Community is the city, county, and state that may provide financial assistance to home owners. Community is the neighbors who participate in a block watch to prevent crime. Community is the feeling of putting down roots by making this your home.

The financial aspects of a city, county, and state vary from area to area. In some areas, senior citizen homeowners are given financial breaks in property tax and financial assistance. Local cities may provide lawn care or snow shoveling for low or no fees to those who are disabled or on fixed incomes. Some areas also provide low cost professional services such as tax preparation and medical assistance for fixed income home owners.

As job losses are on the increase, many communities are providing some financial assistance for home owners in need. This can be in the way of food

CLICK ON THIS:

Go to www.ginniemae.gov in the section Homeownership 101. Select "Are you ready to buy?" This is an online calculator that will help review your income, savings, expenses, and debt responsibilities. Use this site now and throughout the rest of this book.

stamps, utility discounts, free food pantry, property tax assistance, and other financial benefits to keep the home owner from losing his or her house to foreclosure.

The intangibles of living in a community are much harder to define. Neighbors can become best friends, especially when their children grow up together. Local churches provide another aspect of membership and additional sources for friendship. Some towns come together to build homes for the disadvantaged or to help some other worthy cause. The intangible of a community is the feeling of belonging with those of like minds. While this feeling could happen in a rental community—those things that are positive in renting—easier to move and no responsibility for property upkeep—stifle this.

CONCLUSION

So now you are excited. You really want to buy a home, but you are a little concerned. Owning a home doesn't seem so scary, but the act of buying a home means dealing with the frightening unknown (the sellers, the agents, the brokers, the insurance agents, and the lawyers).

Relax and keep reading. By the time you reach the last chapter of this book, you will know what to expect and as a result, buying a home will become a less confusing experience.

chapter two

Qualifying Yourself for a Mortgage

The reason this is one of the first chapters, is that it is something that should be started before you actually go out and look at houses on the market. Unless you are one of the lucky few people who has enough funds to pay cash for your home, your ability to purchase the home of your dreams depends on your ability to qualify for a sizeable loan—a *mortgage*.

YOUR CREDIT HISTORY

When do you start financially qualifying yourself for a mortgage? When you took out that very first credit card, your student loans, or co-signed for someone else's purchase. Anything that deals with loans, credit, or savings is part of your financial history. Your financial history is a primary piece used by lenders in deciding to issue a mortgage.

If someone else is buying a home with you, their credit history may cause problems. This is sometimes the case for the newly married or engaged who want to start off life in their own

ATTORNEY TIP:

Three things to do to improve your credit history today:
- make all payments ON TIME;
- pay an extra $20 toward each charge card payment this month; and,
- don't apply for any new charge accounts.

home. Your spouse or fiancé may have unpaid child support or other court ordered judgements on his or her record, large outstanding credit card debts, or overdue student loans. If one person has a significant negative credit history, you may not be able to obtain a mortgage at a preferred rate or may not be able to obtain any mortgage without a significant down payment.

While not having any credit cards is a great way to keep from temptation, a person without credit cards or loans has no credit history. Having no credit history can be as bad as having a poor credit history. This is because your credit worthiness is determined by comparing your borrowing history with that of other consumers. That is the basis of how a *credit score* is computed. If you have a low or no credit score, you may not be able to obtain that preferred rate mortgage.

Credit worthiness also takes into account the length of time a person has used credit. This can really hurt the younger home buyer who has only had credit cards for a short period of time or who has never used credit cards.

CREDIT REPORTS

Your credit history is captured in a *credit report*. Every lender uses credit reports to qualify a person. Your credit report will show all debts (credit card, loans, mortgages), *payment history* (including late payment instances), amounts currently owed to each creditor, tax liens, bankruptcies, foreclosures, judgments against you, and other public records which would have an impact on a person's financial history.

There are currently three private credit bureaus that electronically keep credit reports:

> **EQUIFAX:**
> Credit Information Services
> P.O. Box 740256
> Atlanta, GA 30374-0256
> 800-685-1111
> www.equifax.com

EXPERIAN:
National Consumer Assistance Center
P.O. Box 2104
Allen, TX 75013-2104
888-397-3742
www.experian.com

TRANS UNION:
National Disclosure Center
PO Box 1000
Chester, PA 19022
800-888-4213
www.tuc.com

Each of these credit bureaus has a facility to provide you with your credit report, for a fee. If you have been denied a job, insurance, or credit because of a negative credit report within the past sixty (60) days, you are entitled to receive a *free* credit report upon request.

Some financial experts suggest that everyone annually get a copy of their own credit report from each of these bureaus. This will alert a person to any fraudulent use of their identity or errors in their credit report.

> **ATTORNEY TIP:**
> Reduce your credit card debt starting today. Try to pay extra on each monthly payment. Tape a picture of a house you like on your wallet so that each time you reach for that credit card, the picture reminds you what you are saving for.

It is very important that you obtain a copy of your own credit report and review it for errors long *BEFORE* applying for a mortgage. If you find errors in your credit report, contact the credit bureau. Each credit bureau has its own procedures for correcting errors. These procedures can take considerable time. Once you discover an error on your credit report in one credit bureau, it is probable that this error will be reflected in the reports at the other two bureaus.

CLICK ON THIS:

For more details on free credit reports, go to:
www.annualcreditreport.com

Go to www.ftc.gov/credit for information on credit scores.

Besides errors, your credit report may show a history of late payments and the amount of outstanding debt that you currently have. While a history of late payments won't totally disqualify you from obtaining a mortgage, it may cause the lender to charge you a higher rate of interest. By reviewing your credit report long before you are ready to get a mortgage, you give yourself time to correct things such as a history of late payments and the pay-off of outstanding bills.

Free Credit Reports

In 2004, the U.S. government passed a law that allows consumers to get one free credit report every twelve months. This program is being phased in across the country. Those in the western states are eligible to get a free credit report as of December 1, 2004; those in the midwest states—as of March 1, 2005; those in the southern states—as of June 1, 2005; and those who live in the eastern states and US territories are eligible beginning September 1, 2005.

The free credit reports law is part of the *Fair Credit Reporting Act* (FCRA) or what is commonly called the FACT Act. This law controls the information that credit reporting companies can release; whom they can release it to; and, how to fix erroneous data.

CREDIT SCORES

A *credit score* is a number computed by the private credit bureaus to indicate the likelihood that a person will pay his or her bills on time. Each credit bureau calculates its own range of scores, so you would probably have three different scores. This score is sometimes referred to as an *FICO score*, because Fair Isaac & Co developed it.

FICO scores take into account a person's credit history. Such things as late payment, amount of credit available, amount of credit used, length of time in a job, length of time living in a location, bankruptcy, and all other financial items are used to calculate this score. FICO scores should not take into account a person's race, religion, national origin, sex, or marital status.

Some mortgage lenders will base the decision to give a person a mortgage loan almost totally on this number. However, FICO is not the only factor that most mortgage lenders use. As with other factors on your credit report, in order to keep your FICO score in an acceptable range pay bills on time, use credit sparingly, and reduce credit card balances.

CLICK ON THIS:

Choose either of the following sites to get a more detailed explanation of FICO scores and ways to put your FICO in an acceptable range:
  www.yourmortgage.net
  www.myfico.com

The FICO number that the mortgage lender is looking for varies by state, by lender, by the state of the economy, any by other variables that only the lender knows. However, here are some generalities that may help.

Scores at 720 or above are considered excellent—the risk of mortgage foreclosure is *very* low. Scores 660 to 719 are good, with the risk of mortgage foreclosure being low. From 620 to 659, the risk of mortgage foreclosure being higher and the lender will look to other information in your credit history. At a score lower than 619, the risk of mortgage foreclosure becomes statistically very high. With a score below 580, you will need to repair your credit score before applying for a loan.

Remember, these numbers are not cast in stone. By the time you read this, the numbers may have significantly shifted. When I wrote the first edition of this book, the low score was 575 and the high was 700. In addition, lenders will look at other things in your credit history, including documented errors in the credit report. The government estimates that about half of the population has FICO scores in the 700s, so your FICO credit score may be significantly better than you think it is.

Improving Your Credit Score

You may want to improve your credit score *now*, so that when it comes time to make that first home purchase you can qualify for a better interest rate. You can do this in a few ways: pay your bills on time, keep your total credit-card balances to no more that 50% of your total debt, pay down the balances, do not apply for more credit, never co-sign for any financial account with a friend or relative, and review your credit report for errors. In general, you should try to improve your credit score at least six month to one year prior to applying for a mortgage.

Be very mindful of managing your credit score between the time that you apply for a mortgage and the date of the closing or sale of the house. Mortgage lenders routinely get a credit report when the borrower first applies for the mortgage and then, again, just before the closing. Most lenders then compare the two reports. If there are significant differences between these two reports you may not get that preferred mortgage rate you wanted. To avoid this, from the date that you apply for the mortgage to the date of the closing do not open any new charge accounts, do not buy a car, do not even buy furniture for that new home. Any credit activity can cause the type of differences which may make the lender review your credit history.

CREDIT REPORT ERRORS

When is a credit report error not really an error? The answer is when the item on the credit report is there because of a misunderstanding.

Example #1

Bob and Jeff are brothers. Bob is going to college and has very little money. Jeff lives near and has held a paying job for years. Bob needs a 'beater' car to drive to classes. He found a great deal at URRIPOFF car dealer, but needs someone who has a job to co-sign for the loan. Jeff, being a good brother, offers to co-sign.

Within months, the car won't run and is abandoned in the school parking lot. Bob drops out of school and is now touring with the rock band "The Purple Drums."

Jeff applies for a mortgage, but is turned down because of a legal judgement on his credit report. That judgment was because URRIPOFF car dealer was never paid for Bob's car. Since Jeff co-signed for the loan, Jeff is legally liable.

Example #2

Suzie had a car accident. She totaled both her car and the one she hit. At the accident scene Suzie was given two tickets and told the accident was her fault. Suzie turned everything over to her insurance company and forgot about the accident.

Later that year, Suzie changed her name to Suzanna Sunshine and moved to Hollywood to be a star. After a few years, she applied for a mortgage and was turned down because of a legal judgment placed against her. Suzie's legal judgement was from the other driver who sued her and the insurance company. Because Suzie could not be located, she was not able to defend herself in court and the judgment was placed on her credit history.

These are just two examples of unexpected things that may appear on a person's credit report. In the first example, Jeff thought that Bob would make the payments on the car and thought nothing more about it. In the second, Suzie figured the insurance company would handle the problem. Had Jeff and Suzie gotten their credit report before they applied for a mortgage, they would have had time to repair the credit report.

Not all financial problems on a person's credit report are because of misunderstandings. Real errors can include a mix up with people of the same name, identity theft, bills for items not received, creditors who promise to reduce or cancel a debt but do not, and computer input errors.

Example:

David is a car enthusiast. He is restoring a collection of 1970's Porsches. David spent $2,500 for a fancy fuel injector system from Puddles Porsche. Unfortunately, the system was defective. David stopped payment on his $2,500 check and wants to return the product.

Puddles believes that David broke the system when he attempted to install it on his Chevy Nova. Puddles will not accept the return. After much arguing over the phone, Mrs. Puddles finally tells David to just return the item and the debt will be forgotten.

Nothing was put in writing. Years later, David finds out that Puddles brought legal action against him for the $2,500, which is now a blemish on his credit report.

ATTORNEY TIP:

Two important things to remember when dealing with any Credit Bureau:

1) BE COURTEOUS.
No matter how big the problem is or how much it is affecting your life, keep your composure. The people at the credit bureau are employees too. They probably did not cause the problem and they can be invaluable in correcting it.

2) DOCUMENT IN WRITING.
Write down whom you spoke to, the date, the time, and what was decided. If you are attempting to repair a problem, send a letter to that person reminding her or him what was said, what needs to be done, and when the agreed action was to take place.

Repairing Your Credit Report

Once you get your credit report, what happens if it has errors? Understand that each credit reporting bureau has its own procedures for correcting error. You MUST follow their instructions to correct error, no matter how dumb the instructions sound. In general, the following will help you deal with the errors on your credit report.

What is the error? Is this a loan you co-signed for? Is this a bill you forgot to pay? Is this something you never heard of? You need to do some detective work *BEFORE* you fix the error.

If you co-signed for a car loan, contact the person you signed for. If the error is an item bought from a store you never went to, call the store. Get copies of receipts for things you supposedly bought. If the error is for something you returned or a debt that you were told was cancelled, find your documentation on that debt.

CLICK ON THIS:

The Federal Trade Commission (FTC) website is www.ftc.gov. This site has helpful information for home buyers in both English and Spanish.

If you are lucky enough to have physical proof that a debt was resolved (cancelled check or other document) let the credit bureau know. If they ask you to send a copy of the document, include a letter saying what the copy is and how it effects the item on your credit report (even if you have already told the credit bureau several times). Remember that the spoken word is usually not enough to resolve a credit bureau error. It must be written down and signed.

State and federal laws regulate credit reporting agencies and procedures. The *Federal Trade Commission (FTC)* is the government agency that monitors credit bureaus.

You have the right to correct items on your credit report. The FTC website provides the information you need to remove false information from your file. Contact the credit bureau for the necessary steps. You can also place your own brief explanation of negative information in your credit file if the bureau investigates and stands by the negative information.

If the error involves a court judgment, you may need to hire an attorney to research and resolve this.

Correcting Credit Report Errors

Take the following steps to correct errors on your credit report.

- Get your credit report from all three credit bureaus—Equifax,

ATTORNEY TIP:

If you determine that a reporting error has occurred on your credit report, do not pay a credit repair agency to correct it. You can do this for free.

Experian, and Trans Union. (Even if this costs a fee, you should begin with information from each place where a lender may review your credit.)

- Make copies of each original report; put the originals away. Review each credit report—line by line. (This will take hours, but it is worth it.) Not only are you reviewing each report, you are comparing each report to the other. For example, one report may list that you paid off a car loan three years ago, while another report may still show that the loan is unpaid.
- Circle each item on the copy of each credit report that you believe is incorrect.
- Find all documentation that proves these items are incorrect. (Locate cancelled checks, receipts, letters from the creditor, a credit contract, and/or proof that a judgment was paid.)
- You will likely find that the negative items on your credit report fall into two categories:
  1. real errors, such as items you knew nothing about, bills you have paid, disputes that were settled or
  2. bills that you legitimately owe, but never resolved. (This can happen when a person moves several times in a short period of time, in returning from college, after a divorce, or for numerous other reasons. These may also show up as court judgments, liens, or collections against you. Generally, the majority of mortgage lenders require these be paid off before the closing.)
- For those items that are legitimate debts, attempt to pay them off or settle with the creditor. This will require contacting the creditor, requesting a copy of the bill they believe you owe, and then either paying the debt off or offering to settle for a lower amount. See the sample letter in **Appendix C.** (Once you pay off or settle a debt,

demand that the creditor inform the credit reporting bureaus—this is what will clear up your credit history. Remember to get everything in writing.)

Be especially concerned with defaulted student loans, as they can dramatically lower your credit score. For problems with student loans, apply for a rehabilitation loan. If you make on-time-payments toward this rehabilitation loan for a period of twelve

CLICK ON THIS:

For more information on Student Loan Rehabilitation administered by the government office of Federal Student Aid go to:

www.fsahelp.ed.gov/rehab.html

months, then the lender for the student loan must erase all negative marks on your credit reports for the defaulted student loans.

If you go into a consumer credit counseling program, it may also lower your credit score until you are totally out of the program.

• For the real errors on the credit report, you will need to write a letter to the creditor and to the credit reporting agency.

To the creditor, inform them of the error that they made and send copies of your documentation. (See the sample letter in **Appendix C**.)

To the credit reporting bureau, send a copy of your credit report with each error circled. In a letter explain each dispute (each item you circled on the copy of the credit report) and

ATTORNEY TIP:

Remember that bankruptcies remain on your credit history for ten years. Lawsuits and unpaid judgments can be reported for more than seven years, depending on the statute of limitation (determined by state laws).

request an investigation to resolve each item. Send along copies of supporting documents with this letter. (See the sample letter in **Appendix C**.)

Both of these letters and documents should be sent by certified mail, return receipt requested. The credit reporting bureaus are required *by law* to investigate these errors within thirty days.

- If the credit reporting bureau verifies that the information is accurate, it will notify you. If you still believe that this is an error, you can ask for another investigation. If the second investigation is not in your favor, you can ask the credit reporting bureau in insert a 100–word explanation next to the erroneous entry that explains your side.

CREDIT COUNSELING

Many people have problems with too much debt. As a result, a new industry has taken hold, the Credit Counseling Organization. These credit counselors can be found everywhere—in financial institutions, through government agencies, at universities, at military bases, at credit unions, and on the Internet.

Recently, several credit counseling companies were accused of committing consumer fraud. These companies charged the consumer high fees and made promises about work they never did. Be careful, not all credit counseling organizations are nonprofit. Besides charging high fees to the consumers, some urge consumer to make contributions to the credit counseling company—all of which causes the consumer to just go deeper into debt.

Reputable credit counseling organizations will help you manage money, debts, and assist you in drawing up a budget. They offer free educational material and may also conduct free credit workshops.

When you are considering a credit counseling organization, consider the following:
- What services are offered to the consumer?
- Does the organization offer free educational material for the consumer?

- Is the organization licensed in your state?
- Is the organization part of a reputable financial institution, credit union, U.S. Cooperative Extension Service, or U.S. government agency?
- Are the counselors certified and trained in consumer credit, money management, or budgeting?
- Does the organization charge a fee or ask for a donation? What happens if a consumer cannot afford to pay?
- Will you be required to sign a written contract with the organization? If yes, can you get a copy of that contract to read before you agree to the service?

CLICK ON THIS:

For more information on credit counseling organizations and what you should know when dealing with them, go to: www.ftc.gov/bcp/conline/pubs/credit/fiscal.htm

chapter three:

Calculating
What You Can Afford

Every lender has a formula to tell how much a person can afford in mortgage payments. Formulas are good because they can give a definitive number. However, most formulas do not factor in a person's lifestyle (what is important to that person), future financial down-turns, or what each person feels comfortable paying for housing.

COMMON DEBT-TO-INCOME RATIOS

Mortgage lenders loan money based on a set of criteria. That criteria rates the property, the neighborhood, the building, and the borrower. This chapter will explore the common criteria used to rate the borrower and how you can use that information to make decisions before you ask for a mortgage.

CLICK ON THIS:

Use the "Affordability Calculator" at www.ginniemae.gov. This allows you to enter your income amount and the amount of your debt to get an estimate of how much house you can afford.

Housing-to-Income Ratio

Lenders usually use a two-part ratio calculation that sets the boundaries of what you can pay for a home. This is currently expressed as the 28/36 formula (but the exact numbers may change by the time you read this).

The first part, the *front-end ratio* or the *housing-to-income ratio* is the total mortgage payment divided by your gross monthly income. The percentage result should be somewhere in the 28% to 33% range. Right now 28% is currently used by the majority of lenders. Depending on your credit history, amount of debts, and amount of potential future income, your lender may change the front end percentage.

The total mortgage payment or *housing costs* includes: monthly loan payment, real estate taxes, home owners insurance, mortgage insurance (if any) and association fees (if any).

Gross monthly income is what you receive each month from every source. This income total is before taxes or any deductions (such as deductions for your 401(k) program) are taken out.

Debt-to-Income Ratio

The second part, *back-end ratio* or *total debts* ratio is the percentage of your gross income that can go towards all of your monthly debt. In the 28/36 formula, a person should not pay more than 36% of his or her monthly gross income for all debts.

CLICK ON THIS:

Choose the Debt-to-Income Ratios path on www.fha.com to get examples of these calculations and how lenders use them.

Again, gross monthly income is what you receive each month from every source. This income total is before taxes or any deductions (such as deductions for your 401(k) program) are taken out.

Monthly debt includes payments on credit card debts, loans, alimony, child support, plus housing costs, but does not include household expenses like utilities, food, clothing.

Monthly housing costs are mortgage payment, real estate taxes, home insurance, mortgage insurance, and association fees.

HOW TO USE THESE RATIOS

So, you are probably looking at these ratios and saying "How does that affect me? All I want to do is to get a mortgage without the hassle of dealing with math equations." Not only do I understand, I feel exactly the same. These ratios were created and are routinely used by lenders, you know, those people who enjoy working with numbers. For the rest of us, these ratios can give us an approximation of what we can afford in a mortgage and for our total debt.

While we can use the ratios like the lenders (as guidelines and generalities to determine if someone qualifies for a mortgage loan), there are two important pieces of information on ratios. First—the ratios can vary by lender, by type of mortgage, and by what the economy is doing. Second—lenders do not only use these numbers, other factors such as your credit history, the size of your down payment, the cost of the home, the appraised value of the home, and other facts about you and the property go into the decision to issue a mortgage.

CLICK ON THIS:

Choose any of the following sites
to check for mortgage calculations:
www.interest.com
www.fha.com
www.mortgageselect.com
www.ginniemae.gov
www.hud.gov
www.freddiemac.com
www.hgtv.com

This can be better explained through examples. Let's follow two potential home buyers as they wade through the ratios. (We will also see how numbers can be deceiving.)

Example 1:

Janet is single. She works as a computer programmer making $42,000 per year. Her gross monthly income is $3,500.

According to the 28/36 formula:
Gross monthly income x 0.28 = Total monthly housing expense
$3,500 x 0.28 = $980

Or, in words, Janet can afford a $980 total monthly housing expense. (Remember that total monthly housing expense includes the mortgage payment, plus homeowners insurance, plus real estate taxes, plus any mortgage insurance payments or association payments.)
Looking at Janet's debts:
Gross monthly income x 0.36 = Total monthly debt expense
$3,500 x 0.36 = $1,260

This shows that Janet's total monthly debts should not exceed $1,260. Again, remember that this does not include those pricey household expenses such as utilities, food, clothing, transportation, and other living expenses.

Looking at Janet's monthly debt, she is paying $150 a month on credit card bills and $100 a month on a student loan. If you add the $980 of a total mortgage payment plus the $250 a month on debts, Janet comes up with a total of $1,230 in obligations. This is $30 less than the maximum debt obligation that the 28/36 ratio allows.

So Janet should be approved to get a mortgage from the lender that uses this ratio. Or should she? The numbers look great, but what if the credit history is not so good? Janet's employment history may be spotty. She may have had several jobs in the past 15 years, never staying longer than two years at each job. Janet's employer may have publicly announced that they are closing. So, Janet may not automatically get the mortgage loan she wanted.

What if Janet's credit worthiness is ok, but the property she wants has problems? Maybe the house is in terrible condition and did not appraise for the amount she is asking the bank to loan her? Janet may not be able to get the mortgage she wanted on that property.

These two scenarios show that although a person can be within the 28/36 ratio, there may still be problems obtaining a mortgage. In both of these cases, Janet may have to provide a larger down payment or she may have to select another property. On the other hand Janet, like many of us, may not feel comfortable with a $980 monthly mortgage payment. She may be planning to buy a new car, plus a house full of new furniture.

So how does the 28/36 ratio relate to *real life?* These numbers are merely maximums. This ratio says that Janet should not take on a total mortgage payment of more than $980 and that she should not have total debt of more than $1,260. So, if Janet can come up with a sizable down payment, or look for a house with a lower total cost, she may be able to get that total monthly mortgage payment down to around $600. This would allow her to go into more debt on other items.

Example #2.

Don and Cheryl are newly married; they have no children. Don is a manager at a major insurance company and makes $80,000 per year. Cheryl is a lab technician with an annual salary of $28,000. Their gross monthly income is $9,000.

According to the 28/36 formula:

Gross monthly income x 0.28 = Total monthly housing expense
$9,000 x 0.28 = $2,520

Don and Cheryl can afford a total monthly housing expense of $2,520. (Again, remember that total monthly housing expense includes, the mortgage payment, plus homeowners insurance, plus real estate taxes, plus any mortgage insurance payments or association payments.

As for debts:

Gross monthly income x 0.36 = Total monthly debt expense
$9,000 x 0.36 = $3,240

This shows that Don and Cheryl's total monthly debts should not exceed $3,240. (This total monthly debt expense does not include those pricey household expenses such as utilities, food, clothing, transportation, and other living expenses.)

Unlike the previous example, these potential home buyers have significantly more monthly debt. Don pays $500 monthly in child support, $100 toward a student loan, and $650 on a new car loan. Cheryl is also paying $100 monthly on a student loan. Their combined monthly payments on credit card debts total $2,000. They are already carrying $3,350 in monthly debt without a mortgage loan. This is over the $3,240 for total indebted that our ratio allows.

If we add the allowable $2,520 in allowable housing expense with the $3,350 of current monthly debts, the total is $5,870— significantly above the total of $3,240. If the lender is merely looking a the 28/36 ratio, Don and Cheryl may be out-of-luck in obtaining a mortgage with this lender.

If we add a few positive facts to these potential home buyers, we may be able to help them get their mortgage. Don's monthly child support payment obligation will end in three months and his monthly car payment obligation will be completed next month. Cheryl has been working part time as a lab technician while she has been taking classes to get her degree in medical research. Cheryl just graduated and will be starting to work full time next month, making an additional $4,000 annually, to start.

As for housing, Don and Cheryl have decided to look for a condominium close to where they both work. They are determined to keep their monthly mortgage payments below $1,200 a month, the amount they currently pay for rent. By looking at things outside most the ratios, our second potential home buyers will probably be able to get the mortgage they want.

This is how to use ratios to determine if you can qualify for a mortgage. Your qualification is more that just two numbers—it is your credit history, what is going on in your financial life, the property you want to buy, and what you are comfortable with paying for total housing expenses.

FROM MONTHLY PAYMENT TO TOTAL MORTGAGE

Homes are not sold by quotes of monthly payments. They have total prices. While knowing what your lender expects your ratio to be is important, in reality, it is how the *total price* of the home computes into monthly payments that means more when looking for a home.

Using the two example home buyers, we can then take the result of the 28% ratio in 28/36 calculation to determine approximately the total price of the house they should be considering.

Potential Home Buyer #1, Janet, ended up with a total monthly house expense of $980 using the 28/36 formula. She was looking for a lower monthly amount.

Potential Home Buyers #2, Don and Cheryl, ended up with a total monthly house expense of $2,520 using the 28/36 formula. They too wanted to keep that amount lower, around $1,200.

In order to determine the total price of a house that would be close to the monthly mort-gage payments our buyers are looking for, go to **www.interest.com**. This calculates of what monthly payments would be on a mortgage loan for a specific amount.

> ## ATTORNEY TIP:
> A down payment lowers the amount of your mortgage. However, taxes and insurance costs will add to the monthly amount.

In order to find the amount that both our potential home buyers would consider, look at the 30-year mortgages in the area of 5% to 6%. These are a few of the findings:

LOAN AMOUNT	MONTHLY PAYMENTS	
	at 6% interest	*at 5% interest*
$160,000	$960	$860
165,000	990	886
170,000	1,020	920
175,000	1,050	940
180,000	1,080	970
185,000	1,110	994
190,000	1,140	1,020
200,000	1,200	1,075

Again, the loan amount is the amount that you get the mortgage on. If you have a down payment of $10,000 the total cost of the house can be $10,000 more than what your loan amount is. For example, if our second potential buyers had $25,000 for down payment they could afford a home that was selling for close to $225,000 and still keep the $1,200 monthly payment they wanted.

These numbers were all based on 30-year mortgages, you can add about $500 to each monthly payment for a 15-year mortgage. (Chapter 8 will explain the differences, in detail.)

These numbers do not include real estate taxes that differs by house, and insurance rates. Your real estate agent and your insurance agent can help you determine these numbers for the property you have selected.

Remember, these are just approximations. For exact calculations, your real estate agent and lender can help you.

COST OF LIVING INCREASES

You should also consider the cost of living. Real estate taxes, insurance costs, and utilities will almost always increase every year. Add to that the cost of food usually increases and, as we get older, so will our annual medical costs. Most of these issues vary by location and are tough for even the experts to predict. In considering what you want to spend for a house make note of the cost of living and decide if you can really live with this mortgage amount.

One way to be sure that you can survive paying a certain mortgage payment is to try it on for a few months. For example, if you are now paying $600 a month for rent and by using the ratios could afford a $1,200 monthly housing payment, try taking that extra $600 a month and putting it in a savings account. That way you are trying out the mortgage without any legal commitments. It is an eye-opening experiment that will increase your savings and may help you decide the type of home you are looking for.

YOUR LIFESTYLE

Up to this point we have been concerned with the routine ratios that lenders use, but that is not all that you should consider in determining how much you can afford to pay every month for that mortgage. Living in your own home is more than just mortgage payments. Just for the home there is upkeep, furniture, decorating, inevitable break-downs, and utility bills. Buying your perfect home, but being unable to afford any furniture or to keep the heat at a comfortable level must also be considered.

Ratios do not know how you and your family want to live. Are vacations important? Do you anticipate college expenses? Do you want to buy a new car every couple of years? These factors are part of your lifestyle and you should not be forced to compromise a lifestyle for a piece of property.

> ## ATTORNEY TIP:
>
> I always use the ratio calculation from the lender as the _maximum_ top end that I will pay on a mortgage. I take their total number and then deduct 20% to come up with a comfortable mortgage payment amount. This translates into buying less of a home than I want, but having a cushion for emergencies, new cars, and living. I can always add improvements to my home as time goes on.

Another issue to consider is emergencies. If the amount of mortgage payment plus other debts leaves little or no money for savings in case of an emergency, you are cutting things too close. In our current economy, downsizing, job loss, and wage cuts have become a reality, and everyone needs to prepare for the worst.

What a person can afford to pay in monthly mortgage payments is a personal amount. This amount cannot be just a cold calculation, but must take into count how you live and what you want to do with your life. Despite what some lenders claim, it is no longer a guarantee that people's income will increase as time goes on.

chapter four

Qualifying the Neighborhood

You have probably heard the old real estate joke—what are the top three things that make a house sell? Location, location, location! This is not just a joke. In reality, when you buy a home you are not just buying a building, you are buying a neighborhood. A good neighborhood is one where homes increase in value. And while being concerned with the *resale value* of your dream house before you even buy it may seem silly, it is that resale value that will determine if you can get the money back you invested in your home when you do sell. It is that resale value that allows you to *refinance* at a lower rate, and even get a loan against the value of your home if you need a large amount of cash. The resale value proves that your choice of a home was a good investment.

HOW TO RESEARCH A NEIGHBORHOOD

To find a good neighborhood, you will need to analyze such things as crime statistics, school ratings, and demographic information. You will also want to explore the actual neighborhood—become familiar with the traffic patterns, identify shopping areas, and evaluate other homes that will be nearby.

On the Internet

One great site is **www.msn.com** in the section called "House and Home." From that site you can search for the right neighborhood by your personal criteria.

Many cities and counties have their own web sites. Some local Chambers of Commerce or other organizations also have websites. Begin by looking up the city and state on your favorite search engine (my personal favorite is **www.google.com**). The results may surprise you.

Many real estate professionals are putting up web sites that contain current homes for sale in an area. Some of these sites are so automated that they contain walking tours of the inside of the house. Most give the reader generalized help in buying a home in addition to the sales pitch. This is a great way to view a home without leaving the comfort of your computer. It is also a way to select a knowledgeable real estate agent or one who concentrates on finding the type of property and mortgage you want.

Field Trips

Field trips are great ways to get information about an area. Find the town's main business district and take a walk. Pick up the local newspapers and flyers. While you are on foot, stop by the local *Welcome Wagon* and *Chamber of Commerce*, to see if they have information on the town.

Besides walking, you should try to drive through the area at rush hour. Calculate how long it will take you to get from this new area to your current job. Look at traffic patterns. Is rush hour a noisy mess with bumper to bumper traffic and public transportation on some streets? Does that make certain streets and driveways almost nonaccessible because you can't make a left turn in the rush hour?

If you live in an area where you are blessed(?) with snow, check to see how the streets are cleared. Does the town spread salt or other ice reducers? Are the streets clean and swept? Are streets in good repair or are you dodging potholes? Besides upkeep, look for abandoned buildings, undesirables, graffiti, gang marks, trash, and signs that the city is not keeping up with trash collection. Some home appraisers look at areas that have a lot of rental properties as not being as desirable. The reason is that most transient people do not keep the property up, as would the property owners.

Once you are close to picking a home, walk the blocks around the home you are considering. Talk to neighbors; check it out at various times of the day and night, weekday and weekends. Check traffic patterns. Remember, a yellow line down the middle of a street is a good indicator of high traffic volume. Check out the parking. Is there enough for both residents and guests. Check out the next door property. Is it well maintained? Are there broken and abandoned vehicles on the property? Don't expect to figure this out in one field trip. Visit your new town often.

On another field trip, visit the village or town hall. Tell them you are interested in the area. You may even be able to get written reports about the property values, restrictions on changing property, and building codes. You can learn a lot about how local government treats the taxpayers by this visit. If you are looking at a big city, the challenge is finding aldermen, local representatives, or others who will actually admit to being part of the government.

In the Library

Many cities and towns have their own library. This is a wealth of information about the area, in addition to being a good field trip for your research. Just thumbing through the local phone book will give you an idea of the availability of doctors, veterinarians, dentists, grocery stores, real estate professionals, etc.

Some libraries may have a history of the town to read. This is usually a place to find those all-important demographics about crime, schools, and property values. Some of the nicest people work at local libraries; many of them are lifelong residents who are anxious to share their knowledge.

Besides libraries, some towns have Historic Preservation Offices, museums, and other local offices that promote the town.

From Your Couch

The greatest tool you can use to learn about real estate in general is to read the real estate section in the newspaper. Big cities (like Chicago) produce large real estate sections weekly or more often, that contain real estate ads, articles, and items of interest to home owners. Even if you are not looking for a home in the big city, these papers are invaluable. The articles alone are worth the price of the paper, plus, reading real estate ads will prepare you for what you want in your own home. If you see that many homes are now advertising central air conditioning, and that increases the value of the home, you may decide to put central air on your "must have" list.

This is also a great way to determine if you can afford to live in a particular town. If all the homes advertised are going for double or triple what you can afford, you may need to rethink that town. On the other hand, if you are set on that expensive area, you may have to compromise in the size, condition, or features of a house.

Besides the larger newspapers, the town or city you are interested in may have its own newspaper. These can be great for researching the benefits of living in that city. They usually have local real estate ads and may even list the actual selling price of property after the deal is done. Once you decide what town you want to live in, it is worth the price of having their local newspaper delivered. Of course, this does not mean that a paperboy will bike miles from home to get you this out of town newspaper. Most out-of-town subscriptions are sent through the mail. You may miss some last minute local sales, but you will learn a lot about the neighborhood. Many newspapers are even available on the Internet.

Another paper listing that you will want to read are the flyers or magazines that list homes for sale. In many towns, they are placed at the entrance of local grocery stores, at community centers, at train stations, and at real estate offices. The contents usually are made up of ads of homes for sale complete with picture, description, and often, asking price.

HOW TO SELECT A LOCATION

What it boils down to—what is important to you and your lifestyle? Remember you want to purchase a home that will increase in resale value. For that alone you should avoid high crime areas, areas where there are many abandoned buildings, and areas where the city services are scarce or nonexistent.

For many people, the length of time it takes to commute to their job will determine where they will live. Some start with a map of the area and calculate how long it takes to get to work from different points. (However, with our economy of lessening job security and companies moving to cheaper areas this may backfire.)

Recent economic studies have shown that the cost of transportation between home and job is rising faster than the cost of a mortgage payment. Higher gas prices, higher costs for public transportation, and the significant population increase in suburbs farther away from large cities are to blame.

Example #1:

David Doodzie loved to drive his bright, safety-orange Porsche to work, but he didn't want to spend more than 45 minutes on the freeway even in bad weather. As an experiment, once a week, David drove to work at the normal time, but took a different freeway and would drive for 45 minutes then exit. After a while, David was able to plot on a map the farthest extent of where he would want to live and he became familiar with the housing choices closest to the off ramps.

Example #2:

David's sister Octavia hated to drive or ride in David's Porsche. She wanted to be near public transportation. Octavia also did not want to limit herself to the company she had been working for which was in a suburb of a medium size city. By doing research on the public transportation available in that area, Octavia found two means of public transportation (bus and train line) that supported both the suburb where she was currently working and the medium size city that had more jobs. She started taking short trips after work on both the bus and train line to learn more about the neighborhoods they served.

You and your family need to decide what is important to you in a neighborhood. Do you need to be in a certain school system, close to an elderly family member, close to other family members, within walking distance to favorite recreational locations?

You should not compromise on schools. The resale value of a home has a connection to the schools in the area. The majority of property tax usually goes towards the local school. In an area where schools must be upgraded to meet state and national guidelines, it is almost a guarantee that property taxes will increase. Many people, even those without children, judge a neighborhood on the quality of the schools.

Besides research on the Internet, you may want to join a service that will evaluate the schools in a particular location. Some real estate offices are offering this service for customers. An independent, well-respected company that provides this service is *School Match*. You can contact it through the Internet at **www.schoolmatch.com** or at 614-890-1573. (This service can be invaluable if your family includes a child with learning disabilities or other special needs.)

Before you decide what is important, ask everyone in your family (especially your spouse) what are the top five things they want in a neighborhood. Then compare lists. **Worksheet 1** in **Appendix B** on page 222 will help you in this decision.

THE FOOD SHOPPING TEST

Once the excitement of getting your first home wears off, the reality of having to live in that neighborhood sets in. Along with day-to-day living comes the usual chores that everyone does. For most of us, weekly food shopping can be one of the most boring and one of the most expensive chores.

While I would like to take credit for this particular test of the neighborhood, I must admit that my husband, Jim, developed this test when we were looking for our first home. We had narrowed the search down to a few different areas in Chicago and its suburbs. He based this test on the fact that living expenses vary from area to area, from suburb to suburb, especially in big cities like Chicago.

The test is simple. Take your regular grocery shopping list and shop at what would be your choice of grocery stores in the new neighborhood. Try to purchase all the items that you would normally get, and make note of the prices for those special items that you buy once in a while. Then compare the prices to what you usually spend or to other neighborhoods under consideration.

When we did the food-shopping test we were able to eliminate two areas because the *cost of living*, just for the weekly food bill, was at least 15% higher than what we had budgeted. Other things that we learned doing this test was that some areas had a limited selection of grocery stores or those that carried what we wanted were a long drive away.

While doing this test, we also ran into stores that had security gates, bars on the windows, barriers from taking the grocery cart to the parking lot, and other high security measures. We decided that if the local business owners felt the neighborhood was so unsafe, it was not the area for us. This did however, eliminate our moving into an area where we could both walk to work and walk to a great city nightlife. These are the type of decisions and trade offs that must be made when looking for an area to live.

OTHER COST OF LIVING AMOUNTS

In addition to groceries, you may wish to check with your automobile insurance agent to see if your rates will change depending upon the area. In some neighborhoods, the large amount of auto thefts and damage will cause higher rates. Most insurance agents will be happy to advise you on this.

While you are talking to your insurance agent, you should ask for an estimate of

> **ATTORNEY TIP:**
>
> Remember to pick up any area flyers that appear in the entrance of many grocery stores. In some areas, the flyer that contains homes for sale extends up to fifty pages or more.

homeowners insurance. Like auto insurance, the neighborhood can cause high rates. In addition, some insurance companies will discount premiums when a person purchases multiple types of policies from one provider.

Again, remember transportation costs. If you drive to work, this is the cost of wear, repairs, and gas in your car, plus the costs of tolls and parking. If you take public transportation, it is your ticket price. Since transportation costs are increasing for across the country, this is an important expense. If you plan to take public transportation, your calculation is as easy as getting the ticket price.

If you drive to work, calculating your costs is more difficult. Begin with monthly car payments, cost of gas (need to know the miles per gallon of gas that your car gets), tolls or highway fees, cost of parking, and wear cost. For wear, take a guess at the cost of repairs that driving daily will cause. Older cars may not take the daily commute, so you may need to figure in the cost of buying a new car.

Another transportation cost that is rarely spoken of is the cost of your wasted time. Most of us have heard that old saying time is money. No place is that truer than in the daily commute. If your dream home requires a one hour commute to your job and a one hour commute back, that calculates to ten hours a week or over twenty days a year. This can be a real waste of your time.

Public transportation may allow you to spend that commuting time dutifully working on your laptop computer, but public transportation puts you at the mercy of someone else's schedule.

Weigh these factors carefully when looking for the right neighborhood. Don't just look at the dollars and cents of commuting, look at how you will feel about that long commute after the excitement of buying your home.

PUBLIC IMPROVEMENT PLANS

Investigate local real estate issues. Is a road about to be widened in your desired neighborhood? Your property value could be reduced. Worse yet, your house could be condemned and purchased at a reduced price by local government if it is in the path of the proposed road. This process is called *eminent domain*.

Eminent domain is invoked when a government unit wants to make a public improvement such as building a new airport, expanding an existing airport, public school, college, or hospital.

In many states, the seller and his realtor have a duty to reveal any public improvements when known. Some states require that the seller and his realtor reveal this information only if you specifically ask. For your protection, always submit the question in writing and insist on a written answer.

OLD VS. NEW

Neighborhoods can generally be classified as either old or new. There are benefits and liabilities in both types. In a new area, the homes are usually modern with the latest extras. You may even be able to select options before the home is built. New areas usually attract younger people and those who are beginning their family.

On the down side, a new area has not established its tax base, so you can expect property tax increases. Property owners may also be charged with assessments to install sidewalks, widen streets, install traffic controls, install sewer system, etc. The mostly younger population may mean lots of children, who will need additional schools to be built, which increases property taxes. If the neighborhood is being built as you move in, there is construction noise, dust, and debris. There is also the additional cost of landscaping that must be considered.

An older, established neighborhood has probably put in the sidewalks, sewers, and streets. However, this is no guarantee that these items will not need replacement and increase taxes through a special assessment. The other pluses of an older neighborhood are that homes are

ATTORNEY TIP:

Read the local newspapers in order to be alerted to any public improvement plans in the area you are searching.

relatively stable in construction and taxes are consistent. (However, taxes may rise if there is a lot of tear-down activity.)

An older neighborhood also has negatives. Some home owners become complacent or become physically unable to keep up their property and houses can suffer from disrepair. City services may go down because the stable tax revenue is not keeping up with the increasing costs for city workers and supplies. An older neighborhood can also become victim to the construction traffic when homes are sold, leveled, and replaced with a very expensive structure.

Section Three:

Searching for Your Home

chapter five

Deciding Which House Features are Important

Before you begin the actual search for your home, you must decide what you would *like* to have and what you really *need*. This is a serious decision that takes into account those things absolutely necessary plus the reality of having to pay for your house.

THE BUILDING, ITSELF

This is not a book on exterior home designs. There are many books and magazines that cover that subject. However, you should be able to tell the difference between a ranch style and a bungalow, but may not want to distinguish an American foursquare from a Victorian.

Following is a short summary of home types and other terms to get you started.

- *ranch* - a home with one level; may or may not have a basement.
- *basement* - lowest level in a home; usually at least half under ground.

> ### ATTORNEY TIP:
> Best way to learn about real estate in general and in a particular area is to read the real estate section of the local newspaper every time it is available. You will become familiar with common real estate terms and learn the types and prices of homes that are available in the area.

- *slab* - some homes do not have a basement level and are built on a level of concrete called a slab.
- *crawlspace* - homes built on a crawlspace do not have a basement level, but do have an area between the floor and the ground where wiring and utilities can be accessed. (A crawlspace is not deep enough to stand up in.)
- *bungalow* - a compact home with a main living level (the first floor), it may have an attic (can be used as living space), and a basement. (These are typically found in the Midwest.)
- *American foursquare* - type of home that has a full first floor, a full second floor, and may also have a basement. (There are few frills on this home. It usually resembles a large square, hence the name.)
- *Victorian* - the name many people call a larger home that has lots of details on the outside, such as wood trims that do nothing but look good.
- *colonial* - a large home usually depicted with tall white columns on the exterior around the front door. (This is usually a stately type of home. Think the White House.)
- *split level* - as the name indicates, this home has several levels. Usually the entry is at the mid-level of the home where you can go up a few steps to one level or down to the lower level. Split level homes are known for the most effective use of space. In many cases, the split level home is built on an incline so that the lower level opens out to a backyard.

In order to learn what these terms mean in your area, read the real estate ads that have pictures. Review classic "House" magazines that show interesting homes.

You may also want to start a file for articles and pictures of homes and decorating ideas that interest you. Review this file often. Add to it frequently. Keep it current and you will begin to see what home design most appeals to you.

Besides the design, you should be concerned with what is on the outside of the structure. Since the majority of first home buyers will be purchasing a previously-owned home, the choice of your home's exterior has already been made for you. Here are some of the popular home exteriors with the pluses and minuses of each.

- *brick/stone:*

    plus = strong construction, durable, low maintenance, looks good

    minus = expensive to add a room or change exterior, can be drafty without sufficient insulation, may be difficult to match

- *stucco:*

    plus = lasts a long time without repair, looks good, durable

    minus = may be difficult to match if you need to repair exterior, will probably require repainting or cleaning

- *aluminum siding:*

    plus = low maintenance

    minus = may fade, can dent, can look old, hard to match if you do any repairs or expansion

- *vinyl siding:*

    plus = low maintenance, keeps its color and finish, can have extra insulation attached right to the siding to keep out drafts

    minus = you are probably stuck with the color, hard to match if you do any repairs or expansion

- *wood siding/paneling:*

    plus = inexpensive, can change the color, can match the style for repairs an expansion

    minus = may require yearly repainting or restaining

There are new options for the exterior of a home coming out every year. Be sure you know both the positives and negatives for any exterior covering on the home you are considering purchasing.

FEATURES

The *features* or the *interior layout* and amenities of a home are usually what a person is mainly concerned with. Do you dream of a winding staircase that your children will scramble down on Christmas morning? Do you dream of a private bath in the master bedroom suite for relaxing after a hard day? Do you need a handicapped accessible kitchen or a home with ramps? How much property or lawn do you want?

You need to decide what you want in a home; how important each feature is to you; and what is absolutely necessary. This is the time to be realistic. If you always wanted an indoor pool, but can barely afford more than two bedrooms, save that pool dream for a future home. There is nothing to stop a person from buying a home with more features in the future, as his or her income increases.

To help you with this decision I have supplied **Worksheet 2** in **Appendix B** on pages 223-226 to prioritize the features you want and which ones you will compromise on. Make lots of copies of this worksheet. As time goes by and you start looking at homes for sale, you will be changing your mind, often. If you are planning to buy a home with another person, make him or her fill one of these forms out and then compare what both parties want in a home. An interesting exercise is to save your final list after you have bought your home. Pull it out in a few years and see if you still feel the same.

ESSENTIALS

Essentials is another word for features, but these are the features that you absolutely MUST have. A lot of essentials vary from area to area. For example, in Southern California, an in-ground pool is an essential (in my mind). In Chicago, an in-ground pool, unless it has a building around it, will cause the home to decrease in value.

Most areas have their own essentials: air conditioning in Las Vegas, heated garage in Minnesota, and so on. Learn about the area to determine what are essentials. If you are moving in from another state, look at the real estate ads to see what features are advertised as part of the homes for sale. What is an essential feature in one state, may be a major problem in another.

As with anything else with your home, you must decide what is important to you, and then determine if that will work in the area you want to live.

HANDY-MAN'S SPECIAL OR FIXER-UPPER

If you have been reading the real estate ads you will see these two terms. The real estate industry has no set definition for what constitutes a *handy-man's special* or a *fixer-upper*. It depends a lot on the area of the country and what the seller thinks can actually be fixed. In reality, these structures range from "an amateur can fix" to "must hire professional contractors" to "should be leveled." The price on one of these homes can be much less than the surrounding area. If you have decided that the neighborhood you want to live in is generally above your price range, this may be one way that you can get into that neighborhood. But realize that this type of home takes a lot of work and you will either have to do it yourself or have to pay someone to do the work. The big question is the quality of the structure of the house. If the structure is poor then renovations will be more expensive.

> **ATTORNEY TIP:**
>
> Rule of thumb when doing home repairs: it will take three times longer and cost three times more than what you originally estimated. Be prepared.

If you are like me and picked the old stately neighborhood with large older homes, you may already be preparing to *rehab* your home. Be sure that you know what you are getting into. Do-it-yourself remodeling requires an infinite amount of patience with construction rubble, a large amount of time and commitment, and the physical ability to do the work.

Several years ago there was a movie, "The Money Pit," about problems and expenses in rehabbing a home. While some of the things that happened to these fictional characters were a bit extreme, (the characters seem to have an unlimited amount of money), the movie is still worth seeing for any potential rehabber.

Before you decide to look for a "needs work" home, honestly asses your abilities to do the work. Take a field trip to one of your local home repair superstores. That will give you some idea of the expenses that even do-it-yourselfers face. Many of the home repair superstores provide free classes and literature on do-it-yourself projects.

As I have mentioned throughout this book, I chose a "needs work" Victorian home in a perfect suburb. My husband, Jim, assured me that he was able to do the repairs since he and his dad had built a family room in his parent's home. However, after we had moved in my mother-in-law told me that my husband's help consisted of going for lunch and passing tools.

The bottom line is that you need to really know your limitations and be willing to learn new trades. Maybe you cannot rewire the house, but you might be a wizard at putting up wallpaper. Over the years Jim has even surprised himself at what he has been able to do. However, he has also learned when to call a professional.

WE ARE ALL GETTING OLDER

As uncomfortable as it may be, we are all aging and so are our families. We all get to that time of our life when health or age dictates that we either stay in our home or go to a place where someone will take care of us. You may have to make that decision for you parents or other relatives. While this may be the farthest thought from your mind when looking at your first home, you may want to take a moment to consider the future.

Houses where all the bedrooms are on the second floor are great—until you break your foot or become sick or are too weak to go up and down the stairs. The same is true for homes that have steep stairs at the entrance without the room to install ramps for handicapped access. A home needs to bend and accommodate you and your family in the future. Take a minute to assess the potential that in a few years elderly parents or relatives may have to move in with you.

Now, I do not advocate buying a huge house on the chance that Grandma Millie or Uncle Pete will move in. However, if there is someone in the family who may be in that situation, it is better to find a home that will accommodate the future changes without complete disruption of your life.

CONDOMINIUMS AND TOWNHOMES

Condominiums are basically personal homes stacked in a larger building. Condos have common areas for the use of all owners and are run by an association. Many of us have been in the situation where an apartment that we live in suddenly turns condo and we are asked to either buy the apartment or get out.

Personally, I felt that the apartments I rented were not even worth the monthly rent. In one of the last apartments that I rented, I told the landlord that I would only buy the condo if he could sound-proof the walls so I didn't hear the next-door noises and guarantee that we had continuous heat in the winter.

If you are buying a condo, make sure that you are not being rushed or pressured to make a decision because your apartment is being converted into condos. Go through the exercises in this book to determine if this is the right choice for you. Condos usually come with association fees that are paid to maintain the common areas of the building. These fees can be very high and can increase every year.

Mortgage lenders may be more inclined to write a mortgage for a first time home buyer who is buying their apartment turned condo, especially if the mortgage payment is about the same as your current rent. Some lenders have requirements regarding the percentage of owners who actually live in their condos in one building. If your apartment complex is going all condo, the owners may even be able to assist you in finding financing or may have already selected a financial institution to handle this.

Condominiums are very popular as a real estate purchase for first time home buyers. It is a way to build up equity while still having the benefits of apartment living. In some areas of the country, especially those in vacation states, that first time condo purchase may be able to be sold as a vacation home when you move up to a single-family home.

Townhouses are usually multi-floored homes that share one or two walls with another townhouse. As with condominiums, they are usually operated by an association that collects fees for the upkeep of common areas. Most townhouses have more living area than condos and may have more land around the building. Townhouses are more resistant to neighbor's noises because neighbors only share walls on the side, not side, top, and bottom. Townhouses usually require the same type of house insurance as a single-family home (which may increase your mortgage payment). As with condominiums, many lenders provide financing programs for townhouses that are directed at first time home buyers.

The reputation of condos and townhouses has increased recently, since the baby boomers have discovered that these homes free the home owner from the upkeep and maintenance of a single-family house. As an added benefit, many condos and townhouses are located in developments that also offer pools, clubhouses, meeting rooms, shuttle service to transportation centers and shopping, and other amenities.

For both condos and townhouses, the most important questions you can ask are:
- What are the monthly assessment fees?
- Are there rules as to how much these fees can increase?
- What do the assessment fees cover?

BUILDING FROM THE GROUND-UP
You may find the perfect neighborhood, but are unable to find a perfect home, and decide to build the home you want. Or you

may find that the only homes available for sale are in a development being built—in either case, you will be making decisions about your home *from the ground-up*.

Building Your House

Building your own home is great and scary because you must decide everything. Assuming you have decided on the neighborhood to build in, do not overbuild for the area. This

ATTORNEY TIP:

The architect designs the home. The builder is the one responsible for putting that design into reality. The contractor is on the job directing the work crew. Many full-service builders will handle all three jobs. This may be the best way for you, however, consider all of your options before making a final decision.

means you should not put a 15 bedroom mansion in an area that has only small homes with two bedrooms. Also, no matter how sure you are that this is the only home you will ever live in, build your home for resale. This means keeping to the *norm*. For example, a one bedroom home with two full kitchens and one bathroom may work for you and your spouse, but will be tough to sell. Finally get the best builder/contractor/architect that your budget can afford.

The best way to begin the search for your building team is to look at newly-built homes in the neighborhood you have selected and find a few that you like. You should be looking not just at the style of the building, but the workmanship. The best scenario would be to observe a home being built and then ask the owners if they would recommend this builder/contractor/architect. Once you find a team that you like, you need to review the references provided. This means looking at several homes they have built and, if at all possible, speaking to the owners about their experience with those professions.

Building your own home is a daunting task, even for experienced home owners. If you decide to go this way—be prepared for delays, going over budget, and frustration.

Buying in a Builder's Development

This is much like building you own home, but easier. First the location has already been selected. Second, the references are on display. New developments usually have a series of different examples of homes this builder is selling. These are great to walk through. You can look at all aspects of the finished building and get tons of ideas for your home. You can also see the craftsmanship of the builder. If this is your first home and you are sure that you want a brand new home, look at the builder's developments. This is a great way to get a new home that is exactly what you want. Also check the builder's references with other home owners, with the local Better Business Bureau, and with any consumer protection agencies in your area.

Another plus for this type of home purchase is that you will be able to determine what goes into the building. Depending upon the builder, you may be able to decide types of wood, roofing materials, landscaping, windows, and options such as fireplaces and kitchen appliances. (Remember that each decision comes with a price.)

Most builders have a set of standard things that come with a home and a set of options that you can add for a price. You may be sure that you really want those expensive granite kitchen counter tops, but your builder may be able to provide something that looks like granite at a lower price. Many builders are willing to make some design changes for your home, but you will pay for any extras.

Advantages/Disadvantages of Building

Building a home or working with a builder allows you to customize the home to your own ideas. All the components are brand new, of the latest design, and are your personal selection. Depending on your builder, you will be able to take an active role in building your home. Some builders even allow the home buyers to save money by doing part of the work themselves. Also, builder's developments are usually in new areas that will probably increase in value over the years.

On the down side, building a house is complex and will probably be subject to several delays. Because so many crafts and materials go into building a home, there will be problems getting materials, problems with the weather, problems in getting the right workers to the building site, and other unexpected delays. Building can also be more expensive than buying a previously-

CLICK ON THIS:

For more information on building your own home and dealing with builders, contractors, and architects go to: www.ourfamily-place.com/homebuyer/build.htm

owned home. Much of the expense is a result of home building products always improving and increasing in price. Buying in a new development may also include additional assessments for streets, sidewalks, and schools.

chapter six:
Working with Real Estate Agents and Brokers

Once you pick out the neighborhood and are really ready to buy a home, you will probably select a real estate agent. The best place to look for your agent is in the neighborhood you want to buy in. The local agent is probably where the current owners will go to sell their property. Local agents also have the advantage of knowing a lot about the community.

REAL ESTATE PROFESSIONALS

The term *real estate professionals* usually refers to *real estate agents* and *real estate brokers*. The primary function of agents and brokers is to assist buyers and sellers in the legal transaction of transferring property from one person to another. Because this is a legal function with great implications on the public, agents and brokers are state licensed. Each state has its own requirements to obtain these licenses. Most require education in real estate, a term of working in the area of real estate, and continuing education.

Appendix D lists the department in each state that controls the licensing of real estate professionals, and their particular Internet site. Many states have Internet sites that provide consumer information about licensed agents and brokers and how to utilize these professionals in buying a home.

Real estate agents work independently (sometimes out of their home), as an employee for a well-known real estate agency, or, even for a large corporation as relocation specialists. No matter what type of office the agent has, it is their experience and commitment to the profession that is important.

The Real Estate Profession

The reality of the real estate profession is that it is plagued with high turnover. This means that many of the real estate agents are relative newcomers. While there is nothing wrong with a newcomer to a job, when someone is helping me with the largest purchase of my life I want a person who has been on the job at least two years in that area.

This profession also attracts the part-time or retired worker who does not want to or cannot work an eight-hour day. Again, that does not make the person incompetent, however in a purchase this large I want to know that my real estate agent is available to return my calls and look at new listings.

Because this type of work is dealing with almost daily changes in listings, real estate law, mortgage rules, and financing, it is important that the real estate agent has made the time commitment to keep up with his or her job.

An agent who views this as his or her only job, not a hobby or extra moneymaker, is able to bring professionalism and commitment to the transaction. He or she wants to keep you as a happy customer because they know that if you are satisfied you will recommend him or her to your friends and family. Most people move several times in their lives. A happy customer can be a source of continued revenue for this agent.

One indicator of commitment is a real estate agent's taking advanced educational courses that provide training in all aspects of the real estate transaction. The

ATTORNEY TIP:

When choosing a real estate agent, look for one who is as committed to his or her job as you have been to finding a home. Look for someone who is knowledgeable, available, and able to work for the commission.

National Association of REALTORS® offers nationwide programs. This organization awards a designation of a GRI to those who have passed the *REALTORS® Graduate* series of courses. Real estate agents who have completed advanced courses use it as a tool for marketing and display such designations on business cards, ads, and at their desk.

PROBLEMS WITH REAL ESTATE AGENTS

Unfortunately, there are real estate agents that conduct themselves as surrogate mothers for their clients. They are so sure that they know exactly what the clients want now and for the future, that they tend to turn a deaf ear to what the potential buyers are actually saying that they want.

In order to defeat this type of person, take control of the situation. Refuse to look at a home that does not meet your qualifications. Insist that the houses the agent wants to show you meet certain criteria. You will have to be firm on this. Most real estate agents mean no harm. They sincerely believe they know what is best for their clients—especially first time buyers. However, the agent will not be there when you have to pay the mortgage bill or realize that your new home is not really what *you* wanted.

I have found that setting the tone of the real estate agent-client relationship at the beginning helps. Tell the agent what you must have and the price range you are looking for. You may even put it in writing for the agent. Tell the agent that you are a busy person and will not waste your time or

CLICK ON THIS:

The National Association of Realtors has a great web site to help find a home:

www.realtor.com

The basic search is by city, state, price range, number of bedrooms and number of bathrooms; more criteria can be added. This site also lets you find a member real estate professional in a particular area. This is a great help if you are moving to another state.

the agent's time by looking at homes that do not match your criteria. Finally, before going to any showing, review the details on the home. Real estate agents have access to detailed info on each home.

Changing Agents

When I first started looking for homes, I was too afraid that I would hurt the real estate agent's feelings if I said that she or he was just not working out and I needed someone else. (It was sort of like dumping a steady boyfriend for no reason.)

After having several near misses in buying the wrong house, I realized that the agent's feelings were not my concern. My priority had to be me and my family. Buying the wrong house can cause financial disaster. It can begin an avalanche of problems for a family, especially if you over-extend yourself financially or buy a house that needs expensive work. It is up to you to insist that the real estate agent respect your wishes, listen to your needs, and understand your financial limitations.

I have found that an honest approach of "I do not think I can work with you" is enough. In most cases, the agent that I rejected would not listen to me about what I could afford and continued to show me homes that were way over my budget.

The only problem with changing agents is that in some states, the agent who showed the house to the buyer first, gets some *or* all of the commission. This depends on local regulations, state laws, and the contract that the seller and the real estate agent signed.

Example:

Sam's brother-in-law, Tom, is a new real estate agent. Sam has been looking for a home with the help of Ms. Green, a local real estate agent. Sam doesn't really like Ms. Green. On Friday, Ms. Green showed him his dream home. On Saturday, Sam told Ms. Green he was no longer interested in working with her. On Monday, Sam made an offer on the dream home using his brother-in-law Tom, so that Tom would get the commission.

In some instances, Tom would not get the commission because Ms. Green showed the buyer the house first. This depends on local regulations, state laws, and the contract that the seller and the real estate agent signed.

WHOSE INTEREST IS PROTECTED BY THE REAL ESTATE AGENT

The biggest misconception with real estate agents is whom they actually work for. In some states, a real estate agent works for the interest of the seller, not the buyer. Again, this depends on local regulations, state laws, and the contract that the seller and the real estate agent signed. This is hard to believe when *your* real estate agent is so friendly and so accommodating to what you want. He or she looks for properties to show you, chauffeurs you to those places, and is ready to assist you in making a selection and getting a mortgage. Your state's Real Estate Commission or licensing board requires that the buyers be treated fairly, but in reality, the motivation is how a real estate agent is paid.

In some states where the real estate agent legally works for the interest of the seller, a home buyer can hire his or her own real estate agent (often called a *buyer's agent*) to represent him or her in finding a home and negotiating its purchase. In order to get this kind of representation, the buyer must pay a percentage or fee to the broker, in much the same way that the seller contracts for a specific commission percentage with an agent.

HOW REAL ESTATE AGENTS GET PAID

When a person wants to sell his or home they usually contact a local real estate agent. The agent views the property, estimates what the selling price should be, and advises the seller of any other things that need to be done to the property to make it more saleable. The seller and the agent then sign a contract that the house will be *listed* by the agent and that the agent will receive a certain percentage of the selling price when the house *closes* (or sells). Generally, the contract will specify the length of time the agent has to sell the house, restrictions as to how it is listed, and any other issues relating to the particular situation.

When the property is sold, the seller's agent or listing agent who contracted with the seller, gets his or her percentage of commission. The seller's agent or listing agent then takes part of that amount and gives it to the buyer's agent. This percentage of the split is determined by prior agreement.

For the real estate agency, it is more profitable for one of its own real estate agents (who represent the buyer) to sell a property that was listed by another one of its real estate agents (who represent the seller). This way, the agency would get the entire percentage of the selling price as listed in the contract, as opposed to having to split it with an agent who works at another agency.

MULTIPLE LISTING SERVICES (MLS)

Many areas of the country have organizations refered to as *Multiple Listing Services*. They were originally created to provide information to all real estate agents that are members of the local MLS, about every house that other MLS agents were selling.

Example:

ABC Real Estate only sells homes that are in town ABC. 250 miles away, XYZ Real Estate only sells homes that are in town XYZ. Everyone worked and stayed in the town they were born in. As life became more mobile, people began to get jobs in the other town and wanted to live near where they worked.

Both real estate offices got together and formed a Multiple Listing Service, where each real estate office would share all the information on houses for sale in their towns. They saved money by printing only one book that had pictures and information on all homes for sales in both towns. This book could be used by both offices.

Most real estate agents in this country belong to a local multiple listing group, which allows all properties for sale in a certain area to be sold by any other licensed agent. In the Chicago area, this produces large phone book size listings of homes on the market by price and location.

The Internet has gone a long way in allowing everyone to see all the homes for sale in every real estate office. No longer does a particular real estate office want a lock on a particular listing, unless there are special circumstances such as a home owned by a celebrity. By letting everyone view these listings, there is a better chance that someone, maybe someone out of town or out of the country, will buy the property. There are some internet sites which will allow you to take advantage of this.

Most of the homes that are listed in the newspapers are sold by an MLS agent. There is nothing a buyer needs to do in order to get the benefit of MLS, in fact MLS is pretty transparent to a buyer. MLS benefits the buyer by allowing many real estate agents to view and show a larger number of homes up for sale.

On the opposite end of MLS is what are usually called *Exclusive listings*. In an exclusive listing, one real estate agent is selling the property. Only he or she is allowed to show the property and the information is not provided to any other agents. With exclusive listings, the real estate agent gets the full commission when the house is sold. (However, this situation is becoming increasingly rare.)

CLICK ON THIS:

For some multiple listing groups across the country, look at:
www.mlslisting.com
www.mls.com

COMPARABLES

The *comparable* is a dollar number that real estate agents use in determining what a particular house is worth. Bankers and home insurance companies also look at this number. The comparable amount is obtained by looking at the selling price of similar houses (judged by square footage, number of rooms, type of construction) in the same area, for a certain time period. The area can be a few blocks within a particular city or the closest properties in the rural areas. This gives the average value of that particular type of home or approximately how much it is worth.

When judging comparables, it is important to use the selling price. If you use the asking price, those sellers who list their homes at an over-inflated amount will skew the result. If you are reading the real estate ads for a particular area over a few months, you will get a feel for what houses are being priced. Some newspapers list the actual sale price a few months after the sale has been completed.

VIEWING A HOUSE UP FOR SALE

Driving in the area you want to live, you see a house with a 'for sale' sign. What do you do? Write down the address, name, and number on the sign. Sometimes there is a box affixed to the sign with an information sheet on the property (if you are just checking out the neighborhood, these sheets can be useful too). If you have an agent working for you, call him or her to obtain the information on price, etc. Your agent may be able to schedule a time for you to see the home.

Notes and Checklists

Your real estate agent will have an *informational sheet* on each house he or she is planning to show you. Ask for your own copy. This sheet should have the *asking price*, number and sizes of rooms, size of the lot, sewage and water information, heating and cooling information, past taxes, and other positives of the

---

ATTORNEY TIP:

Decide what are the top three items you MUST have in a house. When the real estate agent calls you to look at a particular house, ask if the house meets the three criteria. For example:

1) How much is the asking price?

2) Number of bedrooms?

3) Number of bathrooms?

If the answers do not conform to what you want, say "no thanks" to seeing that house.

house. Many of these listings include a picture of the property. Most times you will be seeing multiple homes each time you go out with your agent, so this information sheet will help you compare properties.

> ## ATTORNEY TIP:
> Insist that your real estate agent give you a copy of the informational sheet on each home you are seeing. This will give you a record of what you have looked at and a way to remind yourself about that particular house. This is also a test to see how cooperative the agent is with your needs.

You should also keep a notebook for your notes on the property. This is something you can write on while actually looking at the home, or just after you have seen it. Keep notes on things that may be serious problems like the toilet does not flush; the water faucet does not shut off completely; one room is too cold or too hot; or, the furnace sounds strange. You may wish to use **Worksheet 3** in **Appendix B**, page 227, in addition to your own notebook.

Home Warranty

People who have bought homes have differing opinions on the value of a home warranty. Some swear by the warranties and will not purchase a home that does not have one. Others (myself included) believe that in most cases, warranties are not worth the costs.

Most home warranties cover repair and replacement of certain items in the house. Not everything in the house is covered.

The common items that are covered in a home warranty are:
- furnace;
- air conditioning system;
- certain electrical work;
- refrigerator;
- stove;
- garage door opener;
- certain plumbing;
- water heater;
- washer;

- dryer;
- dishwasher;
- garbage disposal;
- trash compactor; and,
- water softener.

(Sounds like a lot of coverage, but remember not every home warranty covers all this, just as not every home will be sold with all the appliances.)

Technically, the home warranty is an insurance policy bought by the sellers for a cost of several hundred to several thousand dollars. As with all insurance policies, there will be a deductible; the warranty will only cover normal use; and, the warranty usually does not last more than a year or two.

Those of us who are not fans of a home warranty feel that there are more reliable ways of determining defects in a house than relying on an insurance policy that is usually just placed on brand new appliances that probably will not fail. One such buyer's protection used in many states is a law that requires that the seller list all the defects of the house that is being sold. This gives the buyer a heads up to problems before the sale is finalized.

ATTORNEY TIP:

Be a concerned consumer and don't rely on just one piece of paper. Read it. Ask questions. Then get that inspection.

Home Inspection

However, the primary protection for the *buyer* of a home is a *home inspection*. There cannot be enough emphasis placed on getting a professional home inspection before buying. This is a must do! (How to obtain an inspector and other inspection details are covered in subsequent chapters, especially Chapter 14.)

Here are a few facts on home inspections:

- Fact 1: Do not buy a home without getting a professional home inspection. This is such a crucial step that the buyer's offer to purchase a home should be contingent on a home inspection that shows no defects with the house.

- Fact 2: Professional home inspections produce a comprehensive written report that details all aspects of the home. This will show defects in the house and evaluate the seriousness of the defects.
- Fact 3: Professional home inspections are so important that your lender may require an inspection of their own in conjunction with a standard appraisal of the property. Lenders do not rely merely on a seller's warranty.

In some areas of the country, a warranty on a house being sold is an expected thing. It is a marketing tool meant to nudge the hesitant buyer to make an offer. However, the buyer cannot merely rely on this piece of paper for protection. You still must look at the home, negotiate for repairing defects, and above all, have that important home inspection.

Home warranties do not cover everything. If the buyer purchases a home that has a defect, which was disclosed by the seller, chances are the home warranty will not pay to have that defect fixed. Warranties, like contracts, are unique and it is impossible to make generalizations about what they cover. Usually a seller pays for the warranty, but may attempt to pass on the cost to the buyer as part of the deal.

WHAT NOT TO SAY TO REAL ESTATE AGENTS AND SELLERS

Never let your real estate agent know that you are willing to go higher in an offer for a home. The higher the selling price, the more commission they make. While it is not ethical, your real estate agent may be tempted to tell the sellers that you are willing to pay more.

As for the sellers, remember this is the seller's home. Do not criticize the decorating, the lay-

ATTORNEY TIP:

Remember that your real estate agent is being paid a percentage of the selling price. Real estate agents really want their clients to buy a home.

out, the furniture, or anything else out loud. Make a note to discuss points later with your agent. In the same vein, do not discuss plans to knock down walls, rip out carpeting, tear down cabinets—out loud. Quietly observe each room and make notes. Do not make an enemy of the sellers. Be polite. If you can't say something nice don't say anything at all.

Most real estate agents will tell their sellers to leave the home while it is being shown. I personally find this practice very insensitive for the sellers and extremely limiting for the buyers. To expect two families to negotiate the cost of a home without ever seeing each other is silly. Having been both seller and buyer, I have found that the deals went smoother when both sides at least saw each other once before the financial dealing.

GAMES PLAYED TO MAKE THE SALE

Be sure to review the earlier section on how real estate agents get paid. This will give you an idea of their motivation. It is more profitable if the same agency that lists the property also sells it. It is more profitable to sell the property at the highest amount possible. The majority of real estate agents do not defraud or purposely act in an irresponsible way in order to get the sale. However, the following are some of the more common *games* used to push a sale.

Inflating the Worth of the House

Real estate agents can inflate the worth of the house in a number of ways. One way is to show you houses listed at a higher price range than the homes are worth. These are the ones where the current owner, for whatever reason, has listed the asking price of the house at an over-inflated, amount. Once you have seen several over-priced houses, the agent shows you a house that is properly priced, but still in the same high price range.

There can be two problems here:
- the high-price range may be beyond what you want to pay and
- the over-priced homes you looked at may not be a good example of what is available for that price.

This manipulation makes the one properly-priced home look like a real steal.

Another way to inflate the worth of the house is to use the asking price of similar homes and not the selling price when making a comparable calculation. This makes homes look like they are worth more than the market value and again may push you into considering property above what you decided was your limit.

If you have questions about the worth of a particular house, ask that the real estate agent show you similar homes that have recently sold at a similar or comparable price. A real estate professional should be able and willing to give you this information. If yours is not, consider getting a different agent.

Another Offer

Real estate agents may also rush you to make an offer on a home by saying that they have heard that someone else is making an offer on that property right now, so you have to hurry. While there are times when a particular piece of property may be so desirable that people are standing in line to make an offer, that is the exception.

It has been my experience that each and every home I have ever considered making an offer on is just about to be snapped up by another person who is coincidentally ready to offer more. There always is another agent in the same office that is just about to seal the deal. While it may seem like gambling with losing a home you want, my response has always been "Good for them. I hope they get the house, but I need time to make a decision." This type of response lets your real estate agent know that they cannot bluff you and it allows you the time you need to decide on this home.

Another time a buyer is rushed is after the offer has been made. The sellers reject the offer and come back with a *counter offer* that is more money than you want to spend. I personally do not like playing games with a real estate purchase. When I make an offer on a property, it is usually fair and in accordance with what I believe the property is worth and what I can afford. If the seller counters with an amount that is outside of my budget or I feel is outrageous for the property, to me that is not acting in good faith and I look for another property.

Many real estate agents will urge you to meet the seller's offer, extend yourself more, and of course, do it right now. The buyer is urged to do this immediately before someone else buys the property—before you get a chance to think. Going up from a first offer, as long as that is appropriate for the house value and within your finances, is fine—as long as you are not pressured to make the decision.

This is one of the biggest decisions of your life and you do not need to be pushed into making it before you are ready. When you find the right home, you will not be asking for time to decide. The decision will feel right.

WHEN DO YOU LEGITIMATELY NEED TO ACT FAST

The fact is that there are some areas of the country where homes are sold within the first forty-eight hours of being put on the market. In that case, the real estate agent is 100% correct in urging the buyer to act fast.

One of the first homes that I bought and rehabbed had an offer within four hours of the home being put on the market—for the full asking price. There was no outward indication that my house would sell fast. Most other houses in that area were not selling in twenty-four hours. My house was correctly priced considering the area and the upgrades put into the house. However, the buyer

ATTORNEY TIP:

What is a buyer's market? What is a seller's market? Indicators of a buyer's market are homes that linger on the market for a long time before being sold; homes where the asking price has been reduced; and/or homes where the selling price is much lower than the asking price. In a seller's market, homes sell quickly—usually for the asking price or above.

lived close; and, had watched the upgrades and improvements made to my house. He was very motivated.

How do you know when to act fast to get a home? If you have been reading the real estate section of the paper for a particular area, you will have some indication as to how fast the homes move. Also, your real estate agent may be able to provide actual listings of homes that sold and how long they were on the market. Of course, remember that a neighbor down the block may have his eye on the place and will be making an offer on the house before you even get a chance to see it.

If you want to buy in an area where homes are selling quickly, be prepared to pay the full asking price. Which, of course, means that when you are looking for a home, you use that asking price as a guide. Do not expect that you will be able to pay less.

chapter seven:
Handling the Emotional Side of a Home Purchase

House hunting and buying is one of those times in your life when you need to be practical, logical, and unemotional. However, as luck would have it, this is the time when emotions often run high. Emotions can sabotage a first-time home buyer and cause mistakes.

Following are the common occasions when emotions can cause problems in buying your first home. Read this section carefully to learn what to expect, how to overcome potential problems, and when to take a time out.

EMOTIONS IN HOUSE HUNTING
Congratulations! You have decided which neighborhood you want to live in. It has everything you want—the schools are good, the people seem friendly, and the resale value of property is going up. The next hurdle—find your home.

Under a Deadline
If you are under pressure due to an expiring lease or problems where you are currently living, you may be eager to make an offer on the first house that is available. Before you make that jump, step back and review your worksheets of what you want to determine whether the house is right for you or if you are just rushing to get out of where you live. You may want to consider putting your belongings in

storage and taking a temporary rental in a month-to-month residence to give you additional time to look for a home.

In my own experience, I had moved into a new city, rented an apartment, and began the search for a home. The rental was a disaster. It had a criminal element and roaches. I was in such a hurry to find a place to live that I made an offer on a home that I could move into it right away because the owners had already moved. Within the first month of my living there, I found out why the previous owners were so anxious to leave. The next door neighbors threw huge parties complete with live bands every weekend.

House is Beautifully Decorated

There is nothing more emotionally satisfying than seeing a home where everything is just perfect. The decorating in each room is exactly what you want. The furniture is exquisite. The kitchen smells of fresh cooked bread, and it looks like a spread in *House Beautiful.*

It shouldn't surprise you to know that real estate agents will work with the seller to present just this picture. What you need to do is look past the decorating, the soft music, and smell of warm bread. What will this house look like with your furniture, your clutter, your children, and the smell of your cooking?

One way to get away from being influenced by the seller's decoration is to concentrate on the size of each room and the square footage of the home. Before you even look at a home, measure the size of your current bedroom, bathroom, kitchen, and living area. These measurements will give you a starting point to judge other homes. If your current bedroom is so cramped with furniture that you only have a path around the

ATTORNEY TIP:

Buy yourself a good tape measure at the hardware store. Measure each room of where you currently live and write the room sizes down on an index card. When you are viewing a house up for sale, refer to this card to determine if you and your furniture will fit into the rooms.

bed, you have a guide as to how big the bedroom in the new house should be. I have found that measuring a room that I am familiar with is a much better gauge than a mere number of feet and inches.

Another way to avoid letting the seller's decorating influence you is to write down what you really liked about a house. If any of your likes include things like paint, furniture, drapes, the smell of fresh baking bread, flowers, or music playing—then you are being influenced by the seller's decorating.

It is important to look at a house and visualize it with your things in it. Practice some exercises in visualization. Using the newspaper's house section or a house magazine, pick out pictures of the interior of a home. Now, in your mind put your furniture in that interior. Too tough, then start with floor plans offered in the same newspapers or magazines. With a pencil put your furniture in the floor plan. This is something that takes practice. Soon, armed with these exercises and the measurements of your current rooms, you can go into a house for sale and be oblivious of the decorating.

It is a Real Steal

We all love sales and sometimes we buy things just because it is such a good price on sale. However, this is not the best advice to use when buying a home. You have selected the neighborhood, chosen the type of house, and then something sort of close to what you want is available at a price that is much less than other homes in this area. This is a very tough one for most of us to ignore.

The first question you need to get an answer for is "Why is this one home selling at such a low cost?" Your real estate agent may be able to get the answer, but don't count on it. Sometimes the sellers themselves will volunteer that they are relocating out of state, are getting a divorce, or have decided to retire. Sometimes the answer lies in the construction problems. If you cannot get an answer to your question and do plan to make an offer on the house, you need to make your offer contingent on the house passing an inspection.

If the inspection shows some defects, it is up to you to decide how important that defect is. Will the current owner fix this before the sale? Are you willing to pay to get the problem fixed or can you fix it yourself? Is the lender willing to loan you the amount you need to pay for the home? Does this home meet your criteria or are you willing to compromise for the low price?

In my case, after two months of looking, the real estate agent showed us a home that had been on the market for over a year—much longer than anything else. The owners were in a panic and had just significantly reduced the asking price. The home had suffered from a lot of neglect. One bedroom was painted all black. Cars were parked on the nonexistent front lawn and every wall needed to be scrubbed with strong detergent. We looked at it from a nonemotional perspective. The neighborhood was right; the home had the number of rooms we wanted; the defects could be fixed; and, it was a good value for the money.

Using the Seller's Emotions

Remember that sellers are proud of their home. If you do encounter the sellers, keep any negative comments to yourself and find something to praise. Sellers want to hear complements—not how you are going to tear out all their decorating. This is one of those times when being nice really counts.

If you know why the sellers are moving, it may help you in dealing with them. Someone who is being forced to move because of finances or divorce is not likely to be very friendly. If you sense that this sale is not to move to a better life—a simple "You have a beautiful home" will do. Sellers who are anxious to start a new life or are happily relocating can be a wealth of information on the house, what they did, what improvements they made, and the neighborhood.

You want the sellers to like you. Every real estate agent has a story of how the seller chose a particular buyer, not because of

ATTORNEY TIP:

If you see the seller's neighbors watching you as you view the house, smile and nod at them. If you are really interested in the area, come back later (without your real estate agent) and speak to the neighbors.

the amount offered, but because of something intangible. Think about it, if two people come to buy your home for the same or close dollar amounts, who will you sell to—the person who is friendly or the one who is itching to strip the home of all of your hard work?

I have looked at homes where the sellers were arguing; where they refused to speak to my real estate agent; and, where they followed me around as if I would take something. None of that kept me from looking at what was important to me and taking sufficient notes to make a decision. When the tour was over, I made sure I said something positive to the sellers; thanked them for letting me intrude; and, left. (Incidentally, the house where the seller followed me around was the one I selected.)

> **ATTORNEY TIP:**
>
> Three things to remember when looking at a house for sale when the sellers are there:
> - smile;
> - say something positive about the house; and,
> - whatever happens, keep your composure.

BUYER'S REMORSE

You have undoubtedly heard the term *buyer's remorse*. It happens to everyone. No matter how unemotional and factual your decision to buy a house is—it will hit you. The feeling when you realize that you have just taken on an enormous debt for the rest of your life. For some people, this hits after you have signed the contract to offer the seller an amount. For some, it is after the sellers accept the offer. For many, it is at the closing. No matter who you are, buyer's regret will get you.

> **ATTORNEY TIP:**
>
> Quick cure for buyer's remorse.
>
> You know you are going to have this, so stock up on something to celebrate when you know that the seller has accepted your offer. A bottle of favorite wine, a box of expensive chocolates, a good steak — something to mark this as a celebration, not a time to be a "Monday morning quarterback."

When this happens, refer back to the notes and information you have made on the property. Go over the reasons why you chose this particular house and try to concentrate on how you will make the place your home.

As to the total amount of money that will be paid over the mortgage, concentrate more on the monthly payments. It is required that a lender tell you how much the total money of principal and interest you will pay over the life of the mortgage. You will be glad to have the knowledge, however the total number is so big it could just as well be the national debt. Chances are that the majority of us who hear that number will sell that home and buy another one—pretty much living our entire lives in debt. As long as we want to move up to a better home this is the way it will be. While it would be great to pay off one mortgage before looking for a new home, don't expect that to happen.

Things that may Promote Buyer's Remorse

- They don't mean to do it, but some people, usually family and friends, will tell you horror stories about their worst home buying experiences just after you have made an offer on the home of your dreams. (These are the same people who will discuss botched surgeries they have heard about as you are about to get your appendix removed.) They mean well, but just don't seem to know how their words can get to you.
- Some people will continue to look at homes for sale even after they have made an offer on another home. Once you make that offer, stop looking. If the contract falls apart, then resume your hunt.
- Your professionals have let you down. The real estate agent that you spoke to every day has not called since you made the offer. The lender that you thought was great has not returned your calls. You have a ton of unanswered questions and no one to ask. This is time to contact your agent, even if that means making lots of calls and leaving messages. (If you have questions, do not sit and suffer in silence.)

When Buyer's Remorse is Legitimate

There are times that you legitimately need to get out of the offer or contract to buy a home.

- You cannot get financing. This should be a *contingency* in the offer contract. (See Chapter 13.)
- The home does not appraise at or above the sales price. This is connected to why you cannot get financing.
- The inspections uncover serious problems.
- The title search uncovers problems with the boundaries of the house or there are liens on the property due to problems with the seller.

All of these are or should be represented as contingencies in the offer contract. Contingencies mean that if this item happens, then there is no sale. These are serious defects that real estate agents and lenders deal with all the time. (See Chapter 13.)

Legal Consequences of Allowing Buyer's Remorse to Run Amuck

If you have severe buyer's remorse that is not legitimately covered by the serious problems as listed above, ignore the urge to cancel the offer contract. Canceling the offer contract without good reason can cause you many legal problems.

When a buyer makes an offer on a house he or she writes up an offer contract and puts up a certain amount of money (called *earnest money*) to show that this is a legitimate or earnest offer. Once the house is bought, that earnest money becomes part of the down payment. Putting up the money is a way for the buyer to prove that this is a legitimate offer.

However, if the buyer backs out of the deal without legitimate cause, that earnest money goes to the seller as payment for their time and for taking their house off the market. This means your buyer's remorse can really cost you. If you back out of a offer contract for no reason other than buyer's remorse, the seller will probably be able to legally keep the total amount of earnest money you put up.

Section Four:

Finances

chapter eight:
Explanation of
Mortgage Basics

This chapter contains basic information and terms used in the mortgage industry. Finding the best mortgage for your situation also requires research.

Your real estate agent may be able to provide a list of lenders in the area who make mortgage loans or you may already have a business relationship with a bank, credit union, or financial institution. Be sure to get information on a mortgage from several lenders in order to make the right decision for you. **Worksheet 4** in **Appendix B**, pages 229–239 lists common points for comparing lenders. Make photocopies of this worksheet and start interviewing lenders.

PREQUALIFYING
Many mortgage lenders will allow a prospective borrower to *prequalify* for an estimated mortgage amount before they select a home. There are several advantages to doing this.

This may eliminate the house sale being held up for problems in obtaining a mortgage, which can make you very desirable from the seller's standpoint. In an area where many mortgages are being written, just the volume of these transactions can hold up house closings for days or even months. A buyer who is prequalified has already eliminated some of the potential for delays. This is a plus for the seller who needs to be out of the house by a certain date. In an area where homes sell fast, prequalification may be the thing that puts your offer ahead of others.

Remember that you are pre-qualifying for an *estimated amount*. If you have had financial problems between the time you prequalify and the actual mortgage application, the lender may lower the amount they are willing to lend.

Additionally, a mortgage is also based on the property that you want to purchase. If the lender believes that the property is not worth the mortgage amount, there are serious defects in the home or serious problems in the neighborhood, the lender may not be willing to base a mortgage on that purchase. A prequalification amount may be stated as a range amount. Remember, a prequalification is NOT a guarantee or a loan commitment.

CLICK ON THIS:

The best general source of mortgage information is the Internet. Look at the following:

- www.fanniemae.com (mortgage calculators; information on loans)
- www.fdic.gov (overview on mortgages; worksheets)
- www.fha.com (information on mortgages, prequalifying, debt-to-income ratios)
- www.ginniemae.gov (mortgage calculators, details on various mortgages)
- www.hud.gov (mortgage calculator, government grants, civil rights)
- www.interest.com (several mortgage calculators, mortgage references)
- www.mortgageselect.com (mortgage calculators, preapproval, current rates)
- www.msn.com (house and home; getting preapproved)

PREAPPROVAL

Preapproval is a more formal process. The lender examines your finances in detail and legally agrees to loan you a certain amount of money. Not all lenders do formal preapprovals, because when you obtain a mortgage the value of the property is a very large factor in the total amount of a loan you can get. In some areas of the country, preapprovals are totally nonexistent.

Preapprovals are more extensive and more detailed than prequalification. More information is required from the potential borrower. The time it takes to process a preapproval is longer than for prequalification. However, borrowers with preapprovals can cut the time waiting for a mortgage approval, considerably.

MORTGAGE LENDER TYPES

For most of us who want a mortgage, the *type* or *classification* of lender is not an issue. Lower interest rates and the increase in mortgage activity has blurred the lines between the traditional classifications. However, you may want to review the types of lenders to see how they fit your needs.

Portfolio Lenders

These are usually banks and savings & loan institutions. The term portfolio comes because the loans are made from the lender's own portfolio of assets and usually not for resale in the secondary market. An example of this would be *Small Town Savings and Loan* that prides itself in only making loans to the residents of *Small Town*. These types of financial institutions usually service limited areas that are not close to large cities. For those who want to keep their financial dealings local, this may be a good choice. However, with the advent of Internet banking and Internet loans, this lender may soon be forced to expand.

You may not know the type of mortgage lender that you are dealing with because these classifications have become blurred. If your real estate agent recommends a particular lender, it will probably be worthwhile to use that lender. Many real estate professionals have developed relationships with mortgage lenders that help in getting their clients approved with the least amount of red tape—in the least amount of time.

However, even true portfolio lenders may sell a mortgage on the secondary market after a year or more of mortgage payments.

Portfolio loans are typically easier to qualify for and as such do not always offer those great competitive rates. As many portfolio lenders have begun to engage in mortgage banking, those things that made this type of lender different have begun to disappear.

Mortgage Bankers

The larger institutions that do much of the volume mortgage work are called *mortgage bankers*. Some mortgage bankers may offer first-time buyer programs through the state and local government programs. While these large institutions have a lot of clout in working with FHA and VA programs, remember you are dealing with a large bureaucratic company.

In general, mortgage bankers will process, underwrite, loan their own money, and close the loan in their own facility. This may mean a quicker response for the buyer. Here you are dealing directly with the facility that has the money, loans it out, and does all the paperwork in one spot. Mortgage bankers may not make loans for any other purpose other than mortgages or offer other services such as checking accounts.

Direct Lenders

Like portfolio lenders, *direct lenders* fund their own mortgage loans from their own portfolio. In the past, direct lenders always used their own name on the loan documents. Now, even the smallest mortgage broker can arrange to fund a loan in their own name. A direct lender can be one of the biggest lenders to the smallest. Some direct lenders are actually mortgage bankers.

The term *direct lender* can indicate the loan officer at your local bank or the mortgage banker who works in the local mortgage company. Again, this is someone who is lending the money of the institution he or she works for and the mortgage is in the name of that institution. (This is another term for Mortgage Banker that is used in some areas of the country.)

Mortgage Brokers

Loan officers who represent several companies that offer mortgage loans are called *mortgage brokers*. The broker has the flexibility to match a buyer with the right lender. If the buyer is denied a mortgage the broker can merely submit the loan documents to another lender.

Mortgage brokers usually do not lend their own money. They are a middle-man who sets up a buyer with a lender. The broker introduces the potential buyer or borrower to a lender, then the broker handles much of the paperwork between the two. However, as opposed to the other categories, the mortgage broker is not the one who decides if the loan goes through. That is up to the actual lender.

Most brokers work on their own or for a small company. Brokers can usually find mortgages for those with unique borrowing requests, such borrowers who are unable to qualify in other situations.

What Does This Mean for You

In this era where bankers, lenders, and brokers have access to much of the same information, many of the old differences among these categories have faded. Generally, *bankers* are those who work for one lending institution and *brokers* are those who are the middle-men between the borrower and numerous lending institutions.

So what does the first-time buyer do? The first-time buyer should look at both bankers and brokers for a mortgage, compare the service and the rates from every lender, and then chose the one that is financially more beneficial. Your real estate agent can assist you in finding financing.

MORTGAGE TYPES

Following are some of the most common mortgage types. These are not all the mortgage types available, as many lending institutions create their own mortgages.

Adjustable Rate Mortgage (ARM)

An *Adjustable Rate Mortgage (ARM)* has varying interest rates depending on a particular *Index*. The Index is a measurement of the economy that is published by reliable financial groups. Common indexes are U.S. Treasury Bills and the Federal Housing Finance Board's Contract Mortgage Rate. The index is not under the control of the lender, but is driven by the economy in general.

Because the interest rate of an *ARM (Adjusted Rate Mortgage)* is tied to an index, the interest rate, and therefore the monthly payments, are variable. ARMs usually have *caps*, which is the highest that the interest can go up to. However, some caps are only set for the amount the interest can rise annually. This means if the cap is 2% annually with no other restriction, the interest could go up that much every year. Most ARMs recalculate on an annual or semi-annual basis after the first couple of years of payment.

The ARM usually starts out at a very low interest rate, which makes it attractive. However, these low rates are only temporary. A borrower with a small down payment or less than stellar credit rating may be able to qualify for an ARM easier than a fixed rate mortgage because of the low initial payments. ARMs are based on the theory that everyone's salary will increase over successive years.

In times when the interest rates are rising, those with adjustable rate mortgages may find themselves paying a much higher monthly mortgage payment than they had ever expected. This makes getting an ARM a gamble and may trouble some potential home buyers—I know it bothered me.

CLICK ON THIS:

The Internet sites www.fha.com and www.interest.com provide a lot of information on the various types of mortgages and will help you select the one right for you.

So, why do people still get an ARM? The benefits are usually lower costs on the front end. This can mean things like zero closing costs and a very low rate at the beginning of the loan. For many, the uncertainty of the interest rate rising is more than offset by these kinds of up front savings.

Experts now suggest that you should look at an ARM if you expect to move in the first five years. Expecting to move and wanting to move are two different things. Many of us would like to move into a bigger home every five years, but logically know we probably won't. Other people routinely move every couple of years due to their profession or employer. Another group of people who should consider an ARM are those who know that they will definitely have a growing salary that will be able to handle any increases in monthly mortgage payments.

> **ATTORNEY TIP:**
>
> Another type of adjustable rate mortgage loan is the *interest-only* mortgage. With this mortgage, the borrower only pays the interest, which adjusts as the prime rate fluctuates. While this will lower the mortgage payments, you are not gaining equity in the home; you are only paying off the loan. It puts you in the same financial situation as renting an apartment— you will be paying money without having anything to show for it.

Assumable Mortgages

When interest rates for mortgages are going up, a mortgage with a lower interest rate becomes very desirable. One way to get a mortgage at this lower rate is to take-over the existing mortgage on a home. This is called *assuming the mortgage* of another.

Traditionally, both *Federal Housing Administration (FHA)* and *Veterans Administration (VA)* loans are assumable. Other lending institutions may also offer assumable loans. In recent years, mortgage interest rates have continued to decrease. If the country ever goes into another period of inflation that causes the interest rates to increase, we will be looking for assumable mortgages with lower interest rates.

Many people think that assumable mortgages are a thing of the past, but I disagree. Interest rates operate on the "what goes up must come down" and visa-versa principle. Mortgage rates can change due to economic indicators, unrest in the world, or a myriad of other influences. Currently, assumable mortgages are not seen as being desirable, but that may change at any time.

Balloon Mortgages

Balloon mortgages are like ARMs because the interest offered may be low. However, the loan is only financed for a short period of time, with the most common being seven years. At the end of the seven years, the borrower must pay a very large *balloon payment*. Because this lump-sum balloon payment is so large, most borrowers will then be forced to find another mortgage.

Balloon mortgages can be written with various terms, some of which only benefit the lender. Before you consider this type of mortgage, know what the terms are and how they will affect your payments.

> **ATTORNEY TIP:**
>
> As with ARMs, only consider a Balloon mortgage if you expect to move in the first five years.

Balloon mortgages have become the ugly step-sisters of ARMs. They have fallen out of favor with lenders and borrowers. The major problem with Balloons is that at a certain time you will be required to pay off your mortgage loan in one large (balloon) payment, which means you must be able to qualify for yet another mortgage when that Balloon is due. Balloons are usually popular when interest rates are on the rise, but not by much. Balloon mortgages usually have monthly payments similar to those of 30-year-fixed rate mortgages. However, with a 30-year-fixed rate mortgage, you will not be faced with having to remortgage the property when the Balloon comes due.

Buy-Down Mortgage

Some lending institutions offer a method to reduce the interest rate and the monthly mortgage payments. This type of *buy-down mortgage* can require a sum of money up front in addition to a down payment or at the end of the mortgage as in a balloon payment. The calculations differ from place to place. This form of mortgage is usually not used when mortgage interest rates are low.

These types of mortgages are not very popular now. However, you should be aware that lenders frequently come up with special programs to help people who have little money to buy a home or who cannot afford high monthly payments.

If you are offered a special mortgage:

- ask lots of questions;
- ask how it compares to a conventional fixed-rate mortgage; and,
- most importantly, how this mortgage will help you get your home.

Convertible ARM

A *Convertible ARM* is an adjustable rate mortgage that can be changed into a fixed rate mortgage upon a certain event. Usually, the ability to convert the mortgage is tied to mortgage interest rates, a government index amount, or a period of time.

Reread the section on adjustable rate mortgages. This mortgage adds the feature of being able to change to a fixed rate mortgage at some point without the problem of having to requalify for a mortgage loan. That point may be determined by time or by a significant jump in interest rates. This type of mortgage is for those who do not like the uncertainly of the regular ARM, but are in a position to get an ARM. (It is not for everyone and you should heed the warnings in the section on adjustable rate mortgages.)

Deferred Interest Mortgage

A *Deferred Interest Mortgage* allows payments made in the beginning of the mortgage to go primarily toward paying down the principal. This is a variation of the balloon mortgage, because at some point the deferred interest amount will need to be paid.

Deferred interest mortgages are special programs that you may or may not see. Because this is a variation on the balloon mortgage, it has lost its popularity. Again, if your lender offers you a special program mortgage—ask lots of questions; ask how it compares to a conventional fixed-rate mortgage; and, most importantly, how this mortgage will help you get your home.

Faith Financing

This is a very new type of mortgage that is being offered to those whose faith will not allow them to participate in any business transaction which involves charging or paying interest. This type of mortgage is offered on a very limited basis in areas where banks and financial institutions are addressing the needs of Muslims and some other faiths that have a ban on paying interest for religious reasons.

Basically, instead of the buyer getting a mortgage from a bank and paying back the bank principal and interest payment, the bank buys the house and immediately sells it to the buyer at a *sizable markup*. The word *interest* is not used or calculated. The bank makes its money in the *markup*. The *markup price* is about what the buyer would be paying for the house in a conventional 30-year mortgage that includes both principal and interest.

To the world, this mortgage appears to be a conventional 30-year mortgage, but to members of the Muslim faith, this is a tremendous step toward honoring their religion and being able to own their own home. In Chicago, Devon Bank and Broadway Bank began "Sharilah Sanctioned Home Buying Programs" in 2004. This has been very well received by both the Muslim community and the mortgage lender's community.

In January 2005, Devon Bank began offering this product in the following states outside of Illinois:
- Alaska
- Arkansas
- California
- Georgia
- Indiana
- Kentucky
- Michigan
- Missouri
- New Hampshire

- Tennessee
- Texas
- Wisconsin

In addition, it hopes to accept requests soon, from the following states:

- Arizona
- Colorado
- Connecticut
- District of Columbia
- Florida
- Idaho
- Kansas
- Louisiana
- Maryland
- Minnesota
- Nebraska
- Nevada
- New Mexico
- New York
- North Carolina
- Ohio
- Oregon
- South Dakota
- Virginia
- Wyoming

Fixed-Rate Mortgage

A *Fixed-Rate Mortgage* is the most popular type of mortgage. The interest stays the same throughout the entire term of the mortgage—usually fifteen or thirty years. The monthly mortgage payments are the same amount over the term of the mortgage. This fixed amount allows the borrower to budget easier and protects the borrower against inflation.

In the real word, a fixed-rate mortgage is the *gold standard* that all other mortgages are compared to. If you can only understand one type of mortgage it should be the fixed rate. Those who lend money for mortgages will always offer this type of loan along with some of the other specialty mortgages we have covered.

This is the mortgage for people, like me, who do not want to gamble with interest rates that are set by the government or with the possibility that I may make more money sometime in the future. A fixed rate is just that—the interest rate cannot change over the life of the mortgage.

So, what happens when current mortgage rates become much lower than your fixed-rate mortgage—you refinance. Several years ago I was able to refinance that 9% fixed-rate mortgage into a nice 5% fixed-rate mortgage. At that time, I also was able to get some equity out of my home to add an addition. Fixed-rate mortgages are the dependable ones—my choice for first-time home buyers.

15-Year Mortgage vs. 30-Year Mortgage

A 15-year mortgage has a lower, overall cost due to the lower interest rate. The short term of the loan means that the home owner will build equity in the home quicker and the debt will only last for fifteen years. On the negative side, 15-year mortgage means higher monthly payments. The lower interest rate means a lesser amount can be deducted from your annual income tax.

A 30-year mortgage has lower monthly payments. This type of mortgage is easier to qualify for and allows the home owner to take more tax deductions over the length of the mortgage. Of course, the big difference is the length of time you will be paying mortgage payments. Because this type of mortgage has a higher interest rate, the home buyer will actually pay more for the home than if the buyer got a 15-year mortgage.

Subprime Mortgage

Subprime mortgage is a confusing term because many lenders use the word *subprime* to indicate borrowers with poor credit, borrowers who refuse to let their income be verified, or borrowers who want a larger loan than the value of the property. Subprime loans will cost the borrower more. That additional cost will be in the points paid or in the interest paid on the loan. Subprimes may also carry hefty prepayment penalties, meaning that if you sell the home before the mortgage is paid off completely, you will be charged a penalty. Subprimes may also include expensive add-ons such as a required life insurance policy on the borrower.

Financial advisers suggest that if a person has poor credit, he or she should first attempt to repair credit history before accepting a subprime mortgage. Also, these borrowers should look for special loan programs that will lower the interest rate after the borrower has made a history of paying the mortgage on time. In addition, some government assistance for first-time home buyers may be able to help. If you are offered a subprime mortgage, ask why, and then be prepared to contact several other mortgage lenders to see what they are willing to offer you.

Wraparound Mortgage

The *Wraparound Mortgage* is the result of an agreement between the seller and the buyer. The buyer pays a certain number of mortgage payments for the seller, plus the buyer obtains his own mortgage. This may also be called *seller financing*.

Buyers who do not qualify for a mortgage on the full selling price of the home benefit from this. The buyer pays the old mortgage for a period of time and then applies for his or her own mortgage on the lower selling price.

If you are considering doing this type of transaction, get the help of a real estate attorney to draft a contract between you and the seller.

A wraparound mortgage can be used in a family sale where one family member is selling property to another and the seller wants to help with the financing. This is not a common first-time home buyers selection. (It should always be entered into cautiously and with professional assistance.)

ATTORNEY TIP:
There are many potential pitfalls with a Wraparound Mortgage. Do not attempt to work with this type of mortgage without the assistance of an experienced attorney.

Zero Down Mortgage

Zero Down Mortgages are also called *100 Percent Loans* and are a creation of the mortgage industry in order to bring home ownership to more people. For some lenders, these mortgages require that the borrowers complete a form of credit counseling class. Other lenders help the borrowers get grants to help with the total mortgage costs.

Conventional wisdom has always been that a person needed a 20% down payment in order to purchase a home. With home prices rising much more than salaries, the mortgage industry has finally come up with a product that debunks that 20% myth. In addition, this loan requires less of a credit history, which will appeal to younger buyers. The types of income that qualify for this type of loan may also be broader, including the newly employed, the part-timers, and those receiving money from another country.

Zero down mortgages can have problems. Because there is no down payment, the borrower spends many years without having built up significant equity in the home. For this reason, only those who intend to stay in a home for many years should consider a zero down mortgage. There may also be a tendency to buy a more expensive home than can be afforded, because a large down payment is not needed.

NECESSARY DOCUMENTS TO APPLY FOR A MORTGAGE

Once you decide on a lender, you will be asked to fill out a mortgage application and provide financial information to the lender. Most lenders ask for certain financial records when you apply for a mortgage. These records fall into two categories: income and expenses. Following is a list of what most lenders require; however, your particular lender may require more information.

Income:
- pay check stubs;
- W-2s for the past two years;

- income tax returns;
- proof of alimony or child support (divorce decree);
- dividends;
- investments;
- bank statements;
- an estimated value of your other assets;
- location of checking and savings accounts; and,
- copy of document indicating how much earnest money you put down.

Expenses:
Lenders will request their own credit report on you, but may also require that you list all your outstanding debts.

Other:
- the address where you lived for the last two years;
- your employer and salary over the last five years;
- number of people who will live in the home; and,
- names of closest relative not living with you.

Remember to check with your lender to see exactly what paperwork is required. While the above list is long, it likely does not cover every situation.

INTERNET MORTGAGES
We have all seen the obnoxious man who pitches Internet mortgages on TV commercials. The question is "Does this really work?" The answer is "sometimes."

While doing your research on the Internet, you will run across many ads for mortgages. You probably should be more cautious with an Internet mortgage com-

CLICK ON THIS:
One way to protect yourself from mortgage fraud (Internet or otherwise) is to learn the warning signs of fraud in lending. The best website for this information is www.stopmortgagefraud.com

pany than you would be in buying software from an Internet company. Do research and ask questions. You may also want to contact the Better Business Bureau or State Consumer Fraud Department. Because this a new area of business, there is not a lot known about the stability of the Internet mortgage companies.

YOUR MORTGAGE IS APPROVED, NOW LOCK-IN THAT RATE

Once you find out that your mortgage has been approved, the next step is to lock-in the interest rate. Get a written agreement that guarantees a specific interest rate on a mortgage, provided that the loan is closed within a certain period of time. That period of time usually is 60 to 90 days, and the date that this guarantee expires is commonly called the *lock-in date*.

What this really means is that the lender is offering you a mortgage at a particular interest rate, and that offer will only stay open for a period of time (the 60 to 90 days). If you are unable to proceed to the closing (where you actually buy the house) within this period of time, you will probably not get this mortgage. In an economy where interest rates are going up, this becomes very important as borrowers who are unable to proceed to the closing may end up with mortgages with higher interest rates than were originally applied for. This type of problem can cause surprises in the actual amount of your monthly mortgage payment.

YOUR MORTGAGE IS NOT APPROVED

What happens if you have done all the hard work in choosing a lender, gone through the torture of filling out the mortgage application, and you are not approved?

First, try to find out why you were denied. Was the property appraised lower than the amount you wanted to borrow? In that case, maybe you should rethink your house selection. If you still want that property, you will need to increase your down payment in order to reduce the amount borrowed.

This is a serious warning. The lender has contracted with a professional to appraise the property. If that professional sees problems with the house, perhaps those problems are something that have been missed. Be wary of proceeding with such a purchase. Make sure that you know why the appraiser valued the property that way, for example, is it the structure or the neighborhood?

Other common reasons for being turned down for a mortgage are:

- a poor credit report or
- insufficient income for the amount of debt.

ATTORNEY TIP:

You just got a call from the lending institution that you were not approved for your mortgage. How do you respond?

The most important thing:

Ask why you were turned down. If the person on the phone cannot tell you why, ask to speak to someone who can tell you, even if that means the bank president.

In order to determine what your next step is, you need to know why you were turned down.

Again, try to get as much information on this denial as possible. Perhaps there was an error on the credit report or you neglected to include all the income you receive. If there are no obvious errors, perhaps the lending institution is seeing a problem in your ability to make that level of payments. You may need to rethink the price of homes you are looking at. You can always go to another lender or increase the down payment so that the loan amount is lower.

A *mortgage broker* can present you to many suitable lenders. The broker knows which lenders accept "slightly tarnished" borrowers. If you decide to work with a broker, choose a reputable one. Ask for references, and **do not** pay any fees to the broker to handle your loan application.

CLICK ON THIS:

The HUD Internet site provides a wealth of information on how to battle discrimination in housing. View this at: www.hud.gov

or

www.ginniemae.gov

Sometimes the lending institution denies someone a mortgage due to discrimination for such things as race, sex, ethnicity, religion, etc. If you feel you may have been discriminated against, you may be able to get assistance from the local HUD office.

POINTS

In obtaining a mortgage you will hear the term *points* or *discount points*. This is an odd term for a totally illogical concept. The point in a mortgage is equivalent to 1% of the loan amount. The borrower usually pays this amount when he or she takes out the mortgage. For example, for a mortgage on a $100,000 home, each point would cost $1,000. The points would reduce the loan's interest rate by 0.125%.

The mortgage lenders use points as a type of up front discount and tie them to the interest rate of the mortgage. Using our $100,000 home example, the lender might offer a mortgage with a rate of 8.0% and no points, or 7.875% with one point, or 7.75% with two points. Points can make a mortgage rate appear low, while in reality the actual amount paid to the lender is higher because of a large number of points that must be paid.

Points are usually an up front payment made at the time you purchase the house. This is *in addition* to the amount of down payment and other closing costs. However, because of borrower's demand, many lenders will allow the borrower to finance all or part of the point's amount over the term of the mortgage.

Should you pay points up front or finance them? The answer is up to the individual. Paying more toward the mortgage up front will lower monthly payments. However, paying more at closing leaves the home buyer with less cash at a time when the costs of moving into a new home can be overwhelming.

chapter nine:

Government Agencies and the Secondary Mortgage Market

HUD, FHA, Fannie Mae, Ginnie Mae, and *Freddie Mac* are names batted around by lenders and real estate professionals as though everyone knows what they are. They all have to do with financing and the very, very lucrative business of providing mortgages.

HOUSING AND URBAN DEVELOPMENT AGENCY (HUD)

HUD's primary purpose is to provide mortgage insurance through the *Federal Housing Administration (FHA).* The FHA will pay the mortgage if the borrower cannot. HUD offers special home buying programs for which you may qualify. Many of these are offered in conjunction with your local government. These programs provide some financial assistance and financial counseling for those who find themselves in trouble because of debt.

HUD provides education and information for everyone who wants to buy a home. HUD may

CLICK ON THIS:

As the name suggests, HUD is a department of the US government. HUD has numerous plans. HUD's website is a wealth of information to anyone who is considering buying a home. Spend some time reviewing information at:
www.hud.gov
(It is well worth it.)

ATTORNEY TIP:

If you are considering buying a HUD home, you will need a real estate agent to process a bid on the home. You may also want to hire an attorney who specializes in this type of transaction.

even be able to pick up some of your closing costs if you buy a HUD home.

A HUD home is a *foreclosure* from someone who had a HUD mortgage and was not able to keep up with the payments. The homes range in price, but can suffer from neglect or be in less desirable neighborhoods. HUD homes are sold on an *as is* basis, which means that HUD will not correct defects even if they are obvious. This is why HUD homes are sold at such a low price. HUD does not have to spend money to fix them.

Before you buy a HUD home, make sure you know what you are doing, especially in repairs. HUD lists these foreclosures at their offices, on their web site, and in local papers.

HUD also helps those have been discriminated in housing to get justice. Additionally, HUD assists the homeless and low-income people by providing vouchers for those with below poverty income and by supporting many nonprofit organizations.

Federal Housing Administration (FHA)

The FHA is actually an agency of HUD. FHA insures mortgage loans for HUD. If you apply for a mortgage that is insured by the FHA, it is called an FHA loan. Both the property and you will be required to qualify.

FHA loans allow a smaller down payment and come in a variety of loan types from the standard fixed-rate to those with interest rates that vary depending upon a financial index. Besides low down payments, an FHA loan places limits on fees and closing costs—all of which are financial benefits for the first-time home buyer.

CLICK ON THIS:

Visit www.hud.gov or www.fha.com for more specific information on FHA loans.

Ginnie Mae

The *Government National Mortgage Association* or *Ginnie Mae* is a government-owned corporation under HUD. Its purpose is to provide assistance to low and moderate income home buyers. As with Fannie Mae, Ginnie Mae is able to generate profits by investing in the secondary mortgage market. The difference is that Ginnie Mae only deals with government-backed securities. This organization also provides money for low cost, affordable housing and community development.

CLICK ON THIS:

For more information about government-backed securities loans, visit the following site:

www.ginniemae.gov

FANNIE MAE

The *Federal National Mortgage Association (FNMA)* or *Fannie Mae* was created by Congress to bolster the housing industry in the 1920s. Now it is a private corporation that receives no government funding.

It is the largest source of home mortgage funds. It receives its profits from investments in the secondary mortgage market. It is also a leader in providing funds for affordable housing and investments in community development, especially in economically disadvantaged areas.

CLICK ON THIS:

For more information about Fannie Mae loans, visit:

www.fanniemae.com

More information for the first-time home buyer can be found at:

www.freddiemac.com

FREDDIE MAC

The *Federal National Mortgage Association (FNMA)* or *Freddie Mac* is a congressionally created corporation that is in the business of buying and selling mortgages. This ultimately puts more funds for mortgages into the market place. Like its sisters Fannie Mae and Ginnie Mae, Freddie Mac provides mortgage money in areas that are economically disadvantaged and has been successful in lowering interest rates.

GOVERNMENT AGENCIES AND THE FIRST-TIME HOME BUYER

As a first-time home buyer, you are probably wondering if HUD, FHA, Ginnie Mae, Fannie Mae, and Freddie Mac will have any effect on your mortgage. In a global sense, any home buyer should know that there is a secondary market that buys and sells mortgages. This secondary market makes profits that in turn are used to create mortgage assistance programs so that more people like you can own their own home.

Mortgage assistance programs are available to first time home buyers who may come face-to-face with the HUD, FHA, Ginnie Mae, Fannie Mae, and Freddie Mac. One of these agencies may be able provide a mortgage assistance program that is right for you. Each agency handles different programs and there is no one agency that is better than the other. Therefore, you may need to examine each one to determine if any one agency currently has assistance that you can use.

In addition, the current presidential administration has supported new government assistance programs and has requested that Congress look seriously at more mortgage reform. All of this is in an effort to make home ownership more affordable. HUD officials are expecting a new, meaningful reform package that will create several fixed-costs mortgage plans that may help first-time home buyers.

In 2004, the *American Dream Downpayment Assistance Act* was

CLICK On THIS:

For more information on the American Dream Downpayment Assistance Act go to www.hud.gov under the affordable housing assistance programs.

passed for fiscal years 2004 through 2007. This Act provides funds to first-time home buyers who are purchasing single-family housing (also includes condominiums). Another HUD program is the *Teacher Next Door Program*. It encourages teachers to buy homes in low to moderate income areas.

Right now the FHA has a program that only requires a 3% down payment for qualified buyers and Fannie Mae has a zero percent down program. There are many programs that will assist with down payments for first-time home buyers. Do not rely on your lender or real estate agent to tell you about these programs. Take the time to visit the websites listed and see if you qualify for any of the assistance programs run by these agencies.

SECONDARY MORTGAGE MARKET

If you are wondering how these companies can afford to stay in business, it is because of investments in the *secondary mortgage market*. To explain this in the easiest of terms, think back to the mortgage contract that a borrower signs with the lender. This contract says that the borrower will pay back the amount loaned, plus a percentage of interest. If the borrower cannot pay back the loan, then the lender takes back the home.

Generally, the loan is not for the full market value of the house. Also, real estate values usually increase over time. Therefore, if the lender does have to take the house back (foreclosure) he or she can resell it for the amount owed on the loan, plus profit.

In addition, the two major parts of a mortgage—the *principal* amount and the *interest*—are paid in *disproportionate* amounts. In the beginning, the mortgage payment is almost all interest with a small amount going against principal. As time goes on, the amount of money that goes against the principal increases, as the amount going against the interest decreases. The majority of the lender's profit comes from the interest. In the way mortgage payments are structured, the lender gets his or her profit first, so in case of a foreclosure the lender has already received a good portion of the expected profit.

ATTORNEY TIP:

The Internet sites mentioned in this chapter attempt to explain the complex world of the secondary mortgage market. While it is not essential that you understand this method of high finance in order to buy a home, you should understand the meaning of the terms that real estate professionals use in their discussions with you.

The mortgage contract is valuable because the holder of this contract gets expected profits, even if there is a foreclosure. The mortgage becomes a thing of value because of what it represents and because it can be bought and sold. Some lenders package or group a certain number of mortgages together and sell them through companies like Freddie Mac. By packaging mortgages in groups the lender can put mortgages made to those with shaky credit history in a group with mortgages for people that are expected to make every payment. That way the mortgage lender gets all of its profit, less discounts, up front. The sale gives the lender more cash to make more mortgages.

Companies like Freddie Mac repackage the mortgages that they bought from multiple lenders and sell this new package to another mortgage lender. This can go on for as many mortgage lenders and companies who invest in the secondary market. Freddie Mac also sells *notes* (financial loans) that are backed by multiple mortgage loans to people who invest in securities. Freddie Mac takes its profits and invests them in purchasing more loans, thus putting more available mortgage money into the economy.

The fact is that as each company or lender makes a sale, it gets funds to invest in more mortgages. This keeps the flow of money for mortgages available, even when the economy has problems.

For the borrower, having your mortgage sold usually only means that you send your payments to a different address. Of course, each lender will provide different services. One may provide envelopes and coupons for each payment; another may send a monthly bill. If a borrower learns that his or her mortgage has been sold, it is the borrower's responsibility to learn what the new lender requires.

chapter ten

Additional Sources of Money

The fact is that the higher the down payment you make, the lower the monthly mortgage payment will be. Since a mortgage payment is not just the amount to repay the loan, (but also usually includes home insurance and taxes which both increase over the years), the less you have to pay on the loan the better. Besides funds for down payments, you may be able to get help with low interest loans or community funds.

LIVING TOGETHER

Can two live as cheaply as one? That depends on how you live, but two working people can usually come up with a larger down payment and can handle a larger monthly mortgage payment than one person.

The biggest potential problem with buying a house with another person (that you are not legally tied to) is what happens to the home if the two of you decide to part ways.

For example, a married couple purchases a home together. If both work, then both of their salaries are taken in to account when obtaining a mortgage. Because they are legally married, they will or should purchase the home in *joint tenancy*. This prevents one person from selling the house without the permission of the other. Also, if one person dies, the house goes directly to the other. If they divorce, the house is either given to one of the parties or sold and the profits split between the two people.

When two unmarried people decide to buy a home together, in order for both salaries to be considered, then both people must be listed as coborrowers, both legally liable to pay the mortgage loan, and both of their credit histories will be looked at. Also, when two unmarried people buy a home there are several ways that they can own it. For the maximum protection for both parties, the unmarried couple should purchase the home in *joint tenancy* in order to get the benefits as discussed earlier.

Many lenders assume that those who are not married will purchase as *tenants in common*. This means that each person can do what they want with their 50% of the house. One partner can sell his or her 50% ownership without permission of the other or one partner can will his or her 50% to whomever they want. This gives little protection to the remaining partner.

If you are considering living with another person, you may want to visit an attorney to get the financial issues addressed in a contract. Just because you are not legally married, does not mean that you will be exempt from those nasty financial fights that married people have. And, just like married people, you may part ways. Buying a home is a big step and you owe it to yourself and your partner to protect your financial health.

Roommates

You may decide that you need an additional source of income, but you are not ready to commit to marriage or living together. Maybe you should consider a roommate.

If you have been successfully renting an apartment with other people and now you want to buy a home, consider making that purchase and then renting part of your home to your current roommates. You and your roommates have already been living together amicably so there should be no surprises.

If you do rent to roommates, you are now not only a home owner, but a landlord. Being a landlord has certain legal requirements and responsibilities. Protect yourself and your property by entering into a legal landlord/tenant agreement that spells out who does what; who is responsible for damage; and, how to end the lease.

FRIENDS AND RELATIVES

One place to get money to increase your down payment is from your relatives. Parents may be willing to give you an amount against a future inheritance, a substantial gift, or even a loan. Along with parents, perhaps a relative may be willing to loan you some money, especially if you sign a *promissory note* that includes a payback with interest.

Many young couples who are about to be married make a deal with their parents to forego the expensive wedding reception *in lieu* of that amount of money toward a down payment. I have been at weddings where the bride and groom requested cash toward their home instead of gifts or where the newlyweds put the money they would have spent on a lavish honeymoon into their down payment.

Example:

Ginny and Leo wanted to get a house within one year after they married. Ginny had saved enough money for a very expensive designer wedding dress and her parents offered to pay for the wedding reception. Leo's parents had very little extra money, but offered to pay for the honeymoon. Ginny and Leo decided that they wanted a home more than a big wedding reception. They went to their relatives and asked for help.

The family offered to all pitch in to give the young couple an old fashioned wedding reception. Uncle Bob donated the Moose hall. Aunt Deedee, Aunt Edith, and Aunt Marian cooked the food. Uncle George got a friend to donate the wedding cake and Uncle Marty provided cases of beer and wine.

Ginny wore her grandmother's wedding dress. They honeymooned in a cottage owned by Leo's cousin, Sam. By including the entire family Ginny and Leo were able to save enough money for a sizeable down payment on their dream home.

RETIREMENT SAVINGS

If your employer has a 401(k), stock incentive, or savings plan, you may be able to use part of that money for your down payment. However, beware of the taxes. Before you make plans to cash-in this retirement nest egg, know what taxes and penalties you will be responsible for. Besides the potential for a sizeable penalty or tax bill, your employer may also have restrictions on how much you can reduce this fund and when you can do it. It may become a loan that will be deducted from your paycheck.

A word about cashing in your retirement funds. A good (sizable) down payment is definitely the way to go, but if it means that you have no retirement savings and nothing except the house to fall back on, make sure you know all consequences. Retirement funds are great sources for major emergencies, death, severe illness, and for that time when you no longer want to or can work. Weigh this before you deplete your entire retirement survival fund.

Many senior citizens are forced to sell their beloved homes because social security payments do not cover normal expenses plus property tax increases. Keep some savings for the senior time of your life.

Some companies provide credit unions for employees. A credit union may be able to handle your mortgage or provide you with a low interest loan for your down payment.

LOCAL GOVERNMENT ASSISTANCE

Some states, counties, and cities offer financial assistance for home buyers under special circumstances. Usually this money is specifically for those areas where the structures are run down and the city wants to rebuild the neighborhood. These are typically the homes that have been abused and neglected. Low cost loans are offered if the buyer commits to rehabbing the structure and then using it as their primary residence. Along with city money for rehabbing, structures that hold certain significance (usually historical) or are in a historical landmark area may qualify for assistance from preservation groups.

Example:

The City of Chicago recently held a seminar for the first-time home-buyer. The seminar was directed toward the buyer who would rehab or fix up a city property. Besides an overview of how much work it takes to rehab a house, the city brought in both lending institutions that were willing to write low cost mortgages and federal agencies that also could provide funding.

The state of Illinois, through the Illinois State Treasurer, has a statewide program called *Our Own Home* that provides assistance for first-time home buyers. The home buyers must meet certain criteria to qualify for this program, but those that qualify will receive financial help from the state. This help is not in the form of money, but in the form of the state backing the home buyer that may not qualify for regular mortgages. Even if you do not live in Illinois, the Internet site **www.ourownhome.net** can be helpful as it contains Mortgage Calculators, Mortgage Glossary, and a list of Consumer Counseling Centers.

California assists home buyers in certain communities with various financial incentives. Buyers employed as teachers are among those eligible. For example, teachers may be eligible to receive a 50% discount on qualified homes for a down payment of $100.

The federal government also has assistance programs. For example, the *Department of Housing and Urban Development* (HUD) has a program called *Community Building* that may provide down payment assistance. Your state housing authorities may also have programs that will offer some assistance.

Again, the Internet is your best source for information on national or federal programs. Your state may have departments for housing authority or resident benefits that can assist you in finding state run programs. Local city government offices should have information on local programs. Real estate professionals should be able to assist you in this within the area that they serve.

ZERO DOWN PAYMENT

Yes, you read that right. Putting nothing down on a 100% mortgage. There are some lenders who are offering to finance 100% of the cost of a home. As with any too-good-to-be-true offer, there are some restrictions.

First, both the buyer and the property need to qualify. For the buyer, this may mean a totally spotless credit record and a really good, secure job. The property will need to be accurately appraised at an amount that is higher than the selling price. (This does happen frequently, especially in an area where house prices are showing steady increases.) Second, the buyer will be required to purchase *Private Mortgage Insurance* or *PMI*.

NOTE: *Many lenders require PMI purchase for anyone who puts down less than 20%. PMI charges an additional amount per month to insure that the mortgage will be paid.*

Example:

Currently, in the Chicago area, the Private Mortgage Insurance monthly payment on a house which sells for $100,000 is approximately $65 per month with a 5% down payment. The same house is approximately $88 per month with a zero down payment on the mortgage.

Zero down payment loans are available in areas where the price of homes are increasing. Experts predict that this type of creative financing will continue to expand as long as housing values continue to be higher than mortgage values.

LOW INTEREST MORTGAGES

Another way to approach this is to get a mortgage that requires less of a down payment. Read Chapters 9 and 11 on government-insured mortgages, *FHA,* and *VA loans.* Both of these require a lower down payment than *conventional mortgages.* There are also some private insurance companies that may allow you to finance your down payment. Real estate agents and brokers should be able to tell you if this is available in your area.

RENTING WITH AN OPTION TO BUY

One way a first-time home buyer can build up a down payment is to get into a *rent with option to buy* agreement. This type of arrangement may be nonexistent where you live. You may want to seek the help of a real estate agent to find this type of situation.

In a *rent with an option to buy*, a percentage of your monthly rent is considered part of the down payment to purchase the home. The rental contract will last for a period of time and at the end of that time the renter then decides if he or she wants to buy. If the decision is not to buy, the renter does not get that percentage of the rent back.

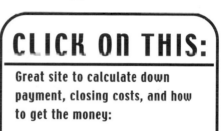

CLICK ON THIS:

Great site to calculate down payment, closing costs, and how to get the money:

www.freddiemac.com

Example:

Sally wanted to buy a new condominium close to her office, but she had saved only a small amount for a down payment. The condominium owner contracted with Sally to rent with an option to buy at the end of three years. The rent amount was a little higher than what Sally would be paying for similar condos. Sally's landlord would credit 25% of each monthly rent payment toward a down payment. At the end of three years, Sally had a credited $15,000 down payment from her rent.

Renting with an option to buy has its pluses and minuses.

Pluses

This type of renting is a forced savings program that will make you put aside money for a down payment. If you have credit problems, this type of program will probably make it easier for you to get a mortgage on your home. It is also a way for you to try-on living in that home and in that neighborhood. The rent may be higher than just renting, so you may also be trying to live with a mortgage.

Minuses

If you rent with an option to buy, make sure to get all the terms in writing. Because you will probably be paying a higher rent, you should have a legal document that clearly spells out how much of each month's rent goes towards the down payment and how much goes toward the rent.

You may find at the end of the lease term that you do not want the buy the home. Unfortunately, that usually means that all of the extra rent you put into that *option* is gone. It is rare that the extra rent will be returned if you decide not to buy.

chapter eleven:
VA Guaranteed Home Loans

One of the benefits of serving our country in the military is the *Veterans Administration Home Loan Guaranty Services.* This is part of the package of veteran's benefits and services that is administered by the Veterans Administration.

CLICK ON THIS:

Website www.va.gov has all the information you will need for a VA loan and lets you download VA forms to apply for the loan.

A VA guaranteed home loan is a regular mortgage or loan made by a lender. The lender can be a mortgage company, bank, or savings and loan. The big difference is that the Veterans Administration (VA) guarantees that the loan will be repaid if the borrower does not make the mortgage payments. This encourages lenders to offer VA loans by limiting their financial risk.

QUALIFYING

To obtain a VA guaranteed loan, the veteran must first qualify. Length of service and the type of discharge determine this. Your local VA office will have the details of qualification. See **Appendix H** on pages 283–287 for specific details of qualification for a VA guaranteed loan.

Generally, service qualifications require active duty of at least ninety days during wartime, 181 days during peacetime, or six years in the selected reserves or National Guard. Discharge from service must not be for dishonorable conditions. Widows and widowers of those killed in action and the spouses of POWs and MIAs may also qualify. (Children of veterans do not qualify for this entitlement.)

Because the details of qualification are very extensive, you should review them on the Internet (at **www.va.gov** in the home loan section) or by requesting VA Pamphlet 26-4 "VA-Guaranteed Home Loans for Veterans" and 26-6 "To the Home-Buying Veteran" from your local VA office. If you are currently on active duty or in the reserves, you can obtain all the information from your benefits coordinator.

If you qualify for a VA loan, the next step is to file VA form 26-1880 *Request of Certificate of Eligibility* (see **Appendix G** on page 280). Many lenders can provide this form. The completed form plus copies of your discharge papers will be submitted to the Veteran's Administration for processing.

If you are currently in the military, you are required to submit a Statement of Service. Statements of Service identify you by social security number, date of entry into the military, and the name of the base or command. It is signed by the appropriate officer, usually the CO, adjutant, personnel officer, or higher headquarters (depending on the branch of service.) The VA will process your request and, if you are indeed eligible, will send you the Certificate.

VA APPRAISAL

Besides the borrower qualifying to be eligible for a VA guaranteed loan, the property must also qualify. The property qualifies on the basis of a VA appraisal. A VA appraisal estimates the value of the property. The appraisal results in a *Certificate of Reasonable Value* or *CRV*. The loan amount cannot exceed the CRV.

The request for a VA appraisal can come from anyone who is involved with the sale. Many lenders automatically do this for the military. You can request a VA appraisal by completing form VA 26-1805 "Request for Determination of Reasonable Value." The form is then sent to the nearest VA office or loan guarantee division. The VA assigns and pays for the appraisal. (A sample of this form with instructions begins in **Appendix G** on pages 272–275.)

This appraisal is similar to that for HUD or FHA. The VA states that the primary reason for this appraisal is to make sure that the loan does not exceed the value of the house. It is not an inspection and does not guarantee that the property is free of problems. In fact, the VA encourages the borrower to get the house inspected prior to committing to an offer. In actual practice, this appraisal does help the borrower determine if the house is really worth the asking price.

> **ATTORNEY TIP:**
>
> The most important requirement for a VA loan is for the veteran to qualify. Those who have been discharged for reasons other than "Honorably" will not even be considered for this benefit.

My own experience with VA loans came when my parents were about to buy what looked like the most beautiful home ever built. Everything looked perfect and we all anticipated a move. That was until the VA appraiser refused to give the property a CRV.

The appraiser found extensive water damage hidden behind brand new wallpaper, plus blatant building code violations. The appraiser would not give the property a CRV unless the owner reduced the price or paid for repairs. (We didn't get the house.)

THE LOAN

The loan itself can be up to a maximum of $240,000 depending on the borrower's income, debts, and the appraised value of the house. VA guaranteed loans can be obtained for buying a house, townhouse, manufactured home, or condominium. This includes building a home and purchasing, plus rehabbing an existing home at the same time. A VA guaranteed loan can also be used to install certain

ATTORNEY TIP:

If you are considering a VA loan, be sure to check for procedures and processes through your local VA office.

energy efficient features or to refinance an existing home loan.

Veterans earn entitlements to VA guaranteed loans of a certain amount. This amount can be spread across two actual mortgages. In some instances, veterans who have prior outstanding VA loans may still be able to get a second loan. Because the entitlement amount has been increased over the years, you may want to check with the VA, even if you already have a VA loan.

Generally, if your prior VA loan was foreclosed on, you will not be able to get another VA loan until that first amount is repaid to the VA. This can also be the case when a veteran's first VA loan was assumed and the person who assumed the loan defaulted.

Approval
Loan approval by the lender for a VA loan is almost identical to that for any other loan, just with a few extra steps.
- The applicant must be eligible and prove it by the Certificate of Eligibility.
- The loan must be for an eligible purpose.
- The veteran must intend to live in the property as his or her primary residence.
- The veteran must be a satisfactory credit risk (the income must be stable and sufficient to meet the current debt plus the loan payments).
- The property must pass a VA appraisal and receive a CRV.

Advantages
A VA guaranteed loan is a good deal for the veteran. While obtaining a VA guaranteed loan on a particular property may take longer than conventional mortgage approval, it is worth the inconvenience for the advantages to the veteran.

Some of the positives of a VA guaranteed loan for the veteran:
- right to repay the loan at anytime without penalty;
- personal loan servicing and financial counseling to avoid foreclosure;
- a small or no down payment is required (as long as the value of the property and the income of the buyer is sufficient);
- low debt-to-income ratio;
- the loan maximum can be 100% of the property value;
- the interest rate can be negotiated;
- monthly mortgage insurance is not required;
- loan is assumable;
- traditional fixed rate with a choice of repayment plans; and,
- limited closing costs to the buyer.

Disadvantages

There are some real estate professionals who prefer not to use a VA loan because of the disadvantages to the seller. Remember this is not a hand out or charity, it is part of a big "thank you for your service" that is well earned by those in the military. If you qualify for and want to use the VA guaranteed loan entitlement, make your real estate agent aware of your intention at the beginning of your search. There are many real estate agents who are willing to cooperate in obtaining a VA loan.

That being said, a large percentage of sellers will list their property with a provision that they are not interested in selling to someone who is using FHA or VA guaranteed loans. In an economy or a neighborhood where homes sell fast, VA loans like FHA loans are not always welcome.

There are several reasons for this dislike of VA and FHA loans. One of the primary reasons is the extra time both of these loans take to close. In some areas of the country where homes do not stay on the market longer than a week, the private mortgage lenders have stepped up their service and can close the deal in about a month.

Besides the additional time it takes to close a VA or FHA loan, it also costs the seller more in closing costs because of the limitations on what closing costs the buyer pays. If the buyer wants the home and the seller does not want to accept a VA or FHA loan, a way to get around the additional closing costs is for the buyer to reimburse the seller for those out of ordinary closing costs in a separate deal.

Both VA and FHA require appraisals that may uncover something about the property which the sellers need to fix. The VA and FHA require that the house be appraised at an amount that is equal to the amount of the loan. While these appraisals result in determining the reasonable value of the home, the home must also adhere to certain construction standards set by VA and FHA.

One interesting thing has come out of the construction standards which the VA and FHA use. More conventional lenders are beginning to look at appraisals for these same items before they agree to write a mortgage on the home.

Even home insurance providers are requiring that certain items meet these tough standards before obtaining full insurance. My own home insurance company would not insure the garage on my property until the exterior walls were repaired, a door put on, and the structure reinforced. The same restrictions that both FHA and VA would have used.

Section Five:
The Buying Process

chapter twelve:
The Legal Side of Real Estate

Real estate transactions are getting more and more complex. More states, counties, and cities are enacting laws which effect what is required to sell the property and how much it will cost. Besides the complexity of the laws, the forms required just to make an offer and those used to apply for a mortgage have become so detailed that it would take hours just to read every word.

This chapter also provides an overview about the common ways to hold title. Each state has enacted laws that govern how title is held. Real estate attorneys are familiar with the requirements of both state and local laws and can advise you accordingly.

DO I NEED AN ATTORNEY

Before you sign an offer on a home, you may want an attorney to review it to make sure that your interests are protected. If you don't have an attorney before you sign the offer, you may ask to have a clause inserted in the offer contract that will allow an attorney to review the document and cancel the contract if there are items detrimental to your interests. Some areas of the country have a legal time period that is allowed for attorney review, the time period is usually a few days.

If you have obtained an attorney at the beginning of your home search, he or she can negotiate the agreement for sale, review the documents, and may be able to hold your escrow amount.

If you obtain an attorney after the offer contract has been accepted by the seller, the attorney can review the documents of the loan, perform title searches, order inspections, obtain land surveys, inform you as to how much money you must bring to closing, review all documents, and assist you in the closing so that you are signing the proper documents.

Many attorneys specialize in real estate closings. Most real estate agents have a list of referrals or you can obtain a referral from your local bar association.

TITLE SEARCHES AND SURVEYS

Depending on the area of the county, your attorney may be the one who orders a *title search* and *survey* of the property. A title search looks at the previous owners of this property and possible liens against the property to determine if the current owner really has the right to sell the property. It determines whether there are any outstanding debts that must be settled before the property can be sold.

Liens on property may occur because an owner did not pay back taxes, remodeling or contract charges, or other debts where the courts allowed a lien to be placed. Before you can buy the property, the person who caused this lien must resolve the debt. Homes with this type of problem are said to have *clouds on title,* which means that the title is not free and clear.

For this type of problem, an industry called *title insurance* has been created. Title insurance protects the buyer and lender against loss resulting from claims by others against your home. The title insurance company does the research to determine if the title is free and clear, and then guarantees the result. Most lenders require title insurance.

In many areas, a few days before the closing, the title insurance company will issue a commitment to insure or a *binder* that summarizes any defect on the title and any exceptions from the title insurance coverage. This document goes to the lender and your attorney. If the defects are sizeable or are contrary to what was in the offer contract, this is the point to resolve the problems. If you have an attorney, he or she will review this document and act accordingly.

In some states, attorneys offer the title insurance through a *title insurance company* as part of their service to the home buyer. The attorney then is the one who deals with the title insurance representative, assists in clearing the title, and provides a title opinion.

Another document that most lenders and title insurance companies insist on is a *land survey*. This marks the boundaries of the property, the structures on it, and any encroachments of the land. Ordering this survey is another service that most real estate attorneys offer the buyers.

HOW TO HOLD TITLE

Your attorney can advise you how you should hold title to your home. Here are the common options.

Joint Tenancy

Most co-owners use *joint tenancy* as the way to take title to a home. It does not matter if the co-owners are married partners, unmarried partners, or just roommates—the rules for joint tenancy apply to all.

In joint tenancy, the co-owners each hold an equal share of the real estate. For simplification let's look at a husband and wife. They would each own 50% of the real estate. They would also share 50/50 in all other decisions having to do with the property, such as living in the home, refinancing, and selling. This can be both a positive and a negative, especially when one of the co-owners is being stubborn or is seriously ill. In some states, one joint tenancy owner can force a property sale.

Joint tenancy ownership is not affected by a person's will—this can be a major positive. When one joint tenancy owner dies, the property automatically goes to the other joint tenancy owner without the delay and expense of going through probate court. The change in ownership is as simple as presenting the lender with a certified death certificate and a signed affidavit that states that the one co-owner has died and that the other owner is asserting her or his rights under joint tenancy.

Tenancy by the Entireties

Another form of joint tenancy recognized in some states is *tenancy by the entireties*. This is strictly for husband and wife. Besides the benefits of a joint tenancy, tenancy by the entireties prevents one spouse from selling their half without the other spouse's knowledge. It also offers some protection from creditors of one spouse.

Tenancy by the entireties was created to protect one spouse from the bad debts and the rash judgments of the other spouse. This method of ownership has all the pluses and minuses of joint tenancy, along with the protections against creditors and against the sale of the home by the other spouse. The protection keeps creditors from putting a financial lien on the home for debts that involve just one spouse. A lien can keep both spouses from selling the house or refinancing until the lien is paid in full.

Tenancy by the entireties is not considered a legal form of property ownership in all states. Also, there are mortgage lenders who are opposed to this type of ownership. Some creditors lobby against this type of ownership because it can prevent the sale of a home for legitimate debts that belong to only one spouse.

A few years ago it appeared that there was going to be universal acceptance of this protection in every state. However, currently, the push to get this type of ownership in every state seems to have slowed down. For married couples, when your mortgage lender asks you "How do you want to take (or own) your house?"—you may want to ask if tenancy by the entireties is available in your state.

Tenancy in Common

While joint tenancy deals with ownership in equal shares, *tenancy in common* is a method for dealing with unequal shares.

Example:

Dad and his two sons decide to buy a house together. Dad is putting in 60% of the down payment and will be paying 60% of the monthly mortgage payments. Son #1 is putting in 15% of the down payment and is responsible for 15% of the monthly mortgage payments. Son #2 is responsible for the remaining 25%. Because of this division of investments, these three will hold the title in tenancy in common in the same percentage split.

Besides using this type of ownership to deal with unequal shares, most commercial real estate is owned in this manner.

Tenancy in common is affected by the owner's will unless there is another agreement connected with the real estate. Most commercial ventures have agreements on how to distribute the percentage of ownership in real estate when one of the owners dies. Many times the solution is that the commercial venture or corporation gets the first opportunity to purchase that percentage of ownership from the deceased's estate at market value.

Because tenancy in common is affected by a will, when one owner dies his or her percentage of the ownership will pass to his or her heirs, which may cause major problems with the other co-owners. If you intend to take ownership as tenancy in common, make sure that your will is updated to reflect your true wishes.

chapter thirteen:
The Offer

After thorough research regarding your neighborhood and comparisons of mortgage lenders, you finally find your dream house. It is everything you want or will compromise for, the neighborhood is perfect, and the schools are great. What is the next step?

THE CONTRACT

Next in the home-buying process is to actually make an *offer* on the house. An offer is legally presenting the sellers with a *contract* to purchase and hoping that they will accept it. Because it is a contract for real estate, the offer is made in writing. Real estate agents and brokers have standard forms for their county that are used to communicate the offer.

The buyers fill in this form with the amount offered, the type of mortgage (conventional, VA, FHA), the estimated closing date, and *contingencies*. Contingencies to a contract say that if this event happens, you are not legally liable to buy the house.

Another area in the contract lists what things other than the house and the property are included in the deal. Most times the window coverings and things permanently affixed to the structure or property come with the home. However, each house is different and the laws in your state may allow a very liberal interpretation of

ATTORNEY TIP:

Some of the most common contingencies are:
- if the buyer cannot get financing, the seller can cancel the sale;
- if the seller does not provide title to the home, the buyer can cancel the sale; and,
- if the inspector finds insect damage, the buyer can cancel the sale.

what is permanently affixed. If you understand that something is to be sold with the house such as window treatments, appliances, sheds, and such, make sure that these things are listed on your contract offer. This will eliminate confusion on both sides.

Once you sign this contract, you agree to proceed through the deal unless one of the contingencies happen.

WHAT IS IN A REAL ESTATE CONTRACT

Each state and most counties have their own version of what is a *standard residential sales contract*. It may be many paragraphs or something closer to a form with each line numbered. It may have additional agreements that are called *riders,* which are required by local law.

Riders usually cover things that the buyer and seller agree on in addition to agreeing to selling the house for a certain price. Common riders cover the seller leaving the appliances in the home for the buyer, the seller paying the buyer a certain amount to repair a defect, and other personal agreements.

Because laws on real estate sales differ by state, it is hard to generalize as to what type of contract you will see. Whatever type of document is used, it will be lengthy, have lots of legal phrases, and be overwhelming, especially to first-time home buyer. It will contain both the

ATTORNEY TIP:

When you start looking for a home, ask your real estate agent for a copy of the standard real estate sale contract for your area. This gives you time to read it and ask questions before the time that you are making the offer.

buyer's and the seller's name and address, the date of the contract, the address of house being sold, the legal description of the house, a section on financing, a section on inspections, a section listing everything included in the sale, and any contingencies to the sale. There will be places for the buyer, seller, and real estate agents to sign.

Since this is a legal document, you may want a lawyer to represent you before you sign it. An alternative could be to ask that the contract not be effective until your lawyer reviews it. Usually a real estate contract will allow for a short period of time for lawyer review. Most states offer two or three days.

Components of a Real Estate Contract

Following are some of the most common parts of a residential sales contract:

- buyer's name and address;
- seller's name and address;
- legal description of property being sold;
- amount that the buyer is offering to pay for the real estate;
- amount of earnest money or good faith deposit that the buyer is putting down;
- specification of who holds the earnest money and how the interest is calculated;
- details of the specific sale (such things as curtains, appliances, garage, garage door openers, etc.);
- length of time the sellers have to respond to the offer with either an acceptance or a counter offer;
- closing date and location;
- contingencies (these things must happen for the contract to be valid):
    - buyer must get a mortgage;
    - home must pass inspection and appraisal;
    - home title must be clear of liens; and,
    - home must pass other inspections such as termites, ant, pests, radon, mold, well and septic;

- date the buyers will take possession of the home;
- whose insurance will cover the property up until the closing date;
- manner in which disputes of the contract will be legally handled; and,
- notices of property disclosures concerning the home.

NEGOTIATION

Most times the home buyer will not want to pay the full price as offered by the sellers. It could be that you feel the home is over priced for the area, there are some problems with the property, or just that you want a bargain. No matter what the reason, most buyers will offer less than the full asking price. *Negotiation* is a process of finding that magic number where both the buyer and seller feel that they are getting a good deal.

In most cases, your real estate agent will help you in this negotiation, but remember, it is in the real estate agent's best interest to make a sale at the highest amount. A real estate attorney can also help you in negotiations.

The real estate agent will help you fill out the proper form and then present it to the seller. In most areas of the country, the buyers put down an amount of *earnest money* (money to show the sellers they are serious about the home) in an *escrow* as a good faith deposit with the offer. The agent will meet with the sellers and their agent and *present the offer*. The sellers then have the option to either turn down the offer or make a *counter offer*. This can go on until either the buyer or the seller turns down an offer and does not make a counter.

Things to Remember in Negotiations

- Be firm on the maximum price you are willing to pay for the property, but do not tell your real estate agent. (Do not let the excitement of the negotiations or the pressures of the real estate agent push you beyond that limit.)

- Use the contingency of an inspection to make sure that the house is as sound as has been advertised and that there is no hidden insect damage.
- Use the contingency of being approved for a mortgage by a certain date just in case you cannot get the mortgage you want.

> **ATTORNEY TIP:**
>
> Make tentative plans with your real estate agent to see other homes. This way, your agent gets the idea that your offer is not a life or death decision. The less interest you display, the better your negotiating position.

- Know why the sellers are moving and use this information to determine whether they are in a hurry to sell. (For example, if the sellers need to move quickly, they may accept a lower offer just to have the property sold.)
- Do not rush in making an offer. In some areas, houses do sell in one day, this is why you need to know the area. In most cases waiting until you have been able to sleep on it is advisable. (Buyers who rush into an offer can seem very anxious for that house. The sellers may then use that to insist on the full asking price.)
- Do not limit the options for mortgages. If you qualify for VA or FHA loans, you may want to write one contract for use of one of these and another for use of a conventional loan at a lower price. This way if the seller refuses the VA or FHA loans, you have an immediate counter offer for a conventional loan at a lower purchase price.
- Insist on a twenty-four-hour walk through the day prior to closing. On occasion, a not-so-ethical seller will remove items, that according to the contract, must be left with the house. (For some sellers this is a game to see how much they can get away with. By insisting on a walk-through the day prior to the closing, a lot of this will be eliminated.)

- Play it cool when making the offer. Even though your insides are churning because you are committing to a huge debt, avoid showing it to your real estate agent.

EARNEST MONEY

Part of most home purchases is the *earnest money*, which is held in *escrow* while the parties negotiate. Earnest money is an amount that indicates that you are a serious buyer. The amount of earnest money varies from one area to another and is usually paid in cash or a *promissory note*. If the buyer decides to back out of the deal for a reason which is not a contingency on the contract, the seller gets the earnest money as payment for their inconvenience. Of course, the seller and the real estate agent want a large amount of earnest money.

The earnest money deposit is supposed to be a reasonable good faith amount that shows that the buyer is interested enough to put up money. Remember, if the buyer backs out of the deal for reasons other than the contingencies mentioned in the contract, the buyer forfeits this amount.

There is no right or wrong amount. Many real estate agents will ask up to 10% of the offer as earnest money, but I personally find that way too high. What is put up for earnest money really depends on how the houses are selling. If you are trying to buy in an area where houses do not stay on the market more than a few days, your offer may be accepted just because you are willing to put up a large amount of earnest money (could be more than 10% of the offer). However, if the home has languished on the market for several months without any offers, a more modest amount may be sufficient. At the closing, the earnest money usually becomes part of or all of the down payment.

Escrow

Earnest money is held in what real estate people call *escrow*. (Also, mortgage companies hold an amount for taxes and home insurance in escrow.) Escrow is another name for money from one person that eventually goes to someone else, but is held by a third person. Some states have licensed escrow agents, some real estate firms have one person in charge of escrow accounts.

Type 1 Escrow

The buyer puts earnest money into a *Type 1 Escrow* account when the offer is made. This account contains the earnest money from the buyer, held by the third party. It will eventually be part of the buyer's payment to the seller. If the offer to purchase the home is refused, the earnest money is returned to the buyer. If the offer to purchase the home fails because the buyer backs out, the seller keeps the money. If the offer to purchase the home fails because of a contingency, the offer contract determines who will keep the money.

Type 1 escrow is what we talk about when we deal with the offer to buy a home. This is the earnest money that a potential buyer puts up as an indication of reasonable good faith in order to get the seller to accept his or her offer.

Type 2 Escrow

Type 2 Escrow is not the same earnest money you put up when buying a home. This is the money you set aside with the lender in order to pay taxes and insurance. (You will see this mentioned in the mortgage documents, but probably will not be required to deal with it until you have lived in your home for at least one year.)

A few years ago, my new mortgage lender sent me a notice that I needed to increase my escrow on my home loan. This sent me furiously running to my mortgage contract to see what they were talking about. Yes, the amount that my mortgage company holds for paying taxes and insurance is called escrow. Although some mortgage companies still refer to this as a fund to pay taxes and insurance, technically and legally, this is an escrow account. As real estate taxes increase in an area, you, too, may be asked to contribute more money to this account in order to pay for the increase—just as I did.

The mortgage company uses a Type 2 Escrow account for payments of insurance and taxes. This account contains money the buyer contributes when he or she purchased the house. It is held by the mortgage company until the taxes and insurance bills come due.

chapter fourteen

Appraisers, Inspectors, and Homeowners Insurance

Besides real estate agents and brokers, the second most important real estate professionals you will deal with are the *appraisers*, *inspectors*, and the *insurance providers*. In most states, these professionals are licensed and are required to complete certain educational courses. In areas where there is a lot of real estate activity, the appraisers and inspectors can have appointments months in advance.

Another important person will be your home insurance provider. This person may also send a professional inspector to view your house before providing you with a home insurance policy.

APPRAISERS

The lender usually hires an *appraiser* to make sure that the property is worth the amount of the loan. Some lenders require that the buyer select the appraiser, while others have appraisers on staff or under contract. Your real estate agent or attorney can help you find an appraiser if you need to provide one.

The appraiser's job is to look at the home for obvious defects, look at comparables for other like homes that have sold in the area, and send a report to the mortgage company.

I have dealt with appraisers who spent hours measuring each room, testing each faucet, listening to the furnace, and checking for

ATTORNEY TIP:

An appraiser is not a home inspector. The appraiser is only attempting to justify the dollar amount of your mortgage. It is very important that you have the potential home inspected by a certified home inspector before you buy.

foundation cracks with a bright light. Others have spent less than fifteen minutes in the house.

What an appraiser looks for is how the sale price (and therefore the loan amount) fits for this type of home in this particular area. If you want to buy a two million-dollar home, in an area where like homes are going for under $50,000, the appraiser is going to ask why.

Let's review some facts:
- the mortgage lender orders the appraisal;
- the appraiser knows the amount the borrower needs to get for a mortgage; and,
- the mortgage lender can be assured of making money on the loan, if the amount of the loan is less than the real value of the home.

As you can imagine, all these conflicting facts make it imperative that the appraiser be both accurate in his or her appraisal of the property, without being so picky that potential borrowers are turned away.

Recently, the *Federal Housing Administration* (FHA) weighed in with blunt messages to both the appraisers and the lenders. The FHA has decided that it will hold both the appraiser and lender responsible for inaccurate appraisals made on FHA mortgages. While this currently only covers FHA mortgages, it has sent a message throughout the real estate industry that appraisals should not be inflated in order to meet the amount being borrowed. Appraisers should not ignore any value-depressing features or flaws with the property.

Ignoring these kinds of flaws can cost the new home owner thousands of dollars in unexpected repair bills; so it is also important to the buyer, that the appraisal be accurate.

INSPECTORS

Inspectors usually have more education and experience than appraisers. Besides being trained in certain fields, inspectors can also be specialists, who only do certain types of inspections. Major home inspection associations certify their inspector's credentials. Some of the bigger associations are the *American Society of Home Inspectors (ASHI)* and the *National Association of Home Inspectors (NAHI)*. Your state may also have its own home inspector association.

> ## CLICK ON THIS:
>
> The Internet site www.msn.com "house and home" section explains in detail many points about home inspections. It has a service that will match inspectors with your zip code.
>
> A comprehensive site for information on home inspections, home inspectors, and home inspections for first time home buyers can be found at:
> www.inspectamerica.com

Specific home inspections are required by the VA and the FHA in order to qualify for the loan. Your offer contract to purchase a house should have a contingent clause in it that requires the house to pass an inspection. Besides your inspection contingency, your mortgage lender and your home insurance provider may also require an inspection. Your real estate agent or attorney may be able to provide you with names of inspectors or you may be able to get a referral from friends, family, or your lender.

The Inspection

Depending upon the inspector, the potential buyer may be able to tag along on the *inspection*. After the inspection is complete, the inspector will write a report and send it to the buyer or his or her attorney for review.

Generally the inspection consists of the following.

- *Drainage.* Rain and snow should drain away from the house to avoid flooding.
- *Electrical wiring.* A house may have to be brought up to the local *building code,* if the electrical system is found to be defective or insufficient.

- *Roof.* Leaks in the roof, patches, and multiple layers of roof are important. Leaks can cause damage to interior walls and weaken the structure of the house.
- *Furnace and air conditioning.* The age of the furnace and air condition unit is very important. Older furnaces are generally inefficient and can cause outlandish heating bills in addition to wasting energy. There are specific tests, especially for CO_2 gas and other leakage, that will be performed on the furnace.
- *Plumbing.* The inspector will check water pressure and be sure that all faucets and toilets properly operate. He or she will also check for sewage leaks and slow moving drains as an indicator of major problems.
- *Bugs.* Most mortgage companies, including FHA and VA, require a termite inspection. Different areas of the country also include other bugs, since termites can destroy a structure without leaving much evidence. Inspectors or exterminators can perform this test.
- *Ventilation.* The inspector will check windows and doors for leaks and inadequate caulking. The inspector will also check for homes that are so airtight that mold could grow in bathrooms with little ventilation.
- *Foundation.* The foundation will be checked for leaks and cracks.
- *Structural damage.* The entire structure of the building will be checked for damage and indicators that it has been poorly maintained.
- *Environmental.* You can obtain special inspections for radon, lead paint, asbestos, formaldehyde, and other environmental hazards. Certain areas require this type of inspection. (If you have done your research on the neighborhood and found that there was a past leak or other environmental problem in the soil or ground water, you may also want to determine if that environmental problem extended to this property.)

Defects

So what happens when the inspector finds a defect? That answer depends on you and the mortgage company. VA and FHA mortgages require that a house pass a certain level of inspection. Both of these organizations will expect the seller to repair the defect prior to issuing the mortgage.

Conventional lenders can vary in their response to defects. The majority will require that the loan amount be reduced to match the value of the home with the defect. This means that you may have to come up with a larger down payment.

> **ATTORNEY TIP:**
>
> Ask your professional inspector if you can go along on the inspection. Some inspectors have no problem with the potential buyer being there so that defects can be explained, while other inspectors and many sellers prefer that only the inspector who produces a written document do the inspection. If you do go along, take your notebook to write down any problems.

If you have written the offer contract to include the contingency that the home passes an inspection, you can negotiate. Technically, if the home does not pass inspection, you can walk away from the deal. You may have to pay for the inspection, but you should be able to get your escrow money returned.

Another approach is to get the seller to either fix the defect and have the home reinspected or pay you an amount to get the defects repaired. This could be the additional down payment money the lender now requires.

Another plus for the buyer is that in some states the seller must disclose known defects of a serious nature. If the sale goes through and then the buyer finds out about a specific defect, the buyer may be able to sue the seller for funds to repair the property.

INSURANCE

Home buyers will have to deal with several kinds of insurance just to get into the home ownership phase. Once you own the home,

CLICK ON THIS:

The following sites contain information on homeowners insurance.

www.iii.org
The Insurance Information Institute provides good, basic information on homeowners insurance; how to determine how much insurance you need; where to buy insurance; how to file a claim; and, great tips for lowering your liability.

www.msn.com (house and home)
This site provides information on lowering insurance costs, preventing damage to your house, and links to insurance companies that will give you a quote on homeowners insurance.

www.insweb.com
This site explains the details of homeowners insurance. (I feel this is the most informative site on insurance.)

While you are at this site, look at Home Insurance Exclusions (things not covered by homeowners insurance). Exclusions talked about range from the common wild animal, water, rats, to the really bizarre occurrences such as religious phenomenon, meteorites, and nuclear irradiation. It is well worth the time to read this section.

you will be dealing with insurance issues until you sell the home and start all over again with another. Here is a overview of the most common insurance issues the first-time home buyer will confront.

Home Insurance

Before you can complete the purchase of your dream house, the mortgage lender will require that you purchase home insurance. You will be required to produce a *Certificate of Insurance, Insurance Binder*, or a document in which the insurance company states that you have insurance on the property at the closing. If you have not obtained insurance by the closing, the closing will stop. You will not be allowed to purchase the home until you obtain insurance.

Home insurance protects the lender's investment and your investment in the property. The mortgage lenders usually require insurance at a certain financial level. In addition, the state in which the property is located may also require that the homeowner get certain types of insurance. If the home is located in a flood plain, you will probably be required to obtain flood insurance.

Standard homeowners insurance policies have two sections. The first covers your property and the second covers your liability to be sued for incidents that happen on your property.

The reimbursement for damage to items or to the house itself is usually identified in terms of *actual cash value* and *replacement cost*. Actual cash value takes into consideration depreciation of the item damaged that would result in the home owner receiving a reduced amount. Replacement cost is the current dollar amount it takes to replace the property with something of a similar type. This may mean that the insurance company has the right to dictate how your house is repaired.

Homeowners insurance is a complex subject. The mortgage lender, the state, where the house is located, and finally the desires of the homeowner dictate the type of policy and the items covered in the policy.

Flood Insurance

Many times the home you have selected will be deemed by the federal or local housing administration as being in a *flood plain* or your mortgage lender will demand that you obtain *flood insurance* on the property. How or why the property has been marked as needing flood insurance is not the issue. (I have tried in vain to get that removed for properties that are no where near waterways.)

The issue here is that flood insurance protects property owners from serious water damage for losses on both the real estate and personal property. This water damage can come from heavy rains, erosion, water back up, or what we usually think of as rising rivers. Most standard home insurance does not cover water damage from these sources.

In 1968, the *National Flood Insurance Program* was created and passed the *Flood Disaster Protection Act* to provide flood insurance at reasonable costs. Flood insurance is offered by private insurance companies in a joint venture with the federal government. Because of this joint venture, the cost is usually not high, but the benefits are great if you suffer from a flood disaster.

Mortgage Insurance

Traditional *mortgage insurance* is usually required by mortgage lenders when the borrower makes a down payment of less than 20% of the total value of the home. The reasoning is that if the lender must foreclose, it will not have much equity in the home if it is sold at a loss. In simple terms, if the borrower cannot pay the mortgage, the mortgage lender may be forced to take back the house and sell it. That is foreclosure.

In foreclosure sales, the mortgage lender wants to make enough money to cover the amount of the outstanding loan plus the costs involved in holding a foreclosure sale. History teaches us that foreclosure sales generally only give the lender 80% of the value of the house. This is why lenders want the borrower to have already paid them 20% as a down payment.

Mortgage insurance is usually calculated as a percentage of the total loan amount. The more money you put towards the down payment, the lower the cost for mortgage insurance. Generally, if the total loan is $100,000 and the borrower puts less than 20% down on the total cost of the house, then mortgage insurance will be in the range of $40 to $60 per month. (This is a very big issue considering the popularity of zero down mortgages.)

Many mortgage lenders will drop the requirement for mortgage insurance once the borrower has paid an amount equal to 20% equity in the home. (You may need to keep track of this yourself and not wait for the lender to let you out of this cost.)

Recently, a new type of mortgage insurance has been introduced as a way to keep more homes out of foreclosure. This one protects the lender by continuing mortgage payments when the borrower is unable to work because of injury, disability, or due to job loss. *Mortgage Payment Protection, Inc.* in Altamonte Springs, Florida provides a mortgage insurance policy called *Mortgage Guardian* that specifically addresses the borrower's loss of job. *GE Mortgage Insurance Corp.* also offers a similar product. This is a new product and the details vary by insurance policy and mortgage lender. (Your mortgage lender can provide you with more information.)

Title Insurance

Lender *title insurance* is usually required by the mortgage lender when the mortgage takes effect. It is in those long documents presented by the lender that most of us just sign without reading. There is also *borrower's, buyer's,* or *owner's title insurance* that is usually paid in a one-time title insurance policy. Title insurance protects the lender, the borrower, the buyer, and the owner from costly problems with the title to the home. Such problems may be title claims by lost heirs of the seller, ex spouses of the seller, mistakes in the deed recording by the state, and most all other risks.

For first time home buyers, this is not an option. Always insist on obtaining an *owner's title policy.* The lender's policy only protects the mortgage lender and offers no protection to the unknowing buyer. Some areas of the country may require title insurance. It is usually offered at a low cost, along with the required title search from professional title insurance companies.

chapter fifteen:
The Closing

The *closing* or the *settlement* occurs when the buyers, the sellers, the agents, the attorneys, the escrow agent, the title company, the mortgage company, and a host of others sit down to finalize the buy-sell agreement. Many of the people on this list will send a representative *or* a legal document. This is what you have been waiting for—the formal proceeding when that dream house becomes yours.

THE WALK THROUGH

The final *walk through* is an activity done shortly before the date of the closing. The purpose is for the buyer and his or her agent to inspect the house to verify that all the items listed in the sales contract are still in place and that there has not been additional damage to the house since the sales contract was signed.

Before you go to the walk through, take the time to review the sales contract. Make a list of items such as drapes, window treatments, appliances, and other fixtures that were specifically listed in the sales contract as part of the sale. You should also list those things that were especially important to you, but were not in the sale contract such a chandelier in the dining room or other items that are mounted to the house. During the walk through, check each item off as you see it.

Your real estate agent should accompany you in the walk through. Systematically, start in one room at a time; keep together; resist the urge for each person to go off to a different room. Use your list to determine if that room still has the items it should. Check the electricity in each room. Note any damage that you did not see when you initially made the offer. Check the water in bathrooms and kitchens. Check that appliances which are to be left in the house are still in good working order. Check to see if the heating system and air conditioning system are in working order.

Check all rooms of the house and any other buildings included in the sale. Watch for damage on floors and walls from the seller moving out. Look for any defects that were covered by the seller's furniture, rugs, or decorating. Make notes of every problem.

Sometimes you will be doing your walk through while the sellers are trying to move out. This is not the best time to do a walk through, but do not let the sellers keep you from looking into each room. If you find that the sellers are taking things that should be left with the house in the sales contract, let your real estate agent handle it. Moving is such a stressful time, do not make it worse by getting emotional with the sellers.

What happens if something is missing or there is damage? Your real estate agent can help you decide what to do. You may insist on the return of the missing item or just take a cash settlement. You may also decide that the item is not important enough to potentially cause the closing to be delayed and just let the issue pass.

While I have found that most people are honest and stick to the sales contract, there are a few who will take items from the house, even though they were required to leave them. In one house, the previous owner took the heavy, custom-made drapes. I ignored this because the rooms looked better without the extra fabric. In another house, there was water damage from snow build up. I took a small financial settlement which was negotiated by my real estate agent at the closing. Never purchase a home without a final walk through. If necessary, stall the closing in order to get the walk through.

WHAT REALLY HAPPENS AT A CLOSING

Legally this is the point when the seller transfers the property to the buyer for money. The buyer will be expected to bring certain documents to the closing. The title company or escrow agent will present the buyer and seller with a *settlement statement* that details exact dollar amounts for each part of the sale. The buyer and seller or their attorneys verify the numbers and sign the statement.

Both the seller and the buyer produce *certified checks* for their portion of the closing costs. The buyer then gets to review the mortgage documents and signs them. The escrow agent, mortgage company, or title agent will establish an escrow account for payment of future property taxes and homeowners insurance. The lender then produces the very large check for the amount of the mortgage loan.

Many other documents are reviewed and signed by both buyer and seller. If appliances or furniture is being sold with the house, a separate document may be required to indicate this. Both buyer and seller then sign the deed. The seller then gives the keys to the buyer.

The final step is done by the escrow agent, title company, or attorney. They will record the newly signed deed with the appropriate city, county, or state office. By recording this deed, the property will be reassessed and the property taxes will probably increase. This is *the* time when you become the owner of your first home.

CLOSING DOCUMENTS

It would be impossible to reproduce the variety of closing documents that real estate professionals use in the United States.

Documents vary by type of mortgage, lender, state, county, city, and real estate professionals. The majority of documents are financial ones from your mortgage lender. The following is a minimum list of what you will probably be required to sign. Most real estate transactions end up with about double the number of documents that are listed here.

- The *Real Estate Settlement Procedure Act* (RESPA) requires that the buyer sign a statement to acknowledge that he or she has been informed about how the closing works.
- HUD-1 *Settlement Statement* form itemizes each payment assigned to both the buyer and seller. (see **Appendix E.**)
- *Truth in Lending Disclosure Statement* will tell the buyer exactly how much it will cost to buy the house. This is the principle amount plus the interest amount.
- *Mortgage Note* or *Contract* is the agreement between the buyer and the mortgage lender to loan the buyer a certain amount. This includes the dates payment is due, interest rates, and other mortgage term information.
- *Security Instrument* (can also be called the *Mortgage* or *Deed*) puts the property up as collateral for the loan.
- *Warranty Deed* transfers the home from the seller to the buyer. In legal terms this then allows the buyer to put the house up as collateral for the mortgage.
- *Escrow papers from the mortgage lender* show the amount of the taxes and insurance escrow.
- *Escrow papers from the earnest money* show the transfer of that amount to the seller.
- *Local tax papers* record the sale to a new homeowner and direct the local taxing authority to send tax bills to your mortgage lender.

Because each closing is different, you will see lots of documents. You, your agent, or your attorney may also have the offer contract, inspection reports, title search results, title insurance documents, proof of insurance, a list of walk through problems and maybe a bill for the sellers for these problems, your attorney's bill, transfer stamps required by the city/state/county, documents required by the city/state/county for recording the deed.

As time goes on the number of documents needed to close a home sale continues to rise with no end in sight. As each document is given to you, your attorney will be able to briefly explain what it is and show you where to sign. At the end of the closing, you will receive a fat envelope with copies of each signed document. Keep these documents for future problems or just to look at when the urge to buy another house hits you.

What to Bring to the Closing

Your attorney and real estate agent will tell you what to bring to your closing. They may also provide some of the documents. General documents include:

- the offer contract;
- escrow document;
- appraisal;
- inspections;
- property survey;
- title search documents;
- title insurance;
- proof of homeowners insurance;
- proof that the final walk-through was ok; and,
- a certified check for the closing costs.

Certified checks are usually required in order to guarantee that the money is available. Some areas of the country do not have this requirement. Check with your attorney or real estate agent to determine what is expected in your situation.

There may be other documents that are required for your closing depending on the area laws, the type of mortgage, and the standards for sale.

CLOSING COSTS

There are no definitive rules as to who pays for what. Buyers and sellers routinely negotiate closing costs as part of the deal. Even in cases of VA and FHA loans where most closing costs are assigned to the seller, the buyer and seller may make a side deal.

Generally, closing costs consist of the following:
- mortgage application fee;
- points;
- inspections;
- state tax;
- city tax;
- title fees;
- insurance;
- escrow fees;
- document preparation fees; and,
- others.

Amounts vary by size and type of loan, state and local taxes, the total price of the home, and area standards.

One of the most annoying things about closing costs is that they are difficult to calculate. Only after the lender, the title company, the inspectors, the insurance company, and others do their processing can closing costs be calculated. Usually, the title company is making the calculations about closing costs a day or even hours prior to the actual closing. That does not give the buyer a whole lot of time to get a certified check. This is especially true in areas where there is a lot of real estate activity.

ATTORNEY TIP:

Schedule your closing for the afternoon so you will have time in the morning to get a certified check from your bank.

PROBLEMS

There are a few things that can hold up the closing process. Any document that is missing, not filled out right, or does not conform to state real estate laws can stall or even postpone the closing. Expect problems and delays in the closing because it is rare that real estate closings go smoothly, no matter how prepared you are. Even without problems, the closing is guaranteed to last longer than what your real estate agent told you.

An experienced real estate attorney can really help the first-time buyer in the area of the closing and its potential problems. Attorneys that have been through many real estate closings can head off some of the most time-consuming problems by obtaining title searches, mortgage documents, and other required documents for your state—and then reviewing these documents. This type of coordination is especially critical if you are moving into another state or must close the real estate deal on a particular date. A delayed closing can cost both buyer and seller in money and time, and it may even cause the sale to be cancelled. While a real estate attorney is another expense, that attorney can avoid delaying the closing.

The primary action the first-time buyer can take in order to prepare for closing is to gather all the documents that he or she is required to bring. Get a letter from the house insurance company certifying that you have insurance on the building. Bring the exact amount of money, usually cashiers or certified check that you are told to bring. Also bring an amount of cash plus your checkbook for last minute calculation errors. (I would advise withdrawing five hundred to one thousand dollars in cash from your bank account for the closing and then returning what is left to your account that same day.)

If you can, take the entire day off work, so that you will not be concerned with getting back to the job. Also, if you can, don't have the move scheduled for the day of closing. Try to schedule the move a few days after you take possession of the house. That will give you time to clean the interior.

So what do you do if you have an eighteen-wheeler loaded with all your furniture and the closing is postponed? Most movers have temporary storage facilities available if your closing is postponed, but your furniture is already in the moving truck. I have been on the bad end of this type of closing and spent three hours looking for a public storage facility so that the truck could unload. Be smart and ask the movers about this before you sign with them.

Problem closings hit almost everyone. Don't let that diminish your enthusiasm for your new home. Years after the closing, you will be able to laugh about it, honestly. It will give you something to warn your apartment-renting friends about and make good stories for your grandchildren.

Section Six:
The Future

chapter sixteen:
Enjoying Your Home

Once you own a home, the hard work begins. Besides keeping up with mortgage payments, you will be required to keep up your property. You probably will redecorate, buy furniture, and spend money making this house your home.

RESPONSIBLE HOME OWNERSHIP

It is not enough that you make your mortgage payments. A responsible home owner is also one who keeps up the property and watches out for problems in the neighborhood before those problems reduce property values. Crime watch is very important nowadays. Your neighborhood may have a group of people who belong to a crime watch organization.

The local police usually sanction organized crime watch groups, so they would be a good source for this information. Some town police departments even offer free services to evaluate your home for break-ins and security. Your local library is also

ATTORNEY TIP:
The best way to keep up with local information is to subscribe to your local town's newspaper and read it. Certain legal notices such as tax increases, referendums, and other serious changes are usually published in advance to get the residents' input.

a good source for crime watch information and for copies of your cities local laws. The best thing you can do is to not turn your head when you see a crime or accident. Keep the police phone number by the phone and don't be afraid to report illegal activity.

You may wish to become involved in other town organizations. Some towns have newcomer groups that provide activities for those new to an area. Most towns support volunteer activities that can be socially beneficial and rewarding.

Keeping-up your property is another way to show responsible home ownership. It is not so much a "keeping up with the Joneses" as keeping your property from deteriorating or making a bad appearance. Pick up trash and litter left on your property, even if you did not put it there. Clear leaves, cut the grass, pull weeds, and trim trees. Obtain proper garbage receptacles and replace them when they break.

Be considerate of your neighbors. Mowing the lawn at six am on a Saturday may get the job done, but you will not be the most-liked person on the block. Even though you own the house, remember that the noise of loud parties can be annoying to your neighbors. Be considerate of others.

Also be considerate of parking. If parking is a problem for residents, you may suggest that guests car pool. Also, make sure that guest's cars are not blocking neighbor's driveways or sidewalks. Some towns have laws against parking on the street overnight, after dark, when it snows, or during scheduled street cleaning. Find out what the local laws are in your new town so that you and your guests won't be ticketed.

KEEPING UTILITY EXPENSES DOWN

As a homeowner you will soon discover that utility bills increase almost on a monthly basis. During the winter you get your family to wear sweaters and in the summers you pass around ice, but the utility bills still hurt.

First, look at your furnace and air conditioner. Newer models are more energy efficient and can pay for themselves with lower utility bills.

My home had a fifteen-year-old furnace with central air. In the winter the gas bill was outrageous and in the summer the electricity bill was so bad I was into candlelight dining just to save money. Both units were frequently breaking down. There was one summer when the repairman was out almost every two weeks. In the fall I spoke to my local heating and cooling repair company regarding a quote on replacing both the furnace and central air. Yes, it was a big expense all at once. However, the cost was made up within eighteen months because of reduced utility bills. It really does work.

Another thing you can do to reduce energy bills is to install a programmable thermostat. This allows you to lower the heat when no one is at home and when you sleep; and run the air conditioner on the same type of schedule. These programmable thermostats are available at home repair stores and some department stores. They come with easy to follow instructions and are directed at the do-it-yourselfer.

Furnaces and central air units require certain maintenance. By keeping up with the maintenance the unit will run more efficiently and therefore cost less. Furnaces usually have filters that should be changed according to the directions on the filter or the furnace itself. Following this schedule keeps the air clean and lets the furnace run at its proper level. Also, you should have an annual check on both these appliances by a certified repairperson. This makes sure that the units are running properly and are not leaking noxious fumes. Ask your neighbors for references of qualified technicians.

Another way to save on utility bills is with insulation and caulking. Outside air that comes pouring in around poorly caulked

CLICK ON THIS:

For more information on energy savings, check out:

www.consumer.gov

doors and windows can cost money in wasted energy. You may have to replace old, poor fitting windows, recaulk, or add foam draft strips on the inside of the window. There are many solutions to this type of problem and some of them are cheap. Go to the local home repair store for more ideas.

As for insulation, you may want to check with your local building code to see what level of insulation is suggested and then make sure the insulation in outside walls and the attic match this level. Your local home repair store will have the supplies and will be able to advise you as to how much insulation is appropriate.

CORRESPONDENCE FROM THE MORTGAGE COMPANY

After you have paid on the mortgage for a while, you may receive a notice that your mortgage has been sold to another lender. This is called the *secondary mortgage market* and it does not mean anything about your creditworthiness. It just means you have a new mortgage company. (see Chapter 9.) The only change you may see is that you will be sending the payment to a new address.

You may also receive a notice that you need to increase the amount of escrow that the mortgage company holds to pay taxes and insurance. This has nothing to do with the escrow that you put down when you made the offer on the house. This is the escrow account that was created at the closing for the purpose of paying taxes and insurance. Because property taxes increase as do insurance premiums, the escrow that was put aside last year may not cover the expenses for this year. This is a legitimate bill, but if you have questions, do not hesitate to contact the new mortgage company.

CONGRATULATIONS— YOU GET A TAX BENEFIT

A person who becomes a homeowner gets a few tax breaks from the IRS. If you paid points when you signed for the mortgage loan, the cost of the points may be deducted in that year's income tax. You can deduct mortgage interest and property tax from your annual income tax. Tax laws may allow additional deductions for the costs of obtaining a mortgage. Plus, if your state has an annual income tax you may get deductions from the state. Certain energy saving devices may also qualify for a tax benefit along with a lower utility bill.

Ask someone who knows the tax laws to do your taxes so that you can take advantage of every deduction available to home owners. Even though it is one more expense, it is financially worth it to hire an income tax professional to do your annual income tax at least for the first year.

There are some people who want our Congress to remove the deduction for mortgages. So far this has been the one strong deduction that remains without tinkering from the lawmakers or IRS. As a home owner, you now have a vested interest in keeping this deduction. Even if you are not a political person, pay attention to this issue.

REDUCING YOUR MORTGAGE DEBT

You can reduce the total amount of your mortgage debt by *prepayment*. Any amount of prepayment goes towards the principal amount, not the interest. Therefore you are shortening the length of time it will take to pay off the mortgage. Reductions can mean up to thousands of dollars to you.

Example:
If you paid an extra $10 per month for a mortgage of $100,000 at 7% interest for thirty years (360 months), it would be paid up in 342 months, and you would save over $8,500.

If you paid an extra $25 per month, the mortgage would be paid up in 320 months at a savings of $18,200 in interest.

The reason prepayment can shorten the life of the mortgage loan goes back to what makes up a mortgage payment: repayment on the principal, paying the interest, paying taxes, and

ATTORNEY TIP:

When you apply for a mortgage, make sure that it does not have a prepayment penalty. This penalty is charged to keep the homeowner from paying ahead on their mortgage or refinancing at a lower interest rate.

Why would a mortgage company not want you to pay ahead? Interest is how the mortgage company makes money. You do not pay interest on the amount that is paid ahead.

paying insurance. When mortgages were invented, it was decided to use a calculation called an *amortization table* to decide how much interest and how much principal is paid in each installment.

Generally, payments made early in the mortgage are mostly toward interest, with little toward the principal amount. However, even while the borrower is paying a lot of interest up front, he or she is also slowly paying down the principal debt.

chapter seventeen:
Foreclosure and How to Avoid It

Just as many more people are able to afford their own homes—our economy has taken several hard hits. These hits have resulted in thousands losing their jobs and being in real danger of losing their homes as well. The Mortgage Bankers Association recently reported a record number of home owners who are behind in their mortgage payments and are facing foreclosure.

PREVENTING FORECLOSURE

Preventing a foreclosure begins when you start your search for a home. Borrow only what you can afford. If this means that you must begin with a home that is less than what you really want, then that is what you must do. That is what many people mean when they use the term *starter home*. It is your first home, the one where you build a good credit rating, experience the joys and problems with home ownership, and then sell it to move up to something closer to what you really want.

Many lenders and real estate agents will encourage you to purchase a home that is on the top end of what you can pay for monthly mortgage payments. What these people forget are ongoing expenses like tuition, illness, a new baby, downsizing, or any other expenses that can drain your income. It is up to you to figure these potentials into what you are willing to borrow.

CLICK ON THIS:

Find out what predatory lending is so that you can avoid it. Look at the following Internet sites for information on this type of fraud:

- www.hud.gov
- www.fdic.gov
- www.stopmortgagefraud.com

Be careful of the type of mortgage you select. Adjustable rate and balloon mortgages may seem great because in the first years of the mortgage you are paying a lower amount. However, when the rates increase or that balloon payment comes due, you may find yourself unable to make the high payments.

Borrowing against the equity in a home can also cause problems leading to foreclosure. People with multiple mortgages or several home loans against their property can find themselves in a financial problem because they are unable to meet these multiple payments. For every additional mortgage or home loan, you are doubling the risk that you may lose your home.

Along with multiple mortgages are those predatory lenders who like to foreclose on a property because they make more money that way. This usually happens to people who are cash strapped, the elderly, and those with bad credit ratings. The lender promises to get a person out of debt and then persuades him or her to take out a high-cost loan that uses the home as collateral.

ATTORNEY TIP:

Before signing with any unfamiliar mortgage lender, check out the company with the Better Business Bureau, or your state's local consumer protection office.

You may wish to invest in mortgage insurance in order to pay the mortgage in cases where you cannot. Each policy has its own terms, such as death of the primary income producer in the family, disability, or another severe financial set back. These policies can be expensive at the beginning when the entire mortgage amount is due, but premiums usually become lower, the longer the policy is in effect. Your lender or insurance agent can probably provide you with information on this type of insurance.

Foreclosure should be avoided at all costs. A foreclosure can cause a problem with a person's credit report for many years. It can cause a person to have major problems whenever they apply for credit cards, car loans, and future mortgages.

WHEN YOU CAN'T PAY THE MORTGAGE

The first thing a home owner needs to know is that a reputable lender who offers mortgages does not want to foreclose on a home. In addition to the legal costs, there are usually costs associated with getting a building in condition to sell after a foreclosure. The reason is simple—if the homeowner cannot afford the mortgage payment, he or she probably has not been able to pay for maintenance to the home. The key here is a "reputable" lender. Unfortunately, there are some lenders who will prey on the elderly, the inexperienced, and the poor. These lenders eagerly provide a loan at high interest, and when the borrower cannot keep up with the payments quickly move to foreclose and resell the home.

What do you do if you find yourself out of a job or faced with bills from a serious illness? This is a two step process—increase money coming in and reduce the expenses. If you have lost your job, you may qualify for unemployment compensation. You may also qualify under your states or federal assistance plans. Most states have assistance for those without jobs and more local cities are supplementing the state's assistance with their own. Some communities will help with food and utility costs. This assistance can help while you look for a permanent job.

Those who find themselves strapped with large bills from their own or their family's serious illness may also be able to get some assistance from their community or state. If you anticipate large medical bills and you know that you probably will not be able to make payments, notify the hospital or doctor immediately. Waiting until the hospital refers the bills to a collection agency is usually too late. Most collection agencies do not have the ability to negotiate the bill amount. However, many hospitals and clinics employ social workers who can help you get state and local assistance. If you anticipate a problem, be willing to work with that person in resolving your bill.

Assess all of your bills and begin to deal with them one at a time. If you have several high interest credit card bills, you may be able to get that interest rate reduced just by contacting the credit card office. Some loans may allow you to postpone payments for several months if you have lost your job, but do expect to pay extra for this ability.

As for your mortgage, the best thing to do is to contact your lender and see if something can be worked out as soon as the problem arises. Waiting until you have missed several mortgage payments will work against you. If you deal honestly with your mortgage lender, it may be willing to modify your loan or even temporarily suspend payments. Of course, if you have been chronically late in making payments, the lender may not want to work with you.

Lenders hear about money problems all the time. Make sure that your problem is serious and legitimate. Do not attempt to get special consideration from your lender because you want to take a year long vacation or because you want to buy that fancy red sports car. Make sure your financial condition is an emergency.

FEDERAL HOUSING AUTHORITY (FHA), FANNIE MAE, AND FREDDIE MAC

In late 2002, these three organizations reported that they had managed to work-out more borrowers in default with loan modifications than ever before. What this means is that people who were about to lose their homes to foreclosure were able to remain in their homes with some creative financing. The FHA actually reported that for the first time in sixty years they had paid more to help borrowers retain their homes, than to foreclose.

These companies plus many privately owned lenders are putting programs into place that will help borrowers before the missed payments get so large than the lenders must foreclose on the property. Each case is looked at on an individual basis so we cannot provide any blanket terms that the borrower must follow at this time.

FHA has done the most with a policy of *loan forbearance* especially for those who have temporarily lost their job. *Loan modification* extends the loan for more time while reducing the amount of payment. *Partial claims* are for those who have very high unpaid balances, but are good credit risks. FHA usually leads the mortgage industry in innovations. It is expected that other private lenders will see the benefit of using these same methods.

Staying Positive

Buying a home, especially your first one, is not an easy task. Home buyers are expected to make major decisions about the future of their finances; about the future of a community; and, about a building that they often have spent less than sixty minutes inside. Through this process, the first-time home buyer is expected to successfully handle the purchase without the aid of a safety net to catch errors or a crystal ball to predict the future economy.

This book was designed to provide first-time home buyers with enough knowledge that their fear could be reduced and they could go into the land of real estate without needing a safety net.

A home buyer who has done research on a community, who has enlisted the help of qualified home inspectors, and who has an understanding of how mortgage financing will work for them can be confident that they have made the right decision when selecting their first home.

The more information that a home buyer can learn on the process of selecting, financing, and actually purchasing a home, the easier it is for the buyer.

• • • • •

A word to those who bought this book with hopes of getting into their first home right away and for some reason have been forced to put that dream on the back burner.

Do not lose your hopes or your dreams of home ownership. This is the best time to increase your knowledge of the real estate world without the pressure of a purchase right away. Use this time, no matter whether it is one, two, or ten years, to learn about real estate, communities, and government housing. Continue to read the real estate sections in the newspaper. Watch those home shows on TV. Take an occasional "field trip" to another community to look around. Keep increasing your knowledge, even if you think that right now it looks like you will never be able to buy a home. Do not give up on your dream.

With knowledge, you will eventually be able to find that special home that fits both your budget and your lifestyle.

Glossary

A

abatement (tax) — lowering of real property tax because the owner filed an appeal.

above par — situation when a mortgage is sold for more than its face value.

abstract of title — legal history of ownership of real property used when doing a title search.

acceleration clause — part of the mortgage contract that allows the lender to legally demand that the entire mortgage be paid in full because the borrower has failed to make a mortgage payment(s).

accommodation party — person who guarantees a loan for another by signing a promissory note, bill, or other negotiable instrument.

accrued interest — interest earned for a specific period of time.

acre — a unit of measure for land, 43,560 square feet. The land that a home sits on is usually expressed in terms of acre (half-acre, quarter-acre, number of acres).

addendum — an agreement or list that is added to a contract. Sometimes a list of items, such as appliances that the seller is leaving is often added as an addendum to the sales contract.

adjustable rate mortgage (ARM) — type of mortgage that has a variable interest rate based on a certain percentage or financial interest.

adjusted basis — original cost of a property, plus the value of improvements to the property, minus any depreciation taken.

administrator — person who has been appointed by the probate court to dispose of the property owned by someone who has died.

adverse possession — right by which someone occupying a piece of land acquires title against the real owner, if that possession has been actual, continuous, hostile, visible, and distinct for a certain time as stated by law.

affidavit — sworn statement in writing, usually notarized.

agency — federal or governmental organization.

agent — one who legally represents another.

agreement for sale — *See purchase and sales agreement.*

air rights — right to control the air space over a property.

air space — space above the surface of land not occupied by a building.

alienation — legal term for transferring title to real estate.

alienation clause — *See acceleration clause.*

all-cash offer — proposal to purchase property without the contingency of needing to get a mortgage.

amenity — describes any of several extras provided with a house.

American Dream Downpayment Assistance Act — law passed that will provide funds for first time home buyers from 2004 to 2007, with some restrictions.

amortization — repayment of the mortgage over a set number of years, which is the term of the mortgage. Lenders will sometimes provide an amortization schedule, which shows the total of each payment and the portion that is put against the principal and the interest amounts.

amortization schedule — a table showing the amounts of principal and interest due at regular intervals and the unpaid mortgage balance after each payment is made.

annual mortgage statement — report prepared by the lender that states the amount of taxes, insurance, and interest that was paid during the year, and the outstanding principal balance.

annual percentage rate (APR) — the cost of a mortgage stated in a yearly term, similar to APRs for cars or credit cards.

application — form used to apply for a mortgage that provides information on both the borrower and the property selected.

application fee — amount charged the borrower by the lender when the borrower fills out the loan application. (It may include the cost of an appraisal, credit report, lock-in fee or other closing costs.)

apportionment — the legal term for how real estate taxes, insurance premiums, and rents are fairly divided between seller and buyer.

appraisal — written analysis of the value of a house as prepared by a qualified professional after sufficient inspection. (A lender will use an appraisal to determine the amount it will provide as a mortgage to the homebuyer.)

appraiser — person who is professionally qualified to estimate the value of a property.

appreciation — increase in financial value of a home. (The economy, the neighborhood, the condition of the home, the property the home sits on, and other intangibles influence this value.)

appurtenance — legal term meaning things attached to land such as a barn, garage, or an easement.

APR — *See annual percentage rate.*

architect — person who designs homes, additions, and remodeling.

architect's inspection certificate — document issued by an independent architect, verifying that a certain portion of construction on a project has been completed in accordance with approved plans and specifications. (Used when building your own home to show the lender that work has been done.)

ARM — *See adjustable rate mortgage.*

arrears — term for paying the mortgage or real estate taxes after the due date.

asbestos — form of insulation or roofing.

asking price — amount for which a house is offered for sale.

assessed value — value placed on a home by the tax assessor for the purpose of calculating the annual property tax.

assessment rolls — public records of taxable property.

assessor — the government official who appraises taxable property.

asset — property owned that has monetary value.

association fee — money paid to a condominium or townhouse association.

assumable mortgage — mortgage contract that can be transferred from one person to another. (Assumable mortgages are desirable when mortgage rates are currently going up and the assumable mortgage has a significantly lower interest rate.)

assumption/assumption of mortgage — taking over the previous borrower's obligation on a mortgage.

assumption agreement — written agreement by one party to pay an obligation of another under the same terms.

assumption fee — amount paid to the lender for the paperwork processing of an assumption of mortgage.

B

balance sheet — financial statement that shows assets, debts, and net worth.

balloon mortgage — a mortgage contract with low monthly payments that do not increase until the final payment. The final payment, due at the end of the term of the mortgage, is usually very large.

balloon payment — a payment on a mortgage that is larger than the others.

bankruptcy — a legal proceeding in federal court in which a person with more debts than assets can reduce the debt under a trustee's direction.

bear market — market characterized by falling prices. (A bear market in the mortgage industry may be triggered by rising interest rates.)

bedroom community — suburban residential area where most residents commute to neighboring metropolitan areas for work.

below market interest rate (BMIR) — type of mortgage insurance programs where the interest rates on the mortgages are below what is charged; used to assist low- and moderate-income families.

beneficiary — person who receives the proceeds from a trust, will, or estate.

bill of sale — legal document that gives title to personal property. (In a real estate closing, this is used to transfer title on other items that are sold separately by the sellers to the home buyers.)

binder — term used to indicate a preliminary agreement. (In real estate, a buyer usually provides a binder of earnest money with his or her offer to purchase a home.)

bona fide — legal term meaning "in good faith;" without fraud.

borrower — the one who receives funds in the form of a loan with the obligation of repaying the loan in full, with interest.

bottom ratio — *See debt-to-income ratio.*

breach — failure to perform under a contract or the violation of a legal obligation.

bridge loan — loan that enables a homebuyer to get financing to make a down payment and pay closing costs on a new home before selling the present house.

broad form — insurance term used to describe insurance coverage that extends beyond "standard" peril insurance policies, *i.e.,* fire and extended coverage, named perils, etc.

broker — person employed as an agent to bring buyers and sellers together and assist in negotiating contracts between them.

bubble, real estate — term used by financial experts to describe an economic condition where there is a lot of positive real estate activity (buying and selling of homes, new homes being built). This situation usually accompanies low interest rates on mortgages. The bubble theory is that real estate activity can only grow to a certain level, then it will stop and that will cause the value of housing to go down.

builder — person or company that is responsible for the construction of a building.

building code — local regulations and laws that define all aspects of a structure.

building permit — written authorization from a local government for the construction of a new building or for extensive repairs or improvements on an existing structure.

built-ins — permanent, immovable appliances or similar features.

business day — days on which a bank or market is open for business or trading; usually excludes Saturdays, Sundays, and legal public holidays.

buy-down mortgage — money paid by the buyer of a house to reduce the monthly mortgage payments.

buyer's agent — real estate agent hired by the buyer to represent him or her in finding a home and negotiating its purchase.

buyer's market — economic conditions in which the supply of housing exceeds demand. (Sellers may be forced to make substantial price concessions.)

buyer's remorse — feeling when the buyer realizes that he or she has taken on a large debt.

C

cancellation clause — provision in a contract that lists the conditions under which each party may end the agreement.

capital improvement — a major investment in a home that becomes part of the home, such as remodeled kitchen, garage, and additional rooms.

capped rate — rate commitment by a lender that locks in a maximum rate, but allows the borrower to relock if market rates decrease.

caps (interest) — a consumer safeguard on an adjustable-rate mortgage that limits the amount that the interest rate may change per year or over the life of the loan.

caps (payment) — a consumer safeguard on an adjustable-rate mortgage that limits the amount monthly payments may change.

carryback financing — agreement whereby the seller takes back a note for part of the purchase price secured by a junior mortgage, wrap-around mortgage, or contract for deed.

certificate of completion — document issued by an architect or engineer stating that construction is completed in accordance with the terms, conditions, approved plans, and specifications.

certificate of deposit index — index commonly used for interest rate changes in ARM mortgages.

certificate of eligibility — used in a VA-guaranteed mortgage to prove that the veteran has legally qualified for the loan.

certificates of insurance — form that shows insurance policy coverage, limits, etc.; generally used as proof of insurance.

certificate of reasonable value (CRV) — used in a VA-guaranteed mortgage, it is the appraisal issued to the Veterans Administration that shows the property's value.

certificate of occupancy — written authorization given by local government that legally allows a newly completed or substantially renovated structure to be used by people.

certificate of title — a document drafted by a title company, attorney, or abstract company that states who is the legal owner of a property.

certificate of veteran status — an FHA form completed by the Department of Veteran Affairs in order to establish a borrower's eligibility for an FHA, Vet Mortgage.

chain of title — the history of who owned or had liens on a property.

Chamber of Commerce — association of merchants for the promotion of commercial interests in the community; provides valuable information on the town.

Chapter 7 — type of bankruptcy filing which gives a trustee the power to distribute a debtor's assets to creditors.

Chapter 11 — type of bankruptcy used by businesses that is a reorganization of debts with a repayment schedule that is acceptable to the creditors.

Chapter 13 — type of bankruptcy where an individual debtor files a budget with the court and agrees to make partial payments to creditors over a three-to-five year period.

child support — a monthly amount of money decided by a court that is paid by the noncustodial parent to the custodial parent for the economic maintenance and education of a child.

clear title — a title to property that does not have liens or legal complications.

closed listing — right of one real estate agent to be the only one who may sell the property during a period of time.

closed period — an interval of time under a mortgage during which the loan cannot be prepaid.

closing — the event where the purchase of the property is completed. It is usually attended by the buyer, seller, and lender (or their legal representatives). Documents are signed, money exchanged, and the buyer gets the keys to the home.

closing costs — expenses in addition to the price of the property that are paid by both buyer and seller.

closing statement — document commonly called a HUD-1 (the number on the form) that lists the final costs incurred to get the mortgage loan and buy the home.

cloud on title — a lien on a title that must be cleared up for the title to pass from the seller to the buyer.

cluster zoning — zoning procedure where there is a limit on the number of houses, structures, or density for an entire area.

coborrower — additional person equally responsible for payments on a mortgage.

collateral — an asset put up to guarantee that a loan will be repaid. (In a mortgage, the property is put up as collateral.)

commission — real estate agent's compensation for negotiating a real estate transaction, often expressed as a percentage of the selling price.

commissioner's adjusted fair market value (CAFMV) — HUD's estimate of the fair market value of a property in foreclosure.

commitment — agreement (often in writing) between a lender and a borrower to accept loaned money at a future date, subject to specified conditions.

commitment (builder) — agreement by a lender to provide long-term financing to a builder, secured by an existing or proposed building(s).

commitment fee — fee paid by a potential borrower to a potential lender for the lender's promise to loan money at a specified date in the future.

commitment letter — promise from a lender to provide the borrower with a mortgage.

community property — in some states, a form of ownership whereby property acquired during a marriage is presumed to be owned jointly.

Community Reinvestment Act (CRA) — federal legislation that requires every financial institution to help meet the credit needs of its entire community, including low- and moderate-income neighborhoods.

comortgagor — second borrower who signs a mortgage loan with a mortgagor.

comparables — similar properties in the same area that have recently sold.

compound interest — situation where interest is computed on both the original principal and accrued interest.

condemnation — taking of private property for public use under the right of eminent domain with just compensation paid the owner.

condominium — form of property ownership where the purchaser receives title to a unit in a multiunit structure and a portion of interest in common areas.

condominium association fee — fee paid by the homeowner to the association that governs a condominium.

condominium conversion — process of changing rental units into a condominium form of ownership.

consideration — something of value offered and accepted in exchange for a promise, without which a contract is unenforceable.

construction contract — agreement between a general contractor and an owner/developer stating the specific duties the general contractor will perform according to blueprints and specifications at a stipulated price and terms of payment.

construction costs — all costs incurred in the construction project, including land, labor, overhead, and builder's profit.

construction loan — short-term, interim loan for financing the cost of construction. The lender advances funds to the builder at periodic intervals as work progresses.

construction loan agreement — written agreement between a lender and a builder or borrower that details the specific terms and conditions of a construction loan, including the schedule of payments.

consumer credit counseling program — a program to help a consumer lower his or her debts, prepare a budget, and clean up any credit score problems.

contingency — a condition that must be met before a contract can be enforced. (In an offer contract for real estate, common contingencies are that the property pass inspections and the buyers are able to obtain financing.)

contract sale or deed — document between the buyer and seller that conveys the title to the property.

contiguous — adjoining or next to.

contract to purchase — *See purchase and sale agreement.*

contractor — person or company who agrees to do work and/or furnish materials for a contracted price. (Subcontractors are often hired by the contractor to perform specialized or technical labor.)

conventional financing — mortgage financing that is not insured or guaranteed by a government agency.

conventional loan — mortgage that is not insured by FHA or VA.

conversion feature — feature of a mortgage that allows the conversion to another interest rate, mortgage term, or type of mortgage instrument.

convertible ARM — an adjustable-rate mortgage that can be converted to a fixed-rate mortgage on certain conditions.

convertible mortgage — type of adjustable-rate mortgage that may be converted to a fixed-rate mortgage.

cooling-off period — period of time, provided by law or by contract, during which a party to a contract can legally back out of a contract.

cooperative (co-op) — form of multiple ownership in which a corporation or business trust entity holds title to a property, (usually an apartment complex) and grants occupancy rights to shareholder tenants through leases.

cosigner — person who agrees to assume a debt obligation if the primary borrower defaults.

Cost of Funds Index (COFI) — an index that may be used to set interest rates in an ARM.

cost of living — cost of the basic necessities of life.

counter offer — home seller's response to buyer's offer on the house.

covenant — legal term for an enforceable promise or a restriction in a mortgage.

credit rating — rating given to a person that establishes credit.

credit report — a professionally created report on a person's credit history.

credit scores — a number calculated by the credit bureaus that represents the likelihood that a person will pay his or her bills on time. *See FICO.*

credit worthiness — a determination done by comparing a person's borrowing history with that of other consumers.

cul de sac — residential street that ends in a large turn around.

cycle (economic) — period of time, such as when the economy is growing or when it is in a recession.

D

debt-to-income ratio — the percentage of a person's income that is already allocated to debts such as, mortgages, loans, utilities, and credit cards.

deed — legal document that conveys title to a property.

deed-in-lieu — deed given by a borrower or mortgagor to a lender or mortgagee to satisfy a debt and avoid foreclosure.

deed of trust — in some states, a legal document is used in place of, or in addition to, a mortgage document to secure the payment.

default — when a person does not pay on the mortgage or any other kind of loan.

default letter — letter sent to the borrower indicating that the mortgage has not been paid or that the borrower has violated one of the requirements of the mortgage (such as keeping the property insured) and asks what the lender is going to do about this issue.

deferred interest — a mortgage that is written so the interest payments are delayed for a period of time.

Department of Housing and Urban Development (HUD) — government agency whose primary purpose is to provide mortgage insurance.

Department of Veterans Affairs (VA) — agency of the U.S. government that manages benefits and other issues for veterans of the military.

depreciation — the decline in value of a property; opposite of appreciation.

deposit — *See earnest money.*

developer — person or entity who prepares raw land for building sites or rehabilitates existing buildings.

direct lender — a mortgage lender of any size that makes loans from the lenders' own portfolio of assets.

discount point — fees used to lower the interest rate on a mortgage. These fees are paid up front, usually at the time of closing.

down payment — the initial amount of money a buyer will pay for a property, in addition to the money from a mortgage.

documentary stamp — mark or actual stamp put on a deed that indicates the proper transfer tax has been paid.

dual agency — person who acts as an agent for two people or entities.

due date — date mortgage payment is required.

due-on-sale clause — legal clause in the mortgage contract that allows the lender to demand immediate payment of the balance on the mortgage when the mortgage holder sells the home.

E

earnest money — a significant amount of money that the potential buyer puts down with the offer to buy that shows that the potential buyer is serious about going through with the deal.

easement — right-of-way given to someone other than the owner of a property that allows some access to the property. (Some examples are a shared driveway, a common fence, and utility poles.)

economic depreciation — loss in the value of real estate due to changes outside the particular property affected, *e.g.*, a decline in the neighborhood or change in zoning.

egress — to go out.

eminent domain — the right of government to take private property for public use after the property owner is paid market value for the property.

encroachment — an improvement that illegally intrudes on someone else's property.

encumbrance — something that limits the ownership of a property, such as mortgage, liens, or easements.

engineer's report — report done by an engineer stating the physical condition of property.

enterprise zone — depressed neighborhood, usually in an urban area, in which businesses are given tax incentives and are not subject to some government regulations. (These advantages are designed to attract new businesses into the particular area or zone.)

environmental impact statement (EIS) — document required by many federal, state, and local environmental land use laws, containing an analysis of the impact that a proposed change may have on the environment of a specific geographic region.

equity — amount of the property that the owner has paid for by mortgage payments, down payment, plus the increase in the value of the home.

Equal Credit Opportunity Act (ECOA) — federal law that requires lenders and other creditors to make credit equally available without discrimination based on race, color, religion, national origin, age, sex, marital status, or receipt of income from public assistance programs.

escrow — in purchasing real estate, a third party holds earnest money in escrow. The third party will deliver the escrow amount upon certain conditions, such as the purchase of the property.

escrow account — the term used by mortgage companies for the funds used to pay the tax on a property.

escrow agent — person or organization that has legal responsibility to both the buyer and seller (or lender and borrower) to see that the terms of the purchase/sale (or loan) are carried out. (This person usually holds the escrow amounts.)

escrow analysis — periodic examination of escrow accounts to determine if current monthly deposits will provide sufficient funds to pay taxes, insurance, and other bills when due.

escrow closing — when the money is taken out of the escrow account.

escrow company — organization established to act as an escrow agent.

escrow contract — three-party agreement between the buyer, seller, and the escrow agent, specifying the rights and duties of each.

escrow overage or shortage — difference, determined by escrow analysis, between escrow funds on deposit and escrow funds required to make a payment when it becomes due.

escrow payment — portion of a mortgagor's monthly payments held by a lender to pay taxes and insurance as they become due.

escrow transfer agreement — document transferring escrow funds held by the lender to a third party upon transfer of property.

estate — ownership an individual has in real property.

evidence of title — proof of ownership of property.

examination of title — review of the chain of title as revealed by an abstract of title or public record.

exclusive listing — *See closed listing.*

exclusive right to sell — *See closed listing.*

F

401(k) — employer-sponsored investment program to set aside tax-deferred money for retirement.

FHA value — value established by the FHA as the basis for determining the maximum mortgage amount that may be insured on a specific property. (The FHA value is the sum of the appraised value of the property plus HUD and FHA's estimate of closing costs.)

Fair Credit Reporting Act — law that protects consumers through federal regulations on the total interest paid over the life of the loan and procedures to repair errors on a person's credit report.

fair market value — the current price for which a property should sell.

faith financing — mortgages, loans, and other financial assistance that is structured to the rules of a person's religion.

Fannie Mae (FNMA) — a corporation created by the government that buys and sells conventional mortgages and mortgages that are insured by the FHA or VA.

Farmers Home Administration (FmHA) — organization that provides loans specifically to farmers who are unable to find other financing.

Federal Home Loan Mortgage Corporation (FHLMC) — *See Freddie Mac.*

Federal Housing Administration (FHA) — division of HUD that insures residential mortgage loans and sets standards for underwriting.

Federal National Mortgage Association — *See Fannie Mae.*

Federal Trade Commission (FTC) — government agency that monitors credit bureaus.

FHA loan — loan insured by the Federal Housing Administration.

FICO — a credit score calculation, developed by Fair Isaac & Co., that private credit bureaus use to indicate the likelihood that a person will pay his or her bills on time.

firm commitment — lender's agreement to provide a mortgage loan.

first mortgage — for those who have multiple mortgages on a home, this one is the first in time. (First mortgages will be paid off first in a foreclosure.)

fixed-rate mortgages — mortgage where the interest and the payment remain the same for the term of the loan.

fixture — personal property that becomes part of the real estate, such as a shed attached to the garage or curtain rods bolted to the wall.

flip mortgage — *See pledged account mortgage.*

flood insurance — insurance for losses due to water damage. (This may be required by the lender.)

flood plain — land that is subject to flooding when a stream or river is at flood stage.

floor plan — architectural drawings showing details of floor design and layout.

forbearance — used when lenders do not take legal action (fore-closure), despite the fact that the mortgage is in arrears. It is usually granted when the borrower makes satisfactory arrangements to pay the amount owed at a future date.

foreclosure — legal process where a lender forces the sale of property because the borrower could not make the mortgage payments.

Freddie Mac (FHLMC) — agency that purchases conventional mortgages from HUD approved bankers.

front-end ratio — *See housing to income ratio.*

G

gap financing — *See bridge loan.*

garnishment — legal notice from the courts to an employer to hold out money from a person's wage in order to pay back a legal debt.

general contractor — party that performs or supervises the construction or development of a property. The general contractor may use his or her own employees for this work or the services of other contractors (subcontractors).

Ginnie Mae (GNMA) — agency of the government that purchases conventional mortgages from HUD approved bankers.

GI loan — old term for a VA guaranteed mortgage loan.

government mortgages — mortgages insured or guaranteed by the government.

Government National Mortgage Association (GNMA) — *See Ginnie Mae.*

grace period — time allowed to get something done.

grantee — person who gets the property (buyer).

grantor — person who gives the property (seller).

gross monthly income — income received each month from every source before taxes deductions for employer incentive savings program 401(k).

groundwater — water that is present in the subsoil.

growing equity mortgage (GEM) — graduated payment mortgage in which increases in a borrower's mortgage payments are used to accelerate reduction of principal on the mortgage.

guaranteed loan — loan that a government agency assures the lender will be paid back even if the borrower defaults.

guarantor — person who is also liable for another's debt or performance.

guaranty — promise to pay the debts of another.

H

handy-man's special — term with no set definition by the real estate industry; usually refers to a home that needs maintenance.

hazard insurance — insurance against specific losses.

hidden defect — a problem with the title that is not apparent in public records. (Examples of hidden defects are unknown heirs, secret marriages, forged instruments, mental incompetence, or infancy of a grantor.)

home equity line of credit loan — open-end loan, usually recorded as a second mortgage, that permits borrowers to obtain cash advances based on an approved line of credit; home is used as collateral.

home improvement loan — mortgage to finance an addition to or rehabilitation of a residence.

home inspection — done by a professional to evaluate structural and mechanical condition of a property.

home loan — mortgage loan secured by a real property.

Home Mortgage Disclosure Act (HMDA) — federal legislation that requires certain types of lenders to compile and disclose data on where their mortgage and home improvement loans are being made.

home warranty — insures a new home against major structural damage for a set period of time, usually ten years.

homeowners association — a group of owners who manage the common areas and set the rules; usually found in condominiums or closed communities.

homeowners insurance — insurance policy that protects the owners and the mortgage holder from loss.

homestead estate — in some states, a legal exemption that prohibits the attachment, lien, or sale of owner-occupied properties to pay the claims of creditors.

house value — determined by upkeep of the home, upgrades made to the home, the neighborhood, and the economy.

housing costs — used in the housing-to-income ratio; includes monthly loan payment, real estate taxes, and insurance.

housing expense ratio — *See debt-to-income ratio.*

Housing Finance Agency (HFA) — state or local agency responsible for the financing of housing and the administration of subsidized housing programs.

housing starts — number of residential units actually under construction. (This is a key economic indicator and is used in analyzing real estate and mortgage trends.)

housing-to-income ration — total mortgage payment is divided by a person's gross monthly income to arrive at a ratio.

HUD-1 Uniform Settlement Statement — standard form used to disclose costs at closing. All charges imposed in the transaction, including mortgage broker fees, must be disclosed separately.

HVAC — real estate term for heating, ventilating, and air-conditioning system.

I

immigrant home buyers — those who are not native to the United States.

impound — that portion of the monthly mortgage payment that is held in escrow by the lender to pay for taxes and insurance.

improved land — land that already has utilities, streets, sewers, or other improvements.

incentive zoning — agreement between public officials and private developers whereby developers are offered an incentive to build a desired public improvement.

income/expense ratio — qualifying ratio used in underwriting a residential mortgage loan that computes the percentage of monthly income required to meet the monthly housing expense.

income limits — income restrictions established for people to qualify for the low- to moderate-income subsidized housing programs.

income property — property such as an apartment building, a condominium, or a house that is rented for money.

index — a rate used to compute the index on adjustable-rate mortgages.

inflation — increase in the general price level of goods and services.

informational sheet — piece of paper real estate agents possess containing the details of a home.

infrastructure — basic public improvements such as roads, sewers, water, drainage, and other utilities that are necessary to prepare raw land for buildings and future development.

ingress — legal term for to go in.

inspection — the act of having a professional inspector look at a property and complete a report on the positives and negatives of that property.

inspector — person hired to complete a thorough examination of the house on behalf of the buyer; credentials certified by major home inspection associations.

installment loan — loan that is repaid in equal payments over a particular time period, such as a mortgage or car loan.

instant sale contract — *See sale-buyback.*

insurable interest — stake that a borrower, lender, or owner must have in real property in order to be able to get insurance against loss of that stake.

insurable title — title to a property for which a title insurance company has agreed to issue a policy.

insurance binder — a document written by an insurance company that states that temporary insurance is in effect. (This is required at a closing to prove that the buyer has contacted the insurance company and they will provide insurance coverage.)

insured closing letter — document issued by a title insurance company that protects a mortgagee against embezzlement or failure to follow specific closing instructions.

intangible property — property that has no intrinsic or marketable value in and of itself, but is merely the evidence of value, such as promissory notes, stock certificates, or certificates of deposits (as distinguished from land, furniture, and equipment).

interest — the cost for borrowing money.

interest rate — percentage paid for the use of money, usually expressed as an annual percentage.

interest rate cap — limit on interest rate increases and/or decreases during each interest rate adjustment (adjustment period cap) or over the term (life cap) of the mortgage.

interim financing — financing used from the beginning of a project to the closing of a permanent loan; usually found in a construction or development loan.

intestate — die without a will.

irrigation district — product of special state laws to provide for water services to property owners. These districts have the power to tax, borrow, and condemn.

J

joint tenancy — ownership of a property by two or more people. Each person holds an undivided part of the property. (For example, a husband and wife can each own 50% of property in joint tenancy.)

jointly-owned property — property held in the name of more than one person in equal portions.

judgment — legal decision issued by a court. (In real estate, it is used to place liens against a property for nonpayment of debts or taxes.)

judicial foreclosure — foreclosure proceeding used in some states that is handled as a civil lawsuit.

jurisdiction — the area where the property is located.

L

land development loan — loan for the acquisition of land to be held in anticipation of zoning, until plans are drawn and construction financing can be obtained.

landscape — used as an activity, to plant foliage and ground cover around a house. As a description on real estate, describes the ground cover, trees, shrubs, and other foliage that is planted around a home.

land-use zones — where local government ordinances dictate permitted land use.

late charge — financial penalty for making a debt payment past the due date.

lease-purchase mortgage loans — *See rent with an option to buy.*

legal description — description of the property that is recorded in public records. (A professional surveyor usually does this.)

lender — bank or financial institution that lends money to buyers.

lender paid mortgage insurance — mortgage insurance program that allows the lender to collect a higher interest rate from the borrower and forward the excess interest to the mortgage insurance company to pay for the mortgage insurance.

letter of credit — letter authorizing a person or company to draw on a bank or stating that the bank will honor their credit up to the stated amount.

letter of intent — letter stating that a buyer or developer is interested in a property.

lien — a legal claim against the property that must be cleared before the owner can sell the property.

life estate — the rights of a person to live in a home until he or she dies.

liquid assets — those things that can quickly be converted to cash. (Stocks and bonds are types of examples.)

lis pendens — legal notice recorded in the official records of a county to indicate that there is a pending suit affecting real property.

listing — commonly used term for the sheet of information on real property that each real estate agent has access to.

listing agent — the real estate agent who signs the contract with the seller to *list* the property for sale.

loan — the amount of money one person or entity lets another borrow.

loan administration — function that includes the receipt of payments, customer service, escrow administration, investor accounting, collections, and foreclosures.

loan forbearance — *See loan modification.*

loan modification — extends the loan for more time while reducing the amount of payment.

loan origination — procedures that a lender follows to produce a mortgage on real property.

loan origination fee — fee charged a borrower by a lender for negotiating a loan.

loan submission — package of pertinent papers and documents regarding a specific property or properties, delivered to a prospective lender to obtain financing.

loan transfer — assumption of existing financing by a new owner when a property is sold.

local housing authority — government agency that monitors and implements programs to satisfy community housing development needs.

location — where the home sits, in terms of neighbors, neighboring structures, city, county, and state.

lockbox — postal address maintained by a mortgagor used solely for the purpose of collecting mortgage checks. (In some areas a lockbox is actually a metal box which locks onto the front door of a home for sale. The real estate agents have keys to the lockboxes. Inside the lockbox is the actual key to the home.)

lock-in — a written contract from the lender that guarantees a particular interest rate on a particular property for a set period of time.

lock-in fee — another fee charged by some lenders at the time the borrower is given a lock-in mortgage rate.

lock-in period — number of days during which a lender guarantees a borrower a specific interest rate and terms on a mortgage.

long-term financing — mortgage or loan with a term of ten years or more.

lot — measured parcel of land having fixed boundaries as shown on the recorded plat.

M

maintenance fee — a charge for work done.

market value — approximate price that a property can get when sold. (It is calculated by looking at comparables and factoring in the potential growth of the area.)

mechanic's lien — lien placed against property by an "unpaid" private contractor.

military indulgence — protection enacted and provided by the Soldier's and *Sailor's Civil Relief Act* to a mortgagor who is about to enter or is in the military and whose ability to keep a loan current has been materially affected by military service.

minimum lot zoning — type of zoning that specifies the smallest lot size permitted per building.

mobile home — factory-assembled residence consisting of one or more modules, in which a chassis and wheels are an integral part of the structure, and can be readied for occupancy without removing the chassis or wheels.

monthly payment — payments of principal and interest collected by mortgage lenders every 30-31 days. This payment may also include escrow items for taxes or insurance and thereby called the housing payment.

moratorium — legal authorization to suspend an activity.

mortgage — a loan for purchase of property where the property is put up as collateral.

mortgage banker — company that exclusively writes mortgages to buyers and sells mortgages to other mortgage bankers.

mortgage broker — a person who finds a mortgage for a buyer for a fee or commission.

mortgage commitment — agreement between lender and borrower detailing the terms of a mortgage loan such as interest rate, loan type, term, and amount.

mortgagee — the lender.

mortgage insurance — an insurance contract that will pay the lender should the borrower default on the mortgage loan.

mortgage life insurance — insurance policy that will pay the rest of the mortgage due if the primary borrower dies.

mortgagor — the borrower.

multiple listing services (MLS) — provides information to all real estate agents that are registered members, about every house that other members are selling.

mutual funds — relatively safe investment in a grouping of bonds and stocks.

N

NAIC (National Association of Insurance Commissioners) — organization whose membership consists of state insurance regulators. (NAIC's objectives are to promote uniformity in regulation by drafting model laws and regulations for adoption by the states and to provide support services to insurance departments such as examinations and statistical information.)

named perils — insurance term for a policy that will specifically list the perils insured against as opposed to an "all risk" policy that covers all perils other than those specifically excluded.

National Association of Home Builders (NAHB) — national trade association that provides support to the building industry through lobbying and educational services.

National Association of Mortgage Brokers (NAMB) — professional society for mortgage brokers that was developed to foster professional business relationships.

National Association of Realtors® (NAR) — trade association representing real estate sales professionals. (Realtors® is a registered trade mark of the National Association, and is properly used only to describe members of the Association, not all real estate brokers or agents.)

negative amortization — unpaid interest that is added to the mortgage principal in a loan where the principal balance increases rather than decreases because the mortgage payments do not cover the full amount of interest due.

net proceeds — amount of cash that the seller gets after expenses are deducted from a home sale.

net worth — value of all the person's assets minus all his or her debts.

nonassumption clause — clause in a mortgage that prohibits the assumption of a mortgage by a third party without approval of the lender.

nonconforming use — permitted use of real property that does not conform to current zoning laws.

note — legal document that obligates a borrower to repay a debt.

notice of default — document sent to defaulting borrowers, required by insurers or guarantors such as FHA, VA, or MIC.

O

offer — legally presenting the seller(s) with a contract to purchase; acceptance is not guaranteed.

off-site improvements — those improvements *outside* the boundaries of a property that enhance its value, such as sidewalks, streets, curbs, and gutters.

on-site improvements — improvements *within* the boundaries of a property that increase its value.

open and notorious — legal description of the use of property that is essential in establishing adverse possession; technically means not hidden.

open equity line — second mortgage that is an open line of credit; the balance can be increased by future draws up to a set amount.

open listing — written contract that does not allow one licensed real estate agent the exclusive right to sell a property for a specified time, but reserving the owner's right to sell the property alone without the payment of a commission.

option — an extra, such as an "renting with an option to buy" or granite counter tops as an option in building a kitchen.

origination date — the date of the mortgage note.

origination fee — *See points.*

over-improvement/overbuild — building, renovation or remodeling that is inappropriate to an area due to excess size, cost, or inadequate return on investment.

owner-occupied purchase — purchase of a property as the primary residence of the owner.

owner financing — seller provides part or all of the financing in the sale of real estate.

P

partial entitlement — the remaining dollar amount of a veteran's entitlement after the veteran has used part of his or her full entitlement of a VA mortgage.

partial payment — payment of only a portion of the required amount due, including payments received without the late charge.

payment cap — limitation on increases or decreases in the payment amount of an adjustable-rate mortgage or fixed-rate mortgage.

payment history — part of a person's credit report; records of late and on-time payments.

payoff letter — statement detailing the unpaid principal balance, accrued interest, outstanding late charges, legal fees, and all other amounts necessary to pay off the lender in full.

percolation test — test performed on soil to determine its ability to absorb liquid, for either septic tank or construction purposes.

perfecting title — elimination of claims against title on real estate.

plat — map representing a piece of land subdivided into lots with streets, boundaries, easements, with legal dimensions shown.

plat book — book showing the lots and legal descriptions of the subdivisions of an area; usually recorded and kept in city and county government offices.

pledged account mortgage (PAM) — graduated payment mortgage in which part of the buyer's down payment is deposited into a savings account; funds are drawn from the account to supplement the buyer's monthly payments during the early years of the loan.

plot plan — layout of improvements on a site, including their location, dimensions, and landscapes. (The plot plan is generally a part of the architectural plan.)

POC — charge that is paid outside of closing. (This would include closing costs such as the appraisal and credit report that an applicant pays up-front to the lender.)

points — an amount paid to the lender for processing the mortgage, with one point equal to one percent of the mortgage amount.

police power — the right by which the state or other governmental authority may take, condemn, destroy, impair the value of, limit the use of, or otherwise invade a person's property.

portfolio lenders — a mortgage lender who makes loans from the lender's own portfolio of assets.

power of attorney — legal document authorizing one person to act on behalf of another.

preapproval — agreement from a lender to loan a buyer a particular amount of money.

prearranged financing agreement — used in some areas of the country to prove that the buyer has been pre-approved for a mortgage loan.

preclosing — in some states there is a meeting preceding formal closing in which documents are reviewed and signed.

prepayment — payment made in addition to the required monthly mortgage payment. (Prepayment allows a borrower to pay down a mortgage loan quicker than originally planned as the payment goes against the principal, not the interest.)

prepayment penalty — charge for paying ahead on a mortgage.

prequalified — buyer who has been preliminarily approved for a loan; not a guarantee and final approval will depend on further investigation.

price level adjusted mortgage (PLAM) — mortgage loan in which the interest rate remains fixed, but the outstanding balance is adjusted periodically for inflation according to a price index like the Consumer Price Index or Cost-of-Living Index. At the end of each period, the outstanding balance is adjusted for inflation and monthly payments are recomputed based on the new balance.

primary residence — home that the owner physically occupies.

prime rate — interest rate commercial banks charge their most creditworthy customers for short-term loans. Prime is a yardstick for trends in interest rates, and it is often a baseline for establishing interest rates on high-risk loans.

principal — amount of debt on a loan that does not include interest.

principal, interest, taxes, and insurance (PITI) — components of a monthly mortgage payment.

private mortgage insurance (PMI) — agreement to give money to the lender, if the buyer defaults on his or her payments.

promissory note — legal agreement to repay a certain amount of money.

proof of loss — a formal statement by an insured to his or her insurance company with information on a loss and the dollar amount of the damage.

property inspection — physical review or evaluation of a property to determine its current structural condition with a report identifying any deferred maintenance or environmental problems.

property tax — tax against the owner of real estate.

pro rate — a method to distribute income, ownership, or debts in a fair manner to both the buyer and the seller.

public auction — process whereby property that has been foreclosed is sold.

purchase and sale agreement — legal document signed by both the buyer and seller to pass property with specific terms for a certain amount of money.

Q

qualification — process that determines whether an applicant can be approved for a mortgage loan.

quick assets — *See liquid assets.*

quiet enjoyment — right of an owner to the use of property without disturbance.

quiet title action — legal action taken to eliminate any interest or claim to property by others.

quit claim deed — a deed that transfers property without warranty; the seller transfers whatever interest he or she has in the property at that point in time to the buyer.

R

radon — radioactive gas found in some homes that may or may not cause health problems.

ratio method — a calculation that mortgage lenders use to determine approximately how much a person can afford to pay for a home. The most common ratio calculation is the 28/36 formula. According to this formula, the total mortgage payment should be no more than 28% of a borrower's gross income. The borrower's total debts should be no more than 36% of his or her gross income.

raw land — land in its natural state, having no physical improvements such as grading, sewers, or structures.

real estate — the term generally used for both buildings and land.

real estate agent — person who is licensed to process the sale of real estate.

real estate attorney — an attorney that works primarily in the area of real estate law.

real estate broker — person who does the same duties as a real estate agent, in addition to searching for homes, arranging funding, and negotiating contracts.

real estate laws — regulations on a city, county, or state level that direct real estate transactions and the actions of real estate agents or brokers.

real estate property taxes — *See real estate taxes.*

Real Estate Settlement Procedures Act (RESPA) — law that provides consumer protection by requiring lenders to give borrowers notice of closing costs.

real estate taxes — local government annual fees levied on the ownership of real estate.

reassessment — revaluation of property for tax purposes.

real property — legal name for the home, the land, other permanent structures, and all other rights included as the property for sale.

realtor® — real estate professional who has membership in a local real estate board that is affiliated with the *National Association of Realtors®.*

recission — cancellation of a transaction or contract.

reconciliation — last step in the appraisal process whereby all data is compared and the approaches to value considered to arrive at a final estimate of value.

recordation fees — the fees charged by a local government to record the documents of a real estate transaction.

recorder — public official or office who legally records the deed after the property has been sold or transferred.

recording — filing a legal document that makes it a matter of public record.

recourse loan — type of mortgage loan whereby the lender's remedies in the event of borrower default are unlimited, extending beyond the property to the borrower's personal assets.

red lining — arbitrary denial of real estate loan applications in certain geographical areas, without considering individual applicant qualifications.

reduced closing cost mortgage — mortgage that carries a higher interest rate in exchange for no points or a credit towards other closing costs from the lender.

refinance — exchanging an old mortgage for a new mortgage with a lower interest rate.

Regulation B — *See Equal Credit Opportunity Act (ECOA).*

Regulation Z — regulation written by the Federal Reserve Board to implement the *Truth in Lending Act*, requiring full written disclosure of the credit portion of a purchase, including the annual percentage rate.

regulatory agency — arm of the state or federal government that has the responsibility to license, pass laws, regulate, audit, and monitor industry related issues (*i.e.*, NAIC, FHLBB, HUD).

rehabilitation — process of reconstructing or improving property that is in a state of disrepair, bringing it back to its full potential or use.

rehabilitation loan — term used by some lenders for a loan that replaces a defaulted student loan and clears up negative credit scores due to defaulting on student loans.

reinstatement — fixing of all mortgage defaults by a borrower to return it to current status.

release — discharge of secured property from a lien.

release of liability — agreement by a lender to terminate personal obligation of a mortgagor in connection with payment of a debt.

release of lien — the document that discharges a secured property from a lien.

release price — dollar amount needed to remove a lien.

remediation — a process that removes contaminants from a building or site.

rent with an option to buy — agreement between the owner of a property and the potential buyer whereby the rent or a portion of the rent will be applied to a down payment on the property at a certain date.

replacement cost — cost to replace a structure with one of an equivalent value and function, but not necessarily identical in design or materials.

replacement cost endorsement — insurance endorsement used with a policy to insure that coverage is on a replacement cost basis.

restrictive covenant — clause in a deed or lease that denies the buyer or lessor full rights to the property in question.

retirement community — planned community for those of retirement age, providing attractively sized and priced dwelling units, and offering construction features, amenities and locations for aging residents.

return on investment (ROI) — percentage of profit returned in relation to the original amount invested in a project.

reverse annuity mortgage (RAM) — mortgage that uses present equity in the property to fund monthly payments from the lender to the borrower *in lieu* of the borrower receiving the proceeds of the loan in a lump sum. (This type of mortgage is popular with the elderly.)

reversionary clause — clause providing that any violations of restrictions will cause title to the property to go back to the party who imposed the restrictions.

revolving credit — open lines of credit that are subject to variable payments in accordance with the balance.

rider — additional clause(s) in a real estate contract that are required by local law.

right of first refusal — right given by an owner stating that if the owner decides to sell the property, this person will have the first opportunity to purchase it.

right of ingress or egress — in real estate, it is the right to enter or leave a portion of the property.

right of redemption — in some states, a right permitting the borrower to reclaim foreclosed property by making full payment of the foreclosure sales price within a specified period of time.

right of survivorship — characteristic of joint tenancy. If one of the owners dies, the other owner gets the deceased's portion without going through probate.

right of way — right to pass over land owned by another. Also, a strip of land used for a street or railway.

riparian rights — rights of owners to the water and land within the normal flow of a river or stream, or below a high water mark. (These rights vary with state laws.)

rural housing service (RHS) — government agency within the U.S. Department of Agriculture that offers various financing programs available for the development of rural America.

S

sale-buyback — financing arrangement where a developer sells a property to an investor then buys it back on a long-term sales contract.

sale-leaseback — sales arrangement where a seller deeds a property to a buyer for consideration. The seller then leases the same property back from its new owner.

sales contract — written agreement between buyer and seller stating terms and conditions of a sale or exchange of property.

seasoned mortgage — mortgage on which payments have been made regularly for a year or longer.

second mortgage — for those who have multiple mortgages, this is the one that is second in time. (In a foreclosure, the second mortgage gets paid off after the first mortgage.)

secondary market — the purchase of existing mortgages by other lenders. (This usually does not increase mortgage payments, but can effect the benefits offered with the mortgage loan.)

section — legal division or parcel of land on a government survey comprising one square or 640 acres.

secured loan — loan that is backed by collateral.

security instrument — mortgage using real estate as collateral for the loan.

seller's agent — the real estate agent who represents the seller of the property in the transaction.

senior mortgage — a first mortgage.

settlement — another name for the closing.

settlement costs — money paid by borrowers and sellers to effect the closing of a mortgage loan, including payments for title insurance, survey, attorney fees, and such prepaid items as taxes and insurance escrow.

settlement statement — *See HUD-1 Uniform Settlement Statement.*

Shariah Program — faith financing that is sanctioned by the Shariah Supervisory Board of America, a panel of ten Islamic scholars that monitors financial products targeting Muslims.

sheriff's deed — deed given by court order when a property is sold to satisfy a judgment or tax lien.

site plan — drawing that shows all improvements to be done on a site, such as clearing, grading, and the installation of public utilities.

site value — value of land without improvements, as if vacant.

sky lease — lease of air rights.

special assessment district — government created subdivision with the power to tax and improve property within its jurisdiction.

special warranty deed — deed containing a covenant whereby the grantor agrees to protect the grantee against any claims arising during the grantor's period of ownership.

spot zoning — government zoning on a lot by lot basis, following no prescribed pattern or plan.

staff appraiser — appraiser who works as an employee for a mortgage company, as opposed to the company hiring an independent firm to appraise properties.

standard metropolitan statistical area (SMSA) — central city area and its surrounding suburbs and small jurisdictions.

starter home — beginning home that is less than what the buyer really wants; typically purchased for the purposes of building credit and experience in home ownership.

starts — number of residential housing units begun within a stated period of time.

statutes of fraud — state laws requiring that certain contracts be in writing; including contracts for the sale of real property.

strict foreclosure — type of foreclosure proceeding used in some states in which title to the foreclosed property is invested directly in the mortgagee by court decree, without holding a foreclosure sale.

student loans — loans taken through an educational institution to pay for that education; these loans are protected by the government and must be repaid.

subcontractor — person or company contracted to perform work for a developer or general contractor.

subdivision — improved or unimproved land divided into a number of parcels for sale, lease financing, or development.

subsurface right — ownership of everything beneath the surface of the earth, such as oil and minerals.

superior lien — lien or encumbrance (for example a mortgage or mechanics lien) on real estate whose priority is greater (or superior) to other's interest in the same property.

survey — measurement of the land by a registered surveyor; produces the legal description of the property with references to known points, dimensions, buildings, and natural items (trees, rocks, and streams).

surveyor's certificate — formal statement, signed, certified, and dated by a surveyor, giving the pertinent facts about a particular property and any easements or encroachments affecting it.

T

take-home pay — borrower's paycheck after taxes and other deductions have been subtracted.

tax deduction — something that the government allows you to subtract from your income before tax liability is computed.

tax deed — deed on property purchased at public sale for nonpayment of taxes.

tax lien — claim against property for unpaid taxes.

tax sale — sale of property by a taxing authority or court acting on a judgment to satisfy the payment of delinquent taxes.

tenancy by the entirety — type of joint tenancy available to married couples; includes the right of survivorship and protection from one spouse selling the home without the permission of the other.

tenancy in common — way to hold title of property where the owners do not have to hold equal shares and do not have the right of survivorship.

term — period of months or years needed to repay a mortgage.

title — document that proves a person's ownership of a property.

title company — company that sells title insurance.

title exception — exclusion appearing in a title insurance policy against which the insurance company does not insure.

title insurance policy — contract by which the insurer agrees to pay the insured a specific amount for any loss caused by defects of title to real estate.

title search — check of records to determine who owned the property and what liens have been placed on the property from the time the property was built.

title theory —- system in which the holder of a mortgage (the lender) has actual title to the mortgaged property until the mortgage loan is repaid.

title update — examination of public records from the date of a previous title search to ascertain the status of title to property since such last search.

Torrens certificate — certificate issued by a public authority called a registrar of titles, establishing title in an indicated owner; used when title to property is registered under the Torrens system of land registration.

total expense ratio — person's debts as a percentage of his or her gross income; usually calculated on a monthly basis.

townhouse — row house on a small lot that has exterior limits common to other similar units. Title to the unit and its lot is vested in the individual buyer with a fractional interest in common areas.

tract — parcel of land.

tract loan — loan to a developer secured by land being subdivided.

transfer of ownership — action whereby ownership of a property changes hands.

transfer tax — state or city tax on the sale of a home.

transmittal form — a form that summarizes the data contained within a loan application.

treasury index — one type of index used in ARMs based on auctions held by the U.S. Treasury for Bills and Securities.

truth-in-lending — *See Regulation Z.*

Type 1 Escrow — account that contains earnest money from the buyer and held by a third party, which will eventually be part of the buyer's payment to the seller.

Type 2 Escrow — account used for payments of insurance and taxes.

U

underwriting — the process of evaluating and investigating a loan application.

unencumbered property — property that is free and clear of debts or liens.

Uniform Residential Appraisal Report (URAR) — form used by appraisers of residential properties to estimate the value to be financed with FHA, VA, or conventional mortgages.

unsecured loan — a loan not backed by collateral.

usury — charging borrowers a rate of interest greater than that permitted by law.

usury ceiling — maximum legal rate, established by some state's laws, for interest, discounts, or other fees that may be charged for the use of money.

usury saving clause — clause in a loan document intended to protect the lender from a claim that an unlawful amount of interest is being charged.

utilities — basic services associated with developed areas that include provisions for electricity, telephone, gas, water, and garbage collection.

V

VA loan — mortgage loan made by an approved lender and guaranteed by the Department of Veterans Affairs. (VA loans are made to eligible veterans and those currently serving in the military, and can have a lower down payment than other types of loans.)

vested — usually used to indicate the percentage of ownership an employee has in his/her retirement account.

valuation — estimation of a property's price through appraisal.

variable rate mortgage (VRM) — *See adjustable rate mortgage.*

variance — approved special change in construction codes, zoning requirements, or other property use restrictions.

verification of deposit (VOD) — document that lists details of a financial transaction.

verification of employment (VOE) — form that requests and secures documentation of a mortgage applicant's work history and occupation, to assist in the lender's credit investigation.

verification of mortgage — form that requests and secures verification of payments made on an applicant's current or past mortgage.

void — used in real estate as phrase "null and void" meaning no longer in effect.

voluntary conveyance — elective transfer of property from a defaulting borrower to the lender, as an alternative to foreclosure. This arrangement saves the lender the expense of foreclosure, and the borrower receives credit for payment in full.

voucher system — in construction lending, a system of *paying* subcontractors vouchers in lieu of cash; they then redeem the documents to the construction lender for actual payment.

W

W-2 — IRS form which reports income paid and taxes withheld by an employer for a particular employee during a calendar year.

W-4 — IRS form which determines the amount of Federal taxes the employer will withhold from a person's paycheck each pay period.

wage-earner plan — *See Chapter 13.*

waiver — legal document used to give another person permission to either do or not do something that was required.

warranty — the insurance policy some sellers get on certain expensive items in the house to pay the buyers in case the item is defective.

Welcome Wagon — a person or group that provides information and gifts from local merchants to new residents; can be a useful source of information.

will — legal document that allows a person to give away his or her possessions after death.

wraparound mortgage — an additional mortgage that includes payments on prior mortgages.

writ of execution — court order authorizing an official to evict a tenant or sell real property.

X

x-mark signature — signature made by a person who is unable to sign his or her name. (This type of signature is only legally valid when witnessed by another person.)

Z

zero down mortgages — also called 100% loans. A mortgage that requires no downpayment.

zero lot line — positioning of a structure on a lot so that one side rests directly on the lot's boundary line.

zoning — creation of districts by local governments whereby specific types of property uses are authorized.

zoning regulations — the laws that a local government enacts regarding zoning.

appendix a:
Internet Sites by Subject

SUBJECT	INTERNET SITE
Affordability Calculator	www.ginniemae.gov
American Dream Down Payment Assistance	www.hud.com
Amortization Tables	www.fha.com
	www.freddiemac.com
	www.ginniemae.gov
	www.hud.gov
	www.interest.com
	www.mortgageselect.com
Building a Home	www.ourfamilyplace.com/
	homebuyer/build.htm
Buy vs. Rent Information	www.ginniemae.gov
Closing Costs Calculator	www.freddiemac.com
Closing Information	www.ginniemae.gov
Credit Bureau Reports	www.annualcreditreport.com
	www.equifax.com
	www.experian.com
	www.ftc.com
	www.tuc.com
Debt-to-Income Ratio	www.fha.com
Decorating	www.hgtv.com

SUBJECT	INTERNET SITE
Discrimination in Housing	www.hud.gov
	www.ginniemae.gov
Down Payment Calculator	www.freddiemac.com
Energy Savings	www.comsumer.gov
Fannie Mae/Federal National Mortgage Association	www.fanniemae.com
FHA/Federal Housing Administration	www.fha.com
FICO/Credit Scores	www.yourmortgage.net
	www.myfico.com
Find a Home for Sale by Area	www.realtor.com
Find a Real Estate Agent by Area	www.realtor.com
Find a Home for Sale by Area	www.msn.com (house & home)
Fraud in Mortgages	www.stopmortgagefraud.com
Freddie Mac	www.freddiemac.com
General Information about Home Buying	www.fha.com
	www.ginniemae.gov
	www.homeloanlearningcenter.com
	www.hud.gov
	www.interest.com
	www.msn.com (house & home)
Ginnie Mae/Government National Mortgage Association	www.ginniemae.gov
Home Buying Road Map	www.msn.com (house & home)
Home Repairs	www.hgtv.com
Housing & Urban Development (HUD)	www.hud.gov

SUBJECT	INTERNET SITE
Inspections	www.inspectamerica.com
	www.msn.com
	(house & home)
	www.ginniemae.gov
Insurance	www.iii.org
	www.insweb.com
	www.msn.com
	(house & home)
Mortgage Calculators	www.ginniemae.gov
	www.hud.gov
	www.interest.com
	www.mortgageselect.com
	www.hgtv.com
	www.ourownhome.net
	www.fanniemae.com
	www.msn.com
	(house & home)
Mortgage Term Glossary	www.ourownhome.net
Mortgage Types	www.fha.com
	www.interest.com
Neighborhood Research	www.msn.com
	(house & home)
Predatory Lending/Fraud	www.fdic.gov
	www.stopmortgagefraud.com
	www.hud.gov
Rehabbing	www.hgtv.com
Schools	www.schoolmatch.com
Taxes	www.freddiemac.com
Veteran's Mortgage Assistance	www.va.gov

appendix b:
Worksheets

Worksheet 1:   **What I Want In My Neighborhood** is used to list all the things that are important to a person about a neighborhood and then prioritize those items.

Worksheet 2:   **Features I Want In My Home** is a four-page worksheet used to rank features that a person wants in their future home.

Worksheet 3:   **Viewing a House For Sale** is a two-page worksheet to be used when looking at a house that is up for sale. It has places for notes and sizes for both interior and exterior.

Worksheet 4:   **Comparing Mortgage Lenders** is a two-page worksheet to be used when comparing four different lenders and the loans that they are offering.

WORKSHEET 1:
WHAT I WANT IN MY NEIGHBORHOOD

STEP 1—Write down all those things that are important to you in a neighborhood; don't mix ideas on the same line. (Ex: Close to a certain church, near recreation, in walking distance from schools, etc.)

WHAT I WANT	RANK

STEP 2—Now go back and rank each item by how important it is to you, with number 1 being most important.

STEP 3—After you have ranked you entire list, go back and put an asterisk * next to the rank number of those items you absolutely MUST HAVE. Try to limit your MUST HAVES to five.

STEP 4—Compare your list with that of the other person you are buying the house with.

WORKSHEET 2:
FEATURES I WANT IN MY HOME

Price Range: from $_____ to $_____

Type/Style of Building: _____

Wheelchair Access: _____ Special Needs: _____

No. of Bedrooms Must Have: _____

No. of Bathrooms Must Have: _____

FEATURES	IMPORTANCE RANK (1 Most—5 Least)				
	1	2	3	4	5
Large yard (1 acre or more)					
Fenced yard					
Outside patio or deck					
In-ground pool					
Professionally landscaped					
Fenced dog run					
Carport					
Garage—No. of cars _____					
Garage attached to house					
Other outside buildings					
Well & septic tank					
City water & sewer					
Personal water source					
Forced-air gas furnace					

FEATURES	IMPORTANCE RANK (1 Most—5 Least)				
	1	2	3	4	5
Baseboard/Radiator heat					
Heat pump					
Central air conditioner					
KITCHEN:					
Eat in					
Appliances remain					
Work island					
New or recently remodeled					
BEDROOMS:					
Master bedroom					
Private bath in master bedroom					
Bedroom on main level					
Sitting room					
Family room					
Great Room					
Den					

FEATURES	IMPORTANCE RANK (1 Most—5 Least)				
	1	2	3	4	5
Library					
Basement					
Laundry room					
Home office					
Computer connections throughout					
Formal living room					
Formal dining room					
Hardwood floors					
Wall to wall carpeting					
Fireplace—In what rooms:					
In-law apartment					
Other features:					

FEATURES	IMPORTANCE RANK (1 Most—5 Least)				
	1	2	3	4	5

WORKSHEET 3:
VIEWING A HOUSE FOR SALE

Date you saw house: _____

Realtor:_____

_____

Asking price: $_____

Taxes: $_____Water source: City _____ Well _____

Address: _____

_____

Description: _____

_____

_____

_____

Lot size: _____   House square footage: _____

Age: _____

<u>INTERIOR:</u>

ROOM	SIZE	NOTES
Kitchen		
Laundry area		
Basement		
Living Room		
Dining Room		
Den		
Great Room		
Master Bedroom		
Bedroom 2		
Bedroom 3		
Bedroom 4		
Bedroom 5		
Bathroom 1		
Bathroom 2		
Bathroom 3		
Bathroom 4		

Appliances and other furniture sold with house:

_____

_____

_____

_____

_____

_____

_____

_____

_____

Heat type: _____

Air conditioning type: _____

EXTERIOR:

Surface of house: _____

_____

Gutters: _____

Deck, patio, outside porch: _____

Garage: _____

Parking: _____

_____

NOTES:

_____

_____

_____

_____

_____

_____

_____

_____

_____

_____

_____

_____

_____

WORKSHEET 4:
COMPARING MORTGAGE LENDERS

MORTGAGE AMOUNT: $_____

LENDER #1:

Name: _____

Contact: _____

Address: _____

_____

Phone/E-mail: _____

_____

LENDER #2:

Name: _____

Contact: _____

Address: _____

_____

Phone/E-mail: _____

_____

LENDER #3:

Name: _____

Contact: _____

Address: _____

_____

Phone/E-mail: _____

_____

LENDER #4:

Name: _____

Contact: _____

Address: _____

_____

Phone/E-mail: _____

_____

	#1	#2	#3	#4
Loan type (fixed rate, adjustable, VA, FHA, other)				
Down payment required				
Length of loan				
Annual Percentage Rate				
Points				
Estimated escrow				
Estimated monthly payment in Total				
Application/Loan processing fee				
Origination/Underwriting fee				
Lender fee/Funding fee				
Appraisal fee				
Document preparation and recording fee				
Points				
Credit report fee				
Other fees charged by lender				
Prepayment available				
Cost of letter to lock-in mortgage rate				

NOTES:

_____

_____

_____

_____

_____

_____

_____

_____

_____

_____

_____

_____

_____

appendix c:
Sample Letters

The following are three sample letters that you may use when you are attempting to clear up credit history errors. You will probably need to change some of the wording in order to make these letters personal to your case.

> *Letter #1*—used in the case where a debt is listed on your credit report and you do not know what the debt is. This letter requests information from the creditor on the debt. Once you get this information, you can determine if the debt is legitimate or if this is an error.

> *Letter #2*—used in the case where a creditor has put a negative listing on your credit report for a debt that you have paid, a debt that the creditor agreed to drop, or a debt that is just not yours. Attach copies of documents that prove your case, such as a copy of cancelled check, a copy of a letter from the creditor that cancelled the debt, or a statement explaining that you are not the proper debtor.

> *Letter #3*—used to send to the credit bureau when you are disputing something on your credit report. You will need to attach a copy of your credit report with the item that you are disputing circled and copies of any documentation that proves your case.

TO A CREDITOR TO DETERMINE WHAT THE DEBT IS

Date

Creditor's Name and Address

RE: your account number or identifying number

Dear Sir or Madam:

It has come to my attention that you have reported an alleged debt in my name to the three major credit reporting agencies.

This is not a refusal to pay, but a notice that your claim is being disputed. This is a formal request for a validation of this alleged debt in accordance with the Fair Debt Collection Practices Act, and in accordance with all related federal and state consumer debt statutes.

Please note that you have thirty (30) days from receipt of this document to either answer this demand or to remove the associated negative notation from all credit reporting bureaus.

Sincerely,

Your Name and Address

TO A CREDITOR TO DISPUTE A DEBT

Date

Creditor's Name and Address

RE: your account number or identifying number

Dear Sir or Madam:

This letter is in regard to a debt that you have erroneously reported to *(name of)* credit reporting agency.

This is not a valid debt because: *(here list the reasons why you believe that the debt is not correct).*

Attached are copies of *(list of documents you are attaching that support your case)* that prove that this debt is no longer owed.

In accordance with the Fair Debt Collection Practices Act, I demand that you remove the associated negative notation from all credit reporting bureaus regarding this debt.

Sincerely,

Your Name and Address

GENERAL LETTER TO CREDIT REPORTING BUREAU:
DISPUTE ENTRY

Date

Name and address of Credit Reporting Bureau

RE: Dispute and Investigation Request

Dear Sir or Madam;

I am writing to dispute information on my file. The am enclosing a copy of my credit report with the disputed items circled.

MY NAME: include former names
MY ADDRESS: include former addresses

ITEM #1
　　　　Creditor name:

　　　　Type of item: Account/ID number:

I am disputing this because (state reasons).

I am enclosing copies of the following that prove my case (list all documents that you are enclosing and how they support your claim).

ITEM #2
　　　　Creditor name:

　　　　Type of item: Account/ID number:

I am disputing this because (state reasons).

I am enclosing copies of the following that prove my case (list all documents that you are enclosing and how they support your claim).

(Repeat this for each circled entry on your credit report.)

I am asking that you investigate the above within thirty days and send me a copy of the results of this investigation. If I disagree with your findings, I want to write a statement and have that statement included in future reports.

If the item is an error I request that you delete the incorrect information from my credit report and send me a free copy of the corrected report.

Sincerely,

Your name

appendix d:
State Offices
of Real Estate Regulation

Following is a list of the state governmental agencies that regulate real estate professionals. This may include agents, brokers, inspectors, and appraisers. Each state issues its own license to the real estate professionals who work there. The requirements for such a license varies from state to state.

The information on the Internet sites listed ranges from things that help the real estate professional renew their license to sites that provide help for the home buyer. The majority of sites list the laws that the real estate professional must follow, and the education required for a license. Many list the names of state-licensed real estate professionals and offer a way to make a complaint against one of these people. Check the Internet site for the state you want to buy a home in. It may provide you with some information on selecting your real estate professional.

- **Alabama Real Estate Commission**
  www.arec.state.al.us
  334-242-5544

- **Alaska Real Estate Commission**
  www.dced.state.ak.us/occ/prec.htm
  907-269-8160

- **Arizona Department of Real Estate**
  www.re.state.az.us
  602-468-1414

- Arkansas Real Estate Commission
  www.state.ar.us/arec
  501-683-8010

- California Real Estate Licensing Board
  www.orea.ca.gov
  916-552-9000

- Colorado Division of Real Estate
  www.dora.state.co.us/real-estate
  303-894-2166

- Connecticut Licensing Department
  www.dcp.state.ct.us/licensing/realestate.htm
  860-566-3290

- Delaware Real Estate Commission
  www.professionallicensing.state.de.us/boards/
  realestate/index.shtml
  302-739-4522

- District of Columbia
  Department of Consumer and Regulatory Affairs
  www.dcra.dc.gov
  202-442-4400

- Florida Department of
  Business and Professional Regulation
  www.state.fl.us/dbpr/re/dre.shtml
  407-245-0800

- Georgia Real Estate Commission
  www.state.ga.us/Ga.Real_Estate
  404-656-3916

- Hawaii Real Estate Commission
  www.state.hi.us/hirec
  808-586-2643

- Idaho Real Estate Commission
  www.idahorealestatecommission.com
  208-334-3285

- **Illinois Office of Banks and Real Estate**
  www.obre.state.il.us
  312-782-3000 or 217-782-3000

- **Indiana Real Estate Commission**
  www.in.gov/pla/bandc/estate
  317-232-2980

- **Iowa Real Estate Commission**
  www.state.ia.us
  515-281-3183

- **Kansas Real Estate Commission**
  www.accesskansas.org/krec
  785-296-3411

- **Kentucky Real Estate Commission**
  www.krec.net
  502-425-4273

- **Louisiana Real Estate Commission**
  www.lrec.state.la.us
  800-821-4529

- **Maine Office of Licensing**
  www.state.me.us/pfr/olr
  207-624-8603

- **Maryland Real Estate Commission**
  www.dllr.state.md.us/license/occprof/recomm.html
  410-230-6200

- **Massachusetts Real Estate Board**
  www.mass.gov
  617-727-2373

- **Michigan Office of Commercial Services**
  www.michigan.gov/cis
  517-241-9288

- **Minnesota Real Estate Comission**
  www.state.mn.us
  651-296-6319

- **Mississippi Real Estate Commission**
  www.mrec.state.ms.us
  601-932-9191

- **Missouri Real Estate Commission**
  www.ded.state.mo.us
  573-751-2628

- **Montana Board of Realty Regulation**
  www.discoveringmontana.com/dli/bsd
  406-444-2961

- **Nebraska Real Estate Commission**
  www.nrec.state.ne.us
  402-471-2004

- **Nevada Real Estate Division**
  www.red.state.nv.us
  775-687-4280 or
  702-486-4033

- **New Hampshire Real Estate Commission**
  www.state.nh.us/nhrec
  603-271-2701

- **New Jersey Department of Real Estate Licensing**
  www.nj.gov/dobi/rec_lic.htm
  609-292-8280

- **New Mexico Real Estate Commission**
  www.nmrealtor.com/2001site/nmrec_frame.htm
  505-841-9120 or 800-801-7505

- **New York Department of State
  Division of Licensing Services**
  www.dos.state.ny.us/lcns/realest.html
  518-473-2728

- **North Carolina Real Estate Commission**
  www.ncrec.state.nc.us
  919-875-3700

- **North Dakota Real Estate Commission**
  www.governor.state.nd.us
  701-328-9749 or 701-328-9737

- Ohio Real Estate and
  Professional Licensing Division
  www.com.state.oh.us/real
  614-466-4100

- Oklahoma Real Estate Commission
  www.orec.state.ok.us
  800-448-4904

- Oregon Real Estate Agency
  www.rea.state.or.us
  503-378-4170

- Pennsylvania Real Estate Commission
  www.dos.state.pa.us/bpoa/cwp
  717-783-4854

- Rhode Island Department of Business Regulation
  www.dbr.state.ri.us/real_estate.html
  401-222-2355

- South Carolina Real Estate Commission
  www.llr.state.sc.us/POL/RealEstateCommission
  803-896-4400

- South Dakota Real Estate Commission
  www.state.sd.us/dcr/realestate
  605-773-3600

- Tennessee Real Estate Commission
  www.state.tn.us/commerce/trec
  800-342-4031

- Texas Real Estate Commission
  www.trec.state.tx.us
  512-459-6544

- Utah Division of Real Estate
  www.commerce.utah.gov/dre
  801-530-6747

- Vermont Real Estate Commission
  www.vtprofessionals.org
  802-828-3228

- Virginia Department of Professional
  and Occupational Regulation
  www.state.va.us/dpor.indexne.html
  804-367-8500

- Washington Department of Professional Licensing
  www.dol.wa.gov/realestate
  360-586-6101

- West Virginia Real Estate Commission
  www.state.wv.us/wvrec
  304-558-3555

- Wisconsin Real Estate Licensing Board
  www.drl.state.wi.us
  608-266-5511

- Wyoming Real Estate Commission
  www.realestate.state.wy.us
  307-777-7141

appendix e:
HUD-1 Settlement Statement

When the real estate agent or broker, attorney, or title company tells you the total amount of the certified check that you must bring to the closing, you may wonder how they arrived at that number. Even those of us who have experience in buying and selling homes have problems understanding how they come up with a total amount. In order to resolve this universal question, the *HUD-1 Settlement Statement* was created. It is used to list, in detail, the costs paid by both the buyer and seller. Besides being an explanation of what you are paying for, this form is also a checklist for those in the title company who are preparing the closing documents to make sure that all costs are covered and that missing costs will not delay the closing. The buyer and seller should use this form to quickly verify, at the closing, that they are not being erroneously charged for something.

This is a sample of a document that is required in every house sale. It breaks down the costs for both buyer and seller at the time of the sale.

A. Settlement Statement

U.S. Department of Housing
and Urban Development

OMB Approval No. 2502-0265

B. Type of Loan

1. ☐ FHA 2. ☐ FmHA 3. ☐ Conv. Unins.	6. File Number:	7. Loan Number:	8. Mortgage Insurance Case Number:
4. ☐ VA 5. ☐ Conv. Ins.			

C. Note: This form is furnished to give you a statement of actual settlement costs. Amounts paid to and by the settlement agent are shown. Items marked "(p.o.c.)" were paid outside the closing; they are shown here for informational purposes and are not included in the totals.

D. Name & Address of Borrower:	E. Name & Address of Seller:	F. Name & Address of Lender:

G. Property Location:	H. Settlement Agent:	
	Place of Settlement:	I. Settlement Date:

J. Summary of Borrower's Transaction		K. Summary of Seller's Transaction	
100. Gross Amount Due From Borrower		**400. Gross Amount Due To Seller**	
101. Contract sales price		401. Contract sales price	
102. Personal property		402. Personal property	
103. Settlement charges to borrower (line 1400)		403.	
104.		404.	
105.		405.	
Adjustments for items paid by seller in advance		**Adjustments for items paid by seller in advance**	
106. City/town taxes to		406. City/town taxes to	
107. County taxes to		407. County taxes to	
108. Assessments to		408. Assessments to	
109.		409.	
110.		410.	
111.		411.	
112.		412.	
120. Gross Amount Due From Borrower		**420. Gross Amount Due To Seller**	
200. Amounts Paid By Or In Behalf Of Borrower		**500. Reductions In Amount Due To Seller**	
201. Deposit or earnest money		501. Excess deposit (see instructions)	
202. Principal amount of new loan(s)		502. Settlement charges to seller (line 1400)	
203. Existing loan(s) taken subject to		503. Existing loan(s) taken subject to	
204.		504. Payoff of first mortgage loan	
205.		505. Payoff of second mortgage loan	
206.		506.	
207.		507.	
208.		508.	
209.		509.	
Adjustments for items unpaid by seller		**Adjustments for items unpaid by seller**	
210. City/town taxes to		510. City/town taxes to	
211. County taxes to		511. County taxes to	
212. Assessments to		512. Assessments to	
213.		513.	
214.		514.	
215.		515.	
216.		516.	
217.		517.	
218.		518.	
219.		519.	
220. Total Paid By/For Borrower		**520. Total Reduction Amount Due Seller**	
300. Cash At Settlement From/To Borrower		**600. Cash At Settlement To/From Seller**	
301. Gross Amount due from borrower (line 120)		601. Gross amount due to seller (line 420)	
302. Less amounts paid by/for borrower (line 220)	( )	602. Less reductions in amt. due seller (line 520)	( )
303. Cash ☐ From ☐ To Borrower		**603. Cash** ☐ To ☐ From Seller	

Section 5 of the Real Estate Settlement Procedures Act (RESPA) requires the following: • HUD must develop a Special Information Booklet to help persons borrowing money to finance the purchase of residential real estate to better understand the nature and costs of real estate settlement services; • Each lender must provide the booklet to all applicants from whom it receives or for whom it prepares a written application to borrow money to finance the purchase of residential real estate; • Lenders must prepare and distribute with the Booklet a Good Faith Estimate of the settlement costs that the borrower is likely to incur in connection with the settlement. These disclosures are manadatory.

Section 4(a) of RESPA mandates that HUD develop and prescribe this standard form to be used at the time of loan settlement to provide full disclosure of all charges imposed upon the borrower and seller. These are third party disclosures that are designed to provide the borrower with pertinent information during the settlement process in order to be a better shopper.

The Public Reporting Burden for this collection of information is estimated to average one hour per response, including the time for reviewing instructions, searching existing data sources, gathering and maintaining the data needed, and completing and reviewing the collection of information.

This agency may not collect this information, and you are not required to complete this form, unless it displays a currently valid OMB control number.

The information requested does not lend itself to confidentiality.

Settlement Charges		Paid From Borrowers Funds at Settlement	Paid From Seller's Funds at Settlement
0. Total Sales/Broker's Commission based on price $ @ % =			
Division of Commission (line 700) as follows:			
1. $ to			
2. $ to			
3. Commission paid at Settlement			
4.			
0. Items Payable In Connection With Loan			
1. Loan Origination Fee %			
2. Loan Discount %			
3. Appraisal Fee to			
4. Credit Report to			
5. Lender's Inspection Fee			
6. Mortgage Insurance Application Fee to			
7. Assumption Fee			
8.			
9.			
0.			
1.			
. Items Required By Lender To Be Paid In Advance			
. Interest from to @ $ /day			
2. Mortgage Insurance Premium for months to			
3. Hazard Insurance Premium for years to			
4. years to			
5.			
0. Reserves Deposited With Lender			
1. Hazard insurance months@ $ per month			
2. Mortgage insurance months@ $ per month			
3. City property taxes months@ $ per month			
4. County property taxes months@ $ per month			
5. Annual assessments months@ $ per month			
6. months@ $ per month			
7. months@ $ per month			
8. months@ $ per month			
0. Title Charges			
1. Settlement or closing fee to			
2. Abstract or title search to			
3. Title examination to			
4. Title insurance binder to			
5. Document preparation to			
6. Notary fees to			
7. Attorney's fees to			
(includes above items numbers:)			
8. Title insurance to			
(includes above items numbers:)			
9. Lender's coverage $			
0. Owner's coverage $			
1.			
2.			
3.			
0. Government Recording and Transfer Charges			
1. Recording fees: Deed $; Mortgage $; Releases $			
2. City/county tax/stamps: Deed $; Mortgage $			
3. State tax/stamps: Deed $; Mortgage $			
4.			
5.			
0. Additional Settlement Charges			
1. Survey to			
2. Pest inspection to			
3.			
4.			
5.			
0. Total Settlement Charges (enter on lines 103, Section J and 502, Section K)			

appendix f:
HUD Offices

For those of us who find ourselves without a computer, this section provides physical addresses and phone numbers for the HUD offices in each state. However, this information is given with a caution—you will not be able to get as much information by writing and calling as you can on the Internet. This is true especially in sites run by the government—with their wealth of information, you will be able to access much, much more online. If at all possible, borrow a computer from someone or go to the library.

Alaska
>   Anchorage Field Office
>   3000 C Street
>   Suite 401
>   Anchorage, AK 99503
>   907-677-9800
>   907-677-9803 (fax)

Alabama
>   Birmingham Field Office
>   950 22nd Street North
>   Suite 900
>   Birmingham, AL 35203-5302
>   205-731-2617
>   205-731-2593 (fax)

Arizona
>   Phoenix Field Office
>   One North Central Avenue
>   Suite 600
>   Phoenix, AZ 85004
>   602-379-7100
>   602-379-3985 (fax)

>   Tucson Field Office
>   160 North Stone Avenue
>   Tucson, AZ 85701-1467
>   520-670-6000
>   520-670-6207 (fax)

Arkansas
Little Rock Field Office
425 West Capitol Avenue
Suite 900
Little Rock, AR 72201-3488
501-324-5931
501-324-6142 (fax)

California
San Francisco Regional Office
600 Harrison Street
3rd Floor
San Francisco, CA 94107-1300
415-489-6400
415-489-6419 (fax)

Fresno Field Office
2135 Fresno Street
Suite 100
Fresno, CA 93721-1718
559-487-5033
559-487-5191 (fax)

Los Angeles Field Office
611 West Sixth Street
Suite 800
Los Angeles, CA 90017
213-894-8007
213-894-8110 (fax)

Sacramento Field Office
925 L Street
Sacramento, CA 95814
916-498-5220
916-498-5262 (fax)

San Diego Field Office
Symphony Towers
750 B Street
Suite 1600
San Diego, CA 92101-8131
619-557-5310
619-557-5312 (fax)

Santa Ana Field Office
1600 North Broadway
Suite 101
Santa Ana, CA 92706-3927
714-796-5577
714-796-1285 (fax)

Colorado
Denver Regional Office
1670 Broadway
23rd Floor
Denver, CO 80202
303-672-5440
303-672-5004 (fax)

Connecticut
  Hartford Field Office
  One Corporate Center
  20 Church Street
  19ᵗʰ Floor
  Hartford, CT 06103-3220
  860-240-4800 ext. 3100
  860-240-4850 (fax)

Washington DC
  Washington, DC Field Office
  820 First Street NE
  Suite 300
  Washington, DC 20002-4205
  202-275-9200
  202-275-9212 (fax)

Delaware
  Wilmington Field Office
  920 King Street
  Suite 404
  Wilmington, DE 19801-3016
  302-573-6300
  302-573-6259 (fax)

Florida
  Miami Field Office
  909 SE First Avenue
  Miami, FL 33131
  305-536-4456
  305-536-5765 (fax)

Jacksonville Field Office
301 West Bay Street
Suite 2200
Jacksonville, FL 32202-5121
904-232-2627
904-232-3759 (fax)

Orlando Field Office
3751 Maguire Boulevard
Room 270
Orlando, FL 32803-3032
407-648-6441
407-648-6310 (fax)

Tampa Field Office
500 Zack Street
Suite 402
Tampa, FL 33602
813-228-2026
813-228-2431

Georgia
Atlanta Regional Office
40 Marietta Street
Five Points Plaza
Atlanta, GA 30303-2806
404-331-4111
404-730-2392 (fax)

Hawaii
Honolulu Field Office
500 Ala Moana Boulevard
Suite 3A
Honolulu, HI 96813-4918
808-522-8175
808-522-8194 (fax)

Iowa
Des Moines Field Office
210 Walnut Street
Room 239
Des Moines, IA 50309-2155
515-284-4512
515-284-4743 (fax)

Idaho
Boise Field Office
Plaza IV
Suite 220
800 Park Boulevard
Boise, Idaho 83712-7743
208-334-1990
208-334-9648 (fax)

Illinois
Chicago Regional Office
Ralph Metcalfe Federal Building
77 West Jackson Boulevard
Chicago, IL 60604-3507
312-353-5680
312-886-2729 (fax)

Springfield Field Office
500 West Monroe Street
Suite 1 SW
Springfield, IL 62704
217-492-4120
217-492-4154 (fax)

Indiana
Indianapolis Field Office
151 North Delaware Street
Suite 1200
Indianapolis, IN 46204-2526
317-226-6303
317-226-6317 (fax)

Kansas
Kansas City Regional Office
400 State Avenue
Room 200
Kansas City, KS 66101-2406
913-551-5462
913-551-5469 (fax)

Kentucky
Louisville Field Office
601 West Broadway
Louisville, KY 40202
502-582-5251
502-582-6074 (fax)

Louisiana
New Orleans Field Office
Hale Boggs Building
501 Magazine Street
9th Floor
New Orleans, LA 70130-3099
504-589-7201
504-589-6619 (fax)

Shreveport Field Office
401 Edwards Street
Room 1510
Shreveport, LA 71101-5513
318-676-3440
318-676-3407 (fax)

Massachusetts
Boston Regional Office
10 Causeway Street
Room 301
Boston, MA 02222-1092
617-994-8200
617-565-5257 (fax)

Maryland
Baltimore Field Office
5th Floor
10 South Howard Street
Baltimore, MD 21201-2505
410-962-2520
410-962-1849 (fax)

Maine
   Bangor Field Office
   Chase Building
   202 Harlow Street
   Suite 101
   Bangor, ME 04401-4919
   207-945-0467
   207-945-0533

Michigan
   Detroit Field Office
   477 Michigan Avenue
   Detroit, MI 48226-2592
   313-226-7900
   313-226-5611 (fax)

   Flint Field Office
   Phoenix Building
   801 South Saginaw
   4ᵗʰ Floor
   Flint, Michigan 48502
   810-766-5112
   810-766-5122 (fax)

   Grand Rapids Field Office
   Trade Center Building
   50 Louis Street, NW
   Grand Rapids, MI 49503-2633
   616-456-2100
   616-456-2114 (fax)

Minnesota
Minneapolis Field Office
Kinnard Financial Center
920 Second Avenue South
Minneapolis, MN 55402
612-370-3000
612-370-3220 (fax)

Missouri
St. Louis Field Office
1222 Spruce Street
Suite 3207
St. Louis, MO 63103-2836
314-539-6583
314-539-6384 (fax)

Mississippi
Jackson Field Office
McCoy Federal Building
100 West Capitol Street
Room 910
Jackson, MS 39269-1096
601-965-4757
601-965-4773 (fax)

Montana
Helena Field Office
7 West 6th Ave
Helena, MT 59601
406-449-5050
406-449-5052 (fax)

North Carolina
Greensboro Field Office
Asheville Building
1500 Pinecroft Road
Suite 401
Greensboro, NC 27407-3838
336-547-4001
336-547-4138 (fax)

North Dakota
Fargo Field Office
657 2nd Avenue North
Room 366
Fargo, ND 58108
701-239-5136
701-239-5249 (fax)

Nebraska
Omaha Field Office
10909 Mill Valley Road
Suite 100
Omaha, NE 68154-3955
402-492-3101
402-492-3150 (fax)

New Hampshire
Manchester Field Office
1000 Elm Street
8th Floor
Manchester, NH 03101-1730
603-666-7510 ext. 3903
603-666-7667 (fax)

New Jersey
   Newark Field Office
   One Newark Center
   13th Floor
   Newark, NJ 07102-5260
   973-622-7900
   973-645-2323 (fax)

   Camden Field Office
   Hudson Building
   2nd Floor
   800 Hudson Square
   Camden, NJ 08102-1156
   856-757-5081
   856-757-5373 (fax)

New Mexico
   Albuquerque Field Office
   625 Silver Avenue SW
   Suite 100
   Albuquerque, NM 87102
   505-346-6463
   505-346-6704 (fax)

Nevada
   Las Vegas Field Office
   300 South Las Vegas Boulevard
   Suite 2900
   Las Vegas, NV 89101-5833
   702-366-2100
   702-388-6244 (fax)

Reno Field Office
3702 South Virginia Street
Reno, NV 89502-6581
775-784-5383
775-784-5005 (fax)

New York
New York Regional Office
26 Federal Plaza
Suite 3541
New York, NY 10278-0068
212-264-8000
212-264-3068 (fax)

Albany Field Office
52 Corporate Circle
Albany, NY 12203-5121
518-464-4200
518-464-4300 (fax)

Buffalo Field Office
Lafayette Court
2nd Floor
465 Main Street
Buffalo, NY 14203-1780
716-551-5755
716-551-5752 (fax)

Syracuse Field Office
128 East Jefferson Street
Syracuse, NY 13202
315-477-0616
315-477-0196 (fax)

Ohio

Columbus Field Office
200 North High Street
Columbus, OH 43215-2463
614-469-2540
614-469-432 (fax)

Cincinnati Field Office
15 East Seventh Street
Cincinnati, OH 45202-2401
513-684-3451
513-684-6224 (fax)

Cleveland Field Office
1350 Euclid Avenue
Suite 500
Cleveland, OH 44115-1815
216-522-4058
216-522-4067 (fax)

Oklahoma
Oklahoma City Field Office
301 NW 6ᵗʰ Street
Suite 200
Oklahoma City, OK 73102
405-609-8509
405-609-8588 (fax)

Tulsa Field Office
1516 South Boston Avenue
Suite 100
Tulsa, OK 74119-4030
918-581-7434
918-581-7440 (fax)

Oregon
Portland Field Office
400 SW 6ᵗʰ Avenue
Suite 700
Portland, OR 97204-1632
503-326-2561
503-326-2568 (fax)

Pennsylvania
Philadelphia Regional Office
The Wanamaker Building
100 Penn Square, East
Philadelphia, PA 19107-3380
215-656-0500
215-656-3445 (fax)

Pittsburgh Field Office
339 Sixth Avenue
Sixth Floor
Pittsburgh, PA 15222-2515
412-644-6436
412-644-4240 (fax)

Puerto Rico
San Juan Field Office
171 Carlos East Chardon Avenue
San Juan, PR 00918-0903
787-766-5201
787-766-5995 (fax)

Rhode Island
Providence Field Office
10 Weybosset Street
Sixth Floor
Providence, RI 02903-2818
401-528-5230
401-528-5312 (fax)

South Carolina
Columbia Field Office
1835 Assembly Street
13ᵗʰ Floor
Columbia, SC 29201-2480
803-765-5592
803-253-3043 (fax)

South Dakota
Sioux Falls Field Office
2400 West 49th Street
Room I-201
Sioux Falls, SD 57105-6558
605-330-4223
605-330-4428 (fax)

Tennessee
Nashville Field Office
235 Cumberland Bend
Suite 200
Nashville, TN 37228-1803
615-736-5213
615-736-7848 (fax)

Knoxville Field Office
710 Locust Street, SW
Suite 300
Knoxville, TN 37902-2526
865-545-4384
865-545-4569 (fax)

Memphis Field Office
200 Jefferson Avenue
Suite 300
Memphis, TN 38103-2389
901-544-3367
901-544-3697 (fax)

Texas

Ft. Worth Regional Office
801 Cherry Street
P.O. Box 2905
Ft. Worth, TX 76102-2905
817-978-5965
817-978-5567 (fax)

Dallas Field Office
525 Griffin Street
Room 860
Dallas, TX 75202-5007
214-767-8300
214-767-8973 (fax)

Houston Field Office
1301 Fannin
Suite 2200
Houston, TX 77002
713-718-3199
713-313-2319 (fax)

Lubbock Field Office
1205 Texas Avenue
Room 511
Lubbock, TX 79401-4093
806-472-7265
806-472-7275 (fax)

San Antonio Field Office
One Alamo Center
106 South Street Mary's Street
San Antonio, Texas 78205
210-475-6806
210-472-6804 (fax)

Utah
Salt Lake City Field Office
125 South State Street
Suite 3001
Salt Lake City, UT 84138
801-524-6070
801-524-3439 (fax)

Virginia
Richmond Field Office
600 East Broad Street
Richmond, VA 23219-4920
804-771-2100
804-771-2090 (fax)

Vermont
Burlington Field Office
159 Bank Street
2nd Floor
Burlington, VT 05401
802-951-6290
802-951-6298 (fax)

Washington
   Seattle Regional Office
   909 First Avenue
   Suite 200
   Seattle, WA 98104-1000
   206-220-5101
   206-220-5108 (fax)

   Spokane Field Office
   U.S. Courthouse Building
   920 West Riverside
   Suite 588
   Spokane, WA 99201-1010
   509-353-0674
   509-353-0682 (fax)

Wisconsin
   Milwaukee Field Office
   310 West Wisconsin Avenue
   Room 1380
   Milwaukee, WI 53203-2289
   414-297-3214
   414-297-3947 (fax)

West Virginia
   Charleston Field Office
   405 Capitol Street
   Suite 708
   Charleston, WV 25301-1795
   304-347-7000
   304-347-7050 (fax)

Wyoming
Casper Field Office
150 East B Street
Room 1010
Casper, WY 82601-1969
307-261-6250
307-261-6245 (fax)

appendix g:
VA Guaranteed Loan

The following sample forms will prepare you for the specific information required to apply for a VA Loan. As stated in Chapter 11, if you are considering applying for this type of a loan, be sure to consult a real estate professional or an attorney who practices in this specific real estate matter. The application is complicated, but is worth the effort if you are eligible.

OMB APPROVED NO. 2900-0█
RESPONDENT BURDEN: 12 █

INSTRUCTIONS FOR PREPARATION OF VA REQUEST FOR DETERMINATION OF REASONABLE VALU█

RESPONDENT BURDEN: VA may not conduct or sponsor, and respondent is not required to respond to this collec█ information unless it displays a valid OMB Control Number. Public reporting burden for this collection of information is es█ to average 12 minutes per response, including the time for reviewing instructions, searching existing data sources, gatheri█ maintaining the data needed, and completing and reviewing the collection of information. If you have comments regardi█ burden estimate or any other aspect of this collection of information, call 1-800-827-1000 for mailing information on where to send your comments.

NOTE: ALL ENTRIES MUST BE TYPED
Remove this instruction page and complete page 1 following the instructions below, using the reverse of this instruction pa█ worksheet. After completion of page 1, detach page 2 for your records and forward the packet, together with any necessary e█ to the VA office having jurisdiction.

Since certain selected data from page 1 is transcribed onto the VA CRV (Certificate of Reasonable Value), we request that th█ be carefully prepared. Incomplete submissions impede timely processing at the expense of both the Government and the request█

This report is authorized by law (38 U.S.C. 3704(a) and 3710(b). Failure to provide the information requested can result in re█ of the property as security for a loan.

REQUIRED EXHIBITS TO BE SENT WITH APPLICATION

SALES CONTRACTS: In cases involving proposed construction or existing construction not previously occupied, a copy█ executed or proposed sales contract must be submitted or, if a previously approved form of contract is to be used, the ap█ contract code number may be shown in Item 37. In those cases in which a veteran is under contract, submission of the contra█ be deferred until a loan application is received.

PROPOSED CONSTRUCTION: Complete working drawings, including plot plan, foundation or basement plans, plans of all█ exterior elevations, grade levels, sectional wall details, heating layout, individual well and septic system layout, and specificat█ VA Form 26-1852, Description of Materials. (Consult local VA office for number of exhibit sets required.) This informa█ subject to reproduction by VA under 38 U.S.C. 3705 (b) and for storage purposes.

EXISTING CONSTRUCTION: 1. ALTERATIONS, IMPROVEMENTS OR REPAIRS - Complete drawings and specifi█ indicating the work to be done and its relation to the house, in the quantity required by the local VA office. 2. NOT PREVIO█ OCCUPIED AND CONSTRUCTION COMPLETED WITHIN 12 CALENDAR MONTHS - Contact local VA office for eli█ criteria and required exhibits.

FORM ENTRIES

NAME, ADDRESS, AND ZIP CODE: Make sure to enter the ZIP code in all blocks which require an address entry.

LEGAL DESCRIPTION: Insert legal description. If necessary, attach 4 copies of a separate sheet showing the legal description.

TITLE LIMITATIONS: Enter known title exceptions. If none are known, enter "None." Include easements, special assessments, mandatory homeowners association membership, etc. Exceptions noted on this application will be considered in reasonable value. Attach separate sheet (4 copies) if necessary.

LOT DIMENSIONS: Show frontage X depth. If irregular, indicate dimensions of all perimeter lot lines.

REMOVABLE EQUIPMENT: Personal property, such as furniture, drapes and rugs, will not be valued and may not be included in the loan. However, wall-to-wall carpeting may be included in value and also included in the loan.

CONSTRUCTION COMPLETED: Insert both month and year when property has been completed less than two years. If over two years old, insert year completed only.

COMMENTS ON SPECIAL ASSESSMENTS A█ HOMEOWNER ASSOCIATION CHARGES: Indicate assessments which are now a lien or will become a lien.█ case of a planned unit development, condominium█ mandatory membership homeowner association, indic█ current monthly or other periodic assessment.

MINERAL RIGHTS: If reserved, explain either in space█ as title exceptions or by separate page.

LEASEHOLD CASES: (Usually Hawaii or Marylar█ property involves a leasehold, insert the ground rent p█ and show whether the lease is for 99 years or ren█ whether it has previously been VA approved, and its ex█ date. Submit two copies of the lease agreement.

SALE PRICE: Enter proposed sale price except█ application involves an individual owner-occupant buil█ himself/herself. In such cases, enter estimated █ construction and the balance owned on the lot, if █ refinancing, enter amount of proposed loan in Item 35.

NOTE: If title is not "fee simple," submit copies in duplicate of all pertinent legal data providing a full explanation of the title involved.

OMB APPROVED NO. 2900-0045
RESPONDENT BURDEN: 12 minutes

REQUEST FOR DETERMINATION OF REASONABLE VALUE (Real Estate)

1. CASE NUMBER	4. TITLE LIMITATIONS AND RESTRICTIVE COVENANTS:

2. PROPERTY ADDRESS (Include ZIP Code and county)	3. LEGAL DESCRIPTION

1. ☐ CONDOMINIUM   2. ☐ PLANNED UNIT DEVELOPMENT

5. NAME AND ADDRESS OF FIRM OR PERSON MAKING REQUEST/APPLICATION (Include ZIP Code)	6. LOT DIMENSIONS:

1. ☐ IRREGULAR: SQ/FT   2. ☐ ACRES:

7. UTILITIES (✓)	ELEC.	GAS	WATER	SAN. SEWER
1. PUBLIC				
2. COMMUNITY				
3. INDIVIDUAL				

8. EQUIP.
1. ☐ RANGE/OVEN   4. ☐ CLOTHES WASHER   7. ☐ VENT FAN
2. ☐ REFRIG.   5. ☐ DRYER   8. ☐ W/W CARPET
3. ☐ DISH WASHER   6. ☐ GARBAGE DISPOSAL   9.

9. BUILDING STATUS	10. BUILDING TYPE	11. FACTORY FABRICATED?	12A. NO. OF BUILDINGS	12B. NO. OF LIVING UNITS	13A. STREET ACCESS	13B. STREET MAINTENANCE
1. ☐ PROPOSED 3. ☐ EXISTING ALTERATIONS, IMPROVEMENTS, 2. ☐ UNDER CONSTRUCTION 4. ☐ OR REPAIRS	1. ☐ DETACHED 3. ☐ ROW 2. ☐ SEMI-DETACHED 4. ☐ APT. UNIT	1. ☐ YES 2. ☐ NO			1. ☐ PRIVATE 2. ☐ PUBLIC	1. ☐ PRIVATE 2. ☐ PUBLIC

14A. CONSTRUCTION WARRANTY INCLUDED?	14B. NAME OF WARRANTY PROGRAM	14C. EXPIRATION DATE (Month, day, year)	15. CONSTRUCTION COMPLETED (Mo.,yr.)
1. ☐ YES 2. ☐ NO (If "Yes," complete Items 14b and 14c also)			

16. NAME OF OWNER	17. PROPERTY:	18. RENT (If applic.)
	☐ OCCUPIED BY OWNER ☐ NEVER OCCUPIED ☐ VACANT ☐ OCCUPIED BY TENANT (Complete Item18 also)	$ / MONTH

19. NAME OF OCCUPANT	20. TELEPHONE NO.	21. NAME OF BROKER	22. TELEPHONE NO.	23. DATE AND TIME AVAILABLE FOR INSPECTION
				☐ AM ☐ PM

24. KEYS AT (Address)	25. ORIGINATOR'S IDENT. NO.	26. SPONSOR'S IDENT. NO.	27. INSTITUTION'S CASE NO.

28. PURCHASER'S NAME AND ADDRESS (Complete mailing address, include ZIP Code)	EQUAL OPPORTUNITY IN HOUSING

NOTE: Federal laws and regulations prohibit discrimination because of race, color, religion, sex, or national origin in the sale or rental of residential property. Numerous State statutes and local ordinances also prohibit such discrimination. In addition, section 805 of the Civil Rights Act of 1968 prohibits discriminatory practices in connection with the financing of housing.

If VA finds there is noncompliance with any antidiscrimination laws or regulations, it may discontinue business with the violator.

29. NEW OR PROPOSED CONSTRUCTION - Complete Items 29A through 29G for new or proposed construction cases only

A. COMPLIANCE INSPECTIONS WILL BE OR WERE MADE BY:	B. PLANS (Check one)	C. PLANS SUBMITTED PREVIOUSLY UNDER CASE NO.
☐ FHA ☐ VA ☐ NONE MADE	☐ FIRST SUBMISSION ☐ REPEAT CASE (If checked complete Item 29C)	

D. NAME AND ADDRESS OF BUILDER	E. TELEPHONE NO.	F. NAME AND ADDRESS OF WARRANTOR	G. TELEPHONE NO.

30. COMMENTS ON SPECIAL ASSESSMENTS OR HOMEOWNERS ASSOCIATION CHARGES	31. ANNUAL REAL ESTATE TAXES	33. LEASEHOLD CASES (Complete if applicable)	
	$	A. LEASE IS:	B. EXPIRES (Date)
	32. MINERAL RIGHTS RESERVED?	☐ 99 YEARS	
	☐ YES (Explain)		C. ANNUAL GROUND RENT
	☐ RENEWABLE		
	☐ NO	$	

34A. SALE PRICE OF PROPERTY	34B. IS BUYER PURCHASING LOT SEPARATELY?	35. REFINANCING-AMOUNT OF PROPOSED LOAN	36. PROPOSED SALE CONTRACT ATTACHED	37. CONTRACT NO. PREVIOUSLY APPROVED BY VA THAT WILL BE
$	☐ YES ☐ NO (If "Yes," see instruction page under "Sale Price")	$	☐ YES ☐ NO	

CERTIFICATIONS FOR SUBMISSIONS TO VA

1. On receipt of "Certificate of Reasonable Value" or advice from the Department of Veterans Affairs that a "Certificate of Reasonable Value" will not be issued, we agree to forward to the appraiser the approved fee which we are holding for this purpose.

2. CERTIFICATION REQUIRED ON CONSTRUCTION UNDER FHA SUPERVISION (Strike out inappropriate phrases in parentheses)

I hereby certify that plans and specifications and related exhibits, including acceptable FHA Change Orders, if any, supplied to VA in this case, are identical to those (submitted to) (to be submitted to) (approved by) FHA inspections, and that FHA inspections (have been) (will be) made pursuant to FHA approval for mortgage insurance on this basis of proposed construction under Sec.

38. SIGNATURE OF PERSON AUTHORIZING THIS	39. TITLE	40. TELEPHONE NUMBER	41. DATE

42. DATE OF ASSIGNMENT	43. NAME OF APPRAISER

WARNING: Section 1010 of title 18, U.S.C. provides: "Whoever for the purpose of . . .influencing such Administration . . .makes, passes, utters or publishes any statement knowing the same to be false . . .shall be fined not more than $5,000 or imprisoned not more than two years or both.

VA FORM **26-1805**
JUN 2001

SUPERSEDES VA FORM 26-1805, DEC 1992, WHICH WILL NOT BE USED.

VA FILE COPY 1

OMB APPROVED NO. 2900-0045
RESPONDENT BURDEN: 12 minutes

REQUEST FOR DETERMINATION OF REASONABLE VALUE (Real Estate)

1. CASE NUMBER	4. TITLE LIMITATIONS AND RESTRICTIVE COVENANTS:

2. PROPERTY ADDRESS (Include ZIP Code and county)	3. LEGAL DESCRIPTION	

1. CONDOMINIUM 2. PLANNED UNIT DEVELOPMENT

5. NAME AND ADDRESS OF FIRM OR PERSON MAKING REQUEST/APPLICATION (Include ZIP Code)	6. LOT DIMENSIONS:

1. IRREGULAR: SQ/FT 2.   ACRES:

7. UTILITIES (✓)   ELEC. GAS WATER SAN. SEWER

1. PUBLIC

2. COMMUNITY

3. INDIVIDUAL

8. EQUIP.
1. RANGE/ OVEN   4. CLOTHES WASHER   7. VENT FAN
2. REFRIG. DISH WASHER   5. DRYER GARBAGE DISPOSAL   8. W/W CARPET 9.

9. BUILDING STATUS 3. EXISTING	10. BUILDING TYPE	11. FACTORY FABRICATED?	12A. NO. OF BUILDINGS	12B. NO. OF LIVING UNITS	13A. STREET ACCESS	13B. STREET MAINTENANCE
1. PROPOSED ALTERATIONS, IMPROVEMENTS,	1. DETACHED 3. ROW APT.				1. PRIVATE	1. PRIVATE
2. UNDER CONSTRUCTION 4. OR REPAIRS	2. SEMI-DETACHED 4. UNIT	1. YES 2. NO			2. PUBLIC	2. PUBLIC

14A. CONSTRUCTION WARRANTY INCLUDED?	14B. NAME OF WARRANTY PROGRAM	14C. EXPIRATION DATE (Month, day, year)	15. CONSTRUCTION COMPLETED (Mo.,yr.)
1. YES 2. NO (If "Yes," complete Items 14b and 14c also)			

16. NAME OF OWNER	17. PROPERTY:	18. RENT (If applic.)
	OCCUPIED BY OWNER NEVER OCCUPIED VACANT OCCUPIED BY TENANT (Complete Item18 also)	$ / MONTH

19. NAME OF OCCUPANT	20. TELEPHONE NO.	21. NAME OF BROKER	22. TELEPHONE NO.	23. DATE AND TIME AVAILABLE FOR INSPECTION
				AM PM

24. KEYS AT (Address)	25. ORIGINATOR'S IDENT. NO.	26. SPONSOR'S IDENT. NO.	27. INSTITUTION'S CASE NO.

28. PURCHASER'S NAME AND ADDRESS (Complete mailing address, Include ZIP Code)	EQUAL OPPORTUNITY IN HOUSING

NOTE: Federal laws and regulations prohibit discrimination because of race, color, religion, sex, or national origin in the sale or rental of residential property. Numerous State statutes and local ordinances also prohibit such discrimination. In addition, section 805 of the Civil Rights Act of 1968 prohibits discriminatory practices in connection with the financing of housing.

If VA finds there is noncompliance with any antidiscrimination laws or regulations, it may discontinue business with the violator.

29. NEW OR PROPOSED CONSTRUCTION - Complete Items 29A through 29G for new or proposed construction cases only

A. COMPLIANCE INSPECTIONS WILL BE OR WERE MADE BY:	B. PLANS (Check one)	C. PLANS SUBMITTED PREVIOUSLY UNDER CASE NO
FHA VA NONE MADE	FIRST SUBMISSION REPEAT CASE (If checked complete Item 29C)	
D. NAME AND ADDRESS OF BUILDER	E. TELEPHONE NO. F. NAME AND ADDRESS OF WARRANTOR	G. TELEPHONE NO.

30. COMMENTS ON SPECIAL ASSESSMENTS OR HOMEOWNERS ASSOCIATION CHARGES	31. ANNUAL REAL ESTATE TAXES	33. LEASEHOLD CASES (Complete if applicable)	
	$	A. LEASE IS:	B. EXPIRES (Date)
	32. MINERAL RIGHTS RESERVED?	99 YEARS	
	YES (Explain)		C. ANNUAL GROUND RENT
		RENEWABLE	
	NO		$

34A. SALE PRICE OF PROPERTY	34B. IS BUYER PURCHASING LOT SEPARATELY?	35. REFINANCING-AMOUNT OF PROPOSED LOAN	36. PROPOSED SALE CONTRACT ATTACHED	37. CONTRACT NO. PREVIOUSLY APPROVED BY VA THAT WILL BE
$	(If "Yes," see instruction page under "Sale Price") YES NO	$	YES NO	

CERTIFICATIONS FOR SUBMISSIONS TO VA

1. On receipt of "Certificate of Reasonable Value" or advice from the Department of Veterans Affairs that a "Certificate of Reasonable Value" will not be issued, we agree to forward to the appraiser the approved fee which we are holding for this purpose.

2. CERTIFICATION REQUIRED ON CONSTRUCTION UNDER FHA SUPERVISION (Strike out inappropriate phrases in parentheses)

I hereby certify that plans and specifications and related exhibits, including acceptable FHA Change Orders, if any, supplied to VA in this case, are identical to those (submitted to) (to be submitted to) (approved by) FHA inspections, and that FHA inspections (have been) (will be) made pursuant to FHA approval for mortgage insurance on this basis of proposed construction under Sec.

38. SIGNATURE OF PERSON AUTHORIZING THIS	39. TITLE	40. TELEPHONE NUMBER	41. DATE

42. DATE OF ASSIGNMENT	43. NAME OF APPRAISER

WARNING: Section 1010 of title 18, U.S.C. provides: "Whoever for the purpose of . . .influencing such Administration . . .makes, passes, utters or publishes any statement knowing the same to be false . . .shall be fined not more than $5,000 or imprisoned not more than two years or both.

VA FORM JUN 2001 26-1805	SUPERSEDES VA FORM 26-1805, DEC 1992, WHICH WILL NOT BE USED.	VA FILE COPY 1

OMB APPROVED NO. 2900-0045
RESPONDENT BURDEN: 12 minutes

REQUEST FOR DETERMINATION OF REASONABLE VALUE (Real Estate)

1. CASE NUMBER	4. TITLE LIMITATIONS AND RESTRICTIVE COVENANTS:

2. PROPERTY ADDRESS (Include ZIP Code and county)	3. LEGAL DESCRIPTION

1. ☐ CONDOMINIUM   2. ☐ PLANNED UNIT DEVELOPMENT

5. NAME AND ADDRESS OF FIRM OR PERSON MAKING REQUEST/APPLICATION (Include ZIP Code)	6. LOT DIMENSIONS:

1. ☐ IRREGULAR: SQ/FT   2. ☐ ACRES:

7. UTILITIES (✓)	ELEC.	GAS	WATER	SAN. SEWER
1. PUBLIC				
2. COMMUNITY				
3. INDIVIDUAL				

8. E Q U I P.	1. ☐ RANGE/OVEN	4. ☐ CLOTHES WASHER	7 ☐ VENT FAN
	2. ☐ REFRIG.	5. ☐ DRYER	8. ☐ W/W CARPET
	3. ☐ DISH WASHER	6. ☐ GARBAGE DISPOSAL	9. ☐

9. BUILDING STATUS		10. BUILDING TYPE	11. FACTORY FABRICATED?	12A. NO. OF BUILDINGS	12B. NO. OF LIVING UNITS	13A. STREET ACCESS	13B. STREET MAINTENANCE
1. ☐ PROPOSED	3. ☐ EXISTING	1. ☐ DETACHED 3. ☐ ROW				1. ☐ PRIVATE	1. ☐ PRIVATE
2. ☐ UNDER CONSTRUCTION	ALTERATIONS, IMPROVEMENTS, 4. ☐ OR REPAIRS	SEMI- 2. ☐ DETACHED APT. 4. ☐ UNIT	1. ☐ YES 2. ☐ NO			2. ☐ PUBLIC	2. ☐ PUBLIC

14A. CONSTRUCTION WARRANTY INCLUDED?	14B. NAME OF WARRANTY PROGRAM	14C. EXPIRATION DATE (Month, day, year)	15. CONSTRUCTION COMPLETED (Mo.,yr.)
1. ☐ YES 2. ☐ NO (If "Yes," complete Items 14b and 14c also)			

16. NAME OF OWNER	17. PROPERTY:	18. RENT (If applic.)
	☐ OCCUPIED BY OWNER ☐ NEVER OCCUPIED ☐ VACANT ☐ OCCUPIED BY TENANT (Complete Item18 also)	$ / MONTH

19. NAME OF OCCUPANT	20. TELEPHONE NO.	21. NAME OF BROKER	22. TELEPHONE NO.	23. DATE AND TIME AVAILABLE FOR INSPECTION
				☐ AM ☐ PM

24. KEYS AT (Address)	25. ORIGINATOR'S IDENT. NO.	26. SPONSOR'S IDENT. NO.	27. INSTITUTION'S CASE NO.

28. PURCHASER'S NAME AND ADDRESS (Complete mailing address, include ZIP Code)	EQUAL OPPORTUNITY IN HOUSING

NOTE: Federal laws and regulations prohibit discrimination because of race, color, religion, sex, or national origin in the sale or rental of residential property. Numerous State statutes and local ordinances also prohibit such discrimination. In addition, section 805 of the Civil Rights Act of 1968 prohibits discriminatory practices in connection with the financing of housing.

If VA finds there is noncompliance with any antidiscrimination laws or regulations, it may discontinue business with the violator.

29. NEW OR PROPOSED CONSTRUCTION - Complete Items 29A through 29G for new or proposed construction cases only

A. COMPLIANCE INSPECTIONS WILL BE OR WERE MADE BY:	B. PLANS (Check one)	C. PLANS SUBMITTED PREVIOUSLY UNDER CASE NO.
☐ FHA ☐ VA ☐ NONE MADE	☐ FIRST SUBMISSION ☐ REPEAT CASE (If checked complete Item 29C)	

D. NAME AND ADDRESS OF BUILDER	E. TELEPHONE NO.	F. NAME AND ADDRESS OF WARRANTOR	G. TELEPHONE NO.

30. COMMENTS ON SPECIAL ASSESSMENTS OR HOMEOWNERS ASSOCIATION CHARGES	31. ANNUAL REAL ESTATE TAXES	33. LEASEHOLD CASES (Complete if applicable)	
	$	A. LEASE IS:	B. EXPIRES (Date)
	32. MINERAL RIGHTS RESERVED?	☐ 99 YEARS	
	☐ YES (Explain)		C. ANNUAL GROUND RENT
		☐ RENEWABLE	
	☐ NO		$

34A. SALE PRICE OF PROPERTY	34B. IS BUYER PURCHASING LOT SEPARATELY?	35. REFINANCING-AMOUNT OF PROPOSED LOAN	36. PROPOSED SALE CONTRACT ATTACHED	37. CONTRACT NO. PREVIOUSLY APPROVED BY VA THAT WILL BE
$	☐ YES ☐ NO (If "Yes," see instruction page under "Sale Price")	$	☐ YES ☐ NO	

CERTIFICATIONS FOR SUBMISSIONS TO VA

1. On receipt of "Certificate of Reasonable Value" or advice from the Department of Veterans Affairs that a "Certificate of Reasonable Value" will not be issued, we agree to forward to the appraiser the approved fee which we are holding for this purpose.

2. CERTIFICATION REQUIRED ON CONSTRUCTION UNDER FHA SUPERVISION (Strike out inappropriate phrases in parentheses)

I hereby certify that plans and specifications and related exhibits, including acceptable FHA Change Orders, if any, supplied to VA in this case, are identical to those (submitted to) (to be submitted to) (approved by) FHA inspections, and that FHA inspections (have been) (will be) made pursuant to FHA approval for mortgage insurance on this basis of proposed construction under Sec.

38. SIGNATURE OF PERSON AUTHORIZING THIS	39. TITLE	40. TELEPHONE NUMBER	41. DATE

42. DATE OF ASSIGNMENT	43. NAME OF APPRAISER

WARNING: Section 1010 of title 18, U.S.C. provides: "Whoever for the purpose of . . .influencing such Administration . . .makes, passes, utters or publishes any statement knowing the same to be false . . .shall be fined not more than $5,000 or imprisoned not more than two years or both.

VA FORM JUN 2001 **26-1805**	SUPERSEDES VA FORM 20-1805, DEC 1992, WHICH WILL NOT BE USED.	**REQUESTOR'S COPY 2**

OMB APPROVED NO. 2900-0045
RESPONDENT BURDEN: 12 minutes

CERTIFICATE OF REASONABLE VALUE

1. CASE NUMBER	4. TITLE LIMITATIONS AND RESTRICTIVE COVENANTS:

2. PROPERTY ADDRESS (Include ZIP Code and county)	3. LEGAL DESCRIPTION	

1. ☐ CONDOMINIUM   2. ☐ PLANNED UNIT DEVELOPMENT

5. NAME AND ADDRESS OF FIRM OR PERSON MAKING REQUEST/APPLICATION (Include ZIP Code)	6. REMAINING ECONOMIC LIFE OF PROPERTY IS ESTIMATED TO BE NOT LESS THAN (Enter number of years)
	YEARS

7. ESTIMATED REASONABLE VALUE OF PROPERTY	8. EXPIRATION DATE
$	

9. SECRETARY OF VETERANS AFFAIRS BY (Signature of authorized agent)

10. DATE ISSUED	11. VA OFFICE

GENERAL CONDITIONS

(NOTE: THE DEPARTMENT OF VETERANS AFFAIRS DOES NOT ASSUME ANY RESPONSIBILITY FOR THE CONDITION OF THE PROPERTY. THE CORRECTION OF ANY DEFECTS NOW EXISTING OR THAT MAY DEVELOP WILL BE THE RESPONSIBILITY OF THE PURCHASER.)

1. This certificate will remain effective as to any written contract of sale entered into by an eligible veteran within the validity period indicated.
2. This dwelling conforms with the Minimum Property Requirements prescribed by the Secretary of Veterans Affairs.
3. The aggregate of any loan secured by this property plus the amount of any special improvements as to which a lien or right to a lien shall exist against the property, except as provided in Item 13 below, may not exceed the reasonable value in Item 7 above.
4. Proposed construction shall be completed in accordance with the plans and specifications identified below, relating to both onsite and offsite improvements upon which this valuation is based and shall otherwise conform fully to the VA Minium Property Requirements. Satisfactory completion must be evidenced by either:
   A. VA Final Compliance Inspection Report (VA Form 26-1839), or
   B. VA Acceptance of FHA Compliance Inspection Reports or other evidence of completion under FHA supervision applicable to proposed construction.
5. By contracting to sell property, as proposed construction or existing construction not previously occupied, to a veteran purchaser who is to be assisted in the purchase by a loan made, guaranteed, or insured by VA, the builder or other seller agrees to place any downpayment received by the seller or agent of the seller in a special trust account as required by section 3706 of title 38, U.S. Code.
6. The VA guaranty is subject to and conditioned upon the lending institution's compliance, at the time of the making, increasing, extending or renewing of the proposed loan, with section 102 of P.L. 93-234, "Flood Disaster Protection Act of 1973."

12. PURCHASER'S NAME AND ADDRESS (Complete mailing address, Include ZIP Code)	13. EXCEPTIONS TO GENERAL CONDITION NO. 3 ABOVE
	☐ ENERGY EFFICIENT MORTGAGE PROGRAM - The buyer may wish to contact a qualified person/firm for a home energy audit to identify needed energy efficiency improvements to the property. In some localities, the utility company may perform this service. The mortgage amount may be increased as a result of making energy efficiency improvements such as: Solar or conventional heating/cooling systems, water heaters, insulation, weather-stripping/caulking, and storm windows/doors. Other energy related improvements may also be considered. The mortgage may be increased by (a) up to $3,000 based solely on documented costs; or, (b) up to $6,000 provided the increase in monthly mortgage payment does not exceed the likely reduction in monthly utility costs; or, (c) more than $6000 subject to a value determination by VA.
	☐ OTHER (Cite and explain in Item 26 below)

SPECIFIC CONDITIONS (Applicable when checked or completed)

14. THE REASONABLE VALUE ESTABLISHED HEREIN FOR THE RELATED PROPERTY IS:	15. PROPOSED CONSTRUCTION TO BE COMPLETED
☐ BASED UPON OBSERVATION OF THE PROPERTY IN ITS "AS IS" CONDITION ☐ PREDICATED UPON COMPLETION OF PROPOSED CONSTRUCTION (If checked, complete Item 15) ☐ PREDICATED UPON COMPLETION OF REPAIRS LISTED IN ITEM 17	

16. INSPECTIONS REQUIRED	17. REPAIRS TO BE COMPLETED
☐ FHA COMPLIANCE INSPECTIONS FOR PROPOSED CONSTRUCTION ☐ VA COMPLIANCE INSPECITONS ☐ LENDER TO CERTIFY	

18. NAME OF COMPLIANCE INSPECTOR

19. HEALTH AUTHORITY APPROVAL - Execution of Health Authority form or letter indicating approval of the individual:	20.
☐ WATER SUPPLY ☐ SEWAGE DISPOSAL SYSTEM	☐ This document is subject to the provisions of Executive Orders 11246 and 11375, and the Rules and Regulations of the Secretary of Labor in effect on this date, and 38 CFR 36.4390 through 36.4393, and also the provisions of the certification executed by the builder, sponsor or developer named herein which is on file in this office.

21. ☐ WOOD DESTROYING INSECT INFORMATION - EXISTING CONSTRUCTION - The seller shall, at no cost to the veteran-purchaser, prior to settlement, obtain a written statement from a qualified pest control operator reporting wood destroying insect information using the NPCA-1, National Pest Control Association form or other form acceptable to VA.

22. WARRANTY	23. NAME OF WARRANTOR	24.
☐ (If checked, complete Item 23)		☐ Since this property is located in a Special Flood Hazard Area as established by FEMA, flood insurance will be required in accordance with 38 CFR 36.4326

25. SAFE DRINKING WATER ACT
☐ Certification required that in construction, any solders and flux did not contain more than 0.2 percent lead and any pipes and pipe fittings did not contain more than 8.0 percent lead.

26. OTHER REQUIREMENTS

VA FORM **26-1843** JUN 2001   SUPERSEDES VA FORM 26-1805, DEC 1992, WHICH WILL NOT BE USED.   REQUESTOR'S COPY 3

CERTIFICATE OF REASONABLE VALUE

1. CASE NUMBER	4. TITLE LIMITATIONS AND RESTRICTIVE COVENANTS:

2. PROPERTY ADDRESS (Include ZIP Code and county)	3. LEGAL DESCRIPTION

1. ☐ CONDOMINIUM   2. ☐ PLANNED UNIT DEVELOPMENT

5. NAME AND ADDRESS OF FIRM OR PERSON MAKING REQUEST/APPLICATION (Include ZIP Code)	6. REMAINING ECONOMIC LIFE OF PROPERTY IS ESTIMATED TO BE NOT LESS THAN (Enter number of years)

YEARS

7. ESTIMATED REASONABLE VALUE OF PROPERTY	8. EXPIRATION DATE
$	

9. SECRETARY OF VETERANS AFFAIRS BY (Signature of authorized agent)

10. DATE ISSUED	11. VA OFFICE

GENERAL CONDITIONS

(NOTE: THE DEPARTMENT OF VETERANS AFFAIRS DOES NOT ASSUME ANY RESPONSIBILITY FOR THE CONDITION OF THE PROPERTY. THE CORRECTION OF ANY DEFECTS NOW EXISTING OR THAT MAY DEVELOP WILL BE THE RESPONSIBILITY OF THE PURCHASER.)

1. This certificate will remain effective as to any written contract of sale entered into by an eligible veteran within the validity period indicated.
2. This dwelling conforms with the Minimum Property Requirements prescribed by the Secretary of Veterans Affairs.
3. The aggregate of any loan secured by this property plus the amount of any assessment consequent on any special improvements as to which a lien or right to a lien shall exist against the property, except as provided in Item 13 below, may not exceed the reasonable value in Item 7 above.
4. Proposed construction shall be completed in accordance with the plans and specifications identified below, relating to both onsite and offsite improvements upon which this valuation is based and shall otherwise conform fully to the VA Minimum Property Requirements. Satisfactory completion must be evidenced by either:
   A. VA Final Compliance Inspection Report (VA Form 26-1839), or
   B. VA Acceptance of FHA Compliance Inspection Reports or other evidence of completion under FHA supervision applicable to proposed construction.
5. By contracting to sell property, as proposed construction or existing construction not previously occupied, to a veteran purchaser who is to be assisted in the purchase by a loan made, guaranteed, or insured by VA, the builder or other seller agrees to place any downpayment received by the seller or agent of the seller in a special trust account as required by section 3706 of title 38, U.S. Code.
6. The VA guaranty is subject to and conditioned upon the lending institution's compliance, at the time of the making, increasing, extending or renewing of the proposed loan, with section 102 of P.L. 93-234, "Flood Disaster Protection Act of 1973."

12. PURCHASER'S NAME AND ADDRESS (Complete mailing address, Include ZIP Code)	13. EXCEPTIONS TO GENERAL CONDITION NO. 3 ABOVE
	☐ ENERGY EFFICIENT MORTGAGE PROGRAM - The buyer may wish to contact a qualified person/firm for a home energy audit to identify needed energy efficiency improvements to the property. In some localities, the utility company may perform this service. The mortgage amount may be increased as a result of making energy efficiency improvements such as: Solar or conventional heating/cooling systems, water heaters, insulation, weather-stripping/caulking, and storm windows/doors. Other energy related improvements may also be considered. The mortgage may be increased by (a) up to $3,000 based solely on documented costs; or, (b) up to $6,000 provided the increase in monthly mortgage payment does not exceed the likely reduction in monthly utility costs; or, (c) more than $6000 subject to a value determination by VA. ☐ OTHER (Cite and explain in Item 26 below)

SPECIFIC CONDITIONS (Applicable when checked or completed)

14. THE REASONABLE VALUE ESTABLISHED HEREIN FOR THE RELATED PROPERTY IS:	15. PROPOSED CONSTRUCTION TO BE COMPLETED
☐ BASED UPON OBSERVATION OF THE PROPERTY IN ITS "AS IS" CONDITION ☐ PREDICATED UPON COMPLETION OF PROPOSED CONSTRUCTION (If checked, complete Item 15) ☐ PREDICATED UPON COMPLETION OF REPAIRS LISTED IN ITEM 17	

16. INSPECTIONS REQUIRED	17. REPAIRS TO BE COMPLETED
☐ FHA COMPLIANCE INSPECTIONS FOR PROPOSED CONSTRUCTION ☐ VA COMPLIANCE INSPECITONS ☐ LENDER TO CERTIFY	

18. NAME OF COMPLIANCE INSPECTOR

19. HEALTH AUTHORITY APPROVAL - Execution of Health Authority form or letter indicating approval of the individual: ☐ WATER SUPPLY ☐ SEWAGE DISPOSAL SYSTEM	20. This document is subject to the provisions of Executive Orders 11246 and 11375, and the Rules and Regulations of the Secretary of Labor in effect on this date, and 38 CFR 36.4390 through 36.4393, and also the provisions of the certification ☐ executed by the builder, sponsor or developer named herein which is on file in this office.

21. ☐ WOOD DESTROYING INSECT INFORMATION - EXISTING CONSTRUCTION - The seller shall, at no cost to the veteran-purchaser, prior to settlement, obtain a written statement from a qualified pest control operator reporting wood destroying insect information using the NPCA-1, National Pest Control Association form or other form acceptable to VA.

22. WARRANTY ☐ (If checked, complete Item 23)	23. NAME OF WARRANTOR	24. ☐ Since this property is located in a Special Flood Hazard Area as established by FEMA, flood insurance will be required in accordance with 38 CFR 36.4326

25. SAFE DRINKING WATER ACT
☐ Certification required that in construction, any solders and flux did not contain more than 0.2 percent lead and any pipes and pipe fittings did not contain more than 8.0 percent lead.

26. OTHER REQUIREMENTS

OMB APPROVED NO. 2900-0045
RESPONDENT BURDEN: 12 minutes

CERTIFICATE OF REASONABLE VALUE

1. CASE NUMBER	4. TITLE LIMITATIONS AND RESTRICTIVE COVENANTS:

2. PROPERTY ADDRESS (Include ZIP Code and county)	3. LEGAL DESCRIPTION	

1. ☐ CONDOMINIUM   2. ☐ PLANNED UNIT DEVELOPMENT

5. NAME AND ADDRESS OF FIRM OR PERSON MAKING REQUEST/APPLICATION (Include ZIP Code)	6. REMAINING ECONOMIC LIFE OF PROPERTY IS ESTIMATED TO BE NOT LESS THAN (Enter number of years)

YEARS

7. ESTIMATED REASONABLE VALUE OF PROPERTY	8. EXPIRATION DATE
$	

9. SECRETARY OF VETERANS AFFAIRS BY (Signature of authorized agent)

10. DATE ISSUED	11. VA OFFICE

GENERAL CONDITIONS

(NOTE: THE DEPARTMENT OF VETERANS AFFAIRS DOES NOT ASSUME ANY RESPONSIBILITY FOR THE CONDITION OF THE PROPERTY. THE CORRECTION OF ANY DEFECTS NOW EXISTING OR THAT MAY DEVELOP WILL BE THE RESPONSIBILITY OF THE PURCHASER.)

1. This certificate will remain effective as to any written contract of sale entered into by an eligible veteran within the validity period indicated.
2. This dwelling conforms with the Minimum Property Requirements prescribed by the Secretary of Veterans Affairs.
3. The aggregate of any loan secured by this property plus the amount of any assessment consequent on any special improvements as to which a lien or right to a lien shall exist against the property, except as provided in Item 13 below, may not exceed the reasonable value in Item 7 above.
4. Proposed construction shall be completed in accordance with the plans and specifications identified below, relating to both onsite and offsite improvements upon which this valuation is based and shall otherwise conform fully to the VA Minimum Property Requirements. Satisfactory completion must be evidenced by either:
   A. VA Final Compliance Inspection Report (VA Form 26-1839), or
   B. VA Acceptance of FHA Compliance Inspection Reports or other evidence of completion under FHA supervision applicable to proposed construction.
5. By contracting to sell property, as proposed construction or existing construction not previously occupied, to a veteran purchaser who is to be assisted in the purchase by a loan made, guaranteed, or insured by VA, the builder or other seller agrees to place any downpayment received by the seller or agent of the seller in a special trust account as required by section 3706 of title 38, U.S. Code.
6. The VA guaranty is subject to and conditioned upon the lending institution's compliance, at the time of the making, increasing, extending or renewing of the proposed loan, with section 102 of P.L. 93-234, "Flood Disaster Protection Act of 1973."

12. PURCHASER'S NAME AND ADDRESS (Complete mailing address, Include ZIP Code)	13. EXCEPTIONS TO GENERAL CONDITION NO. 3 ABOVE
	☐ ENERGY EFFICIENT MORTGAGE PROGRAM - The buyer may wish to contact a qualified person/firm for a home energy audit to identify needed energy efficiency improvements to the property. In some localities, the utility company may perform this service. The mortgage amount may be increased as a result of making energy efficiency improvements such as: Solar or conventional heating/cooling systems, water heaters, insulation, weather-stripping/caulking, and storm windows/doors. Other energy related improvements may also be considered. The mortgage may be increased by (a) up to $3,000 based solely on documented costs; or, (b) up to $6,000 provided the increase in monthly mortgage payment does not exceed the likely reduction in monthly utility costs; or, (c) more than $6000 subject to a value determination by VA.
	☐ OTHER (Cite and explain in Item 26 below)

SPECIFIC CONDITIONS (Applicable when checked or completed)

14. THE REASONABLE VALUE ESTABLISHED HEREIN FOR THE RELATED PROPERTY IS:	15. PROPOSED CONSTRUCTION TO BE COMPLETED
☐ BASED UPON OBSERVATION OF THE PROPERTY IN ITS "AS IS" CONDITION ☐ PREDICATED UPON COMPLETION OF PROPOSED CONSTRUCTION (If checked, complete Item 15) ☐ PREDICATED UPON COMPLETION OF REPAIRS LISTED IN ITEM 17	

16. INSPECTIONS REQUIRED	17. REPAIRS TO BE COMPLETED
☐ FHA COMPLIANCE INSPECTIONS FOR PROPOSED CONSTRUCTION ☐ VA COMPLIANCE INSPECITONS ☐ LENDER TO CERTIFY	

18. NAME OF COMPLIANCE INSPECTOR

19. HEALTH AUTHORITY APPROVAL - Execution of Health Authority form or letter indicating approval of the individual:	20.
☐ WATER SUPPLY ☐ SEWAGE DISPOSAL SYSTEM	☐ This document is subject to the provisions of Executive Orders 11246 and 11375, and the Rules and Regulations of the Secretary of Labor in effect on this date, and 38 CFR 36.4390 through 36.4393, and also the provisions of the certification executed by the builder, sponsor or developer named herein which is on file in this office.

21.
☐ WOOD DESTROYING INSECT INFORMATION - EXISTING CONSTRUCTION - The seller shall, at no cost to the veteran-purchaser, prior to settlement, obtain a written statement from a qualified pest control operator reporting wood destroying insect information using the NPCA-1, National Pest Control Association form or other form acceptable to VA.

22. WARRANTY	23. NAME OF WARRANTOR	24.
☐ (If checked, complete Item 23)		☐ Since this property is located in a Special Flood Hazard Area as established by FEMA, flood insurance will be required in accordance with 38 CFR 36.4326

25. SAFE DRINKING WATER ACT
☐ Certification required that in construction, any solders and flux did not contain more than 0.2 percent lead and any pipes and pipe fittings did not contain more than 8.0 percent lead.

26. OTHER REQUIREMENTS

VA FORM 26-1843 JUN 2001	SUPERSEDES VA FORM 26-1805, DEC 1992, WHICH WILL NOT BE USED.	PURCHASER'S COPY 5

OMB APPROVED NO. 2900-0045
RESPONDENT BURDEN: 12 minutes

REQUEST FOR DETERMINATION OF REASONABLE VALUE (Real Estate)

1. CASE NUMBER	4. TITLE LIMITATIONS AND RESTRICTIVE COVENANTS:
2. PROPERTY ADDRESS (Include ZIP Code and county) 3. LEGAL DESCRIPTION	

1. ☐ CONDOMINIUM   2. ☐ PLANNED UNIT DEVELOPMENT

5. NAME AND ADDRESS OF FIRM OR PERSON MAKING REQUEST/APPLICATION (Include ZIP Code)

6. LOT DIMENSIONS:

1. ☐ IRREGULAR: SQ/FT   2. ☐ ACRES:

7. UTILITIES (✓)	ELEC.	GAS	WATER	SAN. SEWER
1. PUBLIC				
2. COMMUNITY				
3. INDIVIDUAL				

8. EQUIP.
1. ☐ RANGE/OVEN   4. ☐ CLOTHES WASHER   7. ☐ VENT FAN
2. ☐ REFRIG.   5. ☐ DRYER   8. ☐ W/W CARPET
3. ☐ DISH WASHER   6. ☐ GARBAGE DISPOSAL   9. ☐

9. BUILDING STATUS		10. BUILDING TYPE	11. FACTORY FABRICATED?	12A. NO. OF BUILDINGS	12B. NO. OF LIVING UNITS	13A. STREET ACCESS	13B. STREET MAINTENANCE
1. ☐ PROPOSED 3. ☐ EXISTING		1. ☐ DETACHED 3. ☐ ROW SEMI- APT.				1. ☐ PRIVATE	1. ☐ PRIVATE
2. ☐ UNDER CONSTRUCTION 4. ☐ ALTERATIONS, IMPROVEMENTS, OR REPAIRS		2. ☐ DETACHED 4. ☐ UNIT	1. ☐ YES 2. ☐ NO			2. ☐ PUBLIC	2. ☐ PUBLIC

14A. CONSTRUCTION WARRANTY INCLUDED?	14B. NAME OF WARRANTY PROGRAM	14C. EXPIRATION DATE (Month, day, year)	15. CONSTRUCTION COMPLETED (Mo.,yr.)
1. ☐ YES 2. ☐ NO (If "Yes," fill in Items 14b and 14c also)			

16. NAME OF OWNER	17. PROPERTY:	18. RENT (If applic.)
	☐ OCCUPIED BY OWNER ☐ NEVER OCCUPIED ☐ VACANT ☐ OCCUPIED BY TENANT (Complete Item18 also)	$ / MONTH

19. NAME OF OCCUPANT	20. TELEPHONE NO.	21. NAME OF BROKER	22. TELEPHONE NO.	23. DATE AND TIME AVAILABLE FOR INSPECTION
				☐ AM ☐ PM

24. KEYS AT (Address)	25. ORIGINATOR'S IDENT. NO.	26. SPONSOR'S IDENT. NO.	27. INSTITUTION'S CASE NO.

28. PURCHASER'S NAME AND ADDRESS (Complete mailing address, Include ZIP Code)

EQUAL OPPORTUNITY IN HOUSING
NOTE: Federal laws and regulations prohibit discrimination because of race, color, religion, sex, or national origin in the sale or rental of residential property. Numerous State statutes and local ordinances also prohibit such discrimination. In addition, section 805 of the Civil Rights Act of 1968 prohibits discriminatory practices in connection with the financing of housing.

If VA finds there is noncompliance with any antidiscrimination laws or regulations, it may discontinue business with the violator.

29. NEW OR PROPOSED CONSTRUCTION - Complete Items 29A through 29G for new or proposed construction cases only

A. COMPLIANCE INSPECTIONS WILL BE OR WERE MADE BY:	B. PLANS (Check one)	C. PLANS SUBMITTED PREVIOUSLY UNDER CASE NO.
☐ FHA ☐ VA ☐ NONE MADE	☐ FIRST SUBMISSION ☐ REPEAT CASE (If checked complete Item 29C)	

D. NAME AND ADDRESS OF BUILDER	E. TELEPHONE NO.	F. NAME AND ADDRESS OF WARRANTOR	G. TELEPHONE NO.

30. COMMENTS ON SPECIAL ASSESSMENTS OR HOMEOWNERS ASSOCIATION CHARGES	31. ANNUAL REAL ESTATE TAXES $	33. LEASEHOLD CASES (Complete if applicable)
	32. MINERAL RIGHTS RESERVED? ☐ YES (Explain) ☐ NO	A. LEASE IS: ☐ 99 YEARS ☐ RENEWABLE B. EXPIRES (Date) C. ANNUAL GROUND RENT $

34A. SALE PRICE OF PROPERTY $	34B. IS BUYER PURCHASING LOT SEPARATELY? ☐ YES ☐ NO (If "Yes," see instruction page under "Sale Price")	35. REFINANCING-AMOUNT OF PROPOSED LOAN $	36. PROPOSED SALE CONTRACT ATTACHED ☐ YES ☐ NO	37. CONTRACT NO. PREVIOUSLY APPROVED BY VA THAT WILL BE

38. REMARKS

ASSIGNMENT OF APPRAISER

| 39. DATE OF ASSIGNMENT | 40. SIGNATURE OF LOAN GUARANTY OFFICER OR DESIGNEE | NOTE TO APPRAISER: You are assigned to make an appraisal of the above-described property and to submit your report to this office. If Item 1, 3 or 4 * of block 9 is checked, you must submit two copies of the report. Your estimate of reasonable value is subject to administrative adjustment. If existing construction is appraised, you must gain access to the interior of the property to be appraised, and two photos (different views) of the subject property must be submitted with your report. A front-view picture of each comparable used in the market data analysis must also be provided with your report unless this appraisal involves a low-rise or high-rise condominium; or a horizontal condominium development or townhouse planned-unit development, provided the comparables are located in the same project as the subject property and are considered substantially identical to the subject property in design (i.e., same unit type constructed by same builder). If you cannot complete this assignment in 5 days, please notify the Loan Guaranty Officer or designee immediately.

*Photos of the subject property are required only if Item 3 or 4 is checked. |
|---|---|---|
| 41. NAME AND ADDRESS OF APPRAISER (Complete mailing address, Include ZIP Code) | | |

VA FORM 26-1805   **APPRAISER'S COPY 6**
JUN 2001

OMB Approved No. 2900-
Respondent Burden: 15 mi...

Department of Veterans Affairs		Department of Veterans Affairs Attn: Loan Guaranty Division
REQUEST FOR A CERTIFICATE OF ELIGIBILITY FOR VA HOME LOAN BENEFITS	**TO**	

NOTE: Please read information on reverse before completing this form. If additional space is required, attach a separate shee...

1. FIRST-MIDDLE-LAST NAME OF VETERAN	2. DATE OF BIRTH	3. VETERAN'S DAYTIME TELEPHONE NO. ( )
4. ADDRESS OF VETERAN (No., street or rural route, city or P.O., State and ZIP Code)	5. MAIL CERTIFICATE OF ELIGIBILITY TO: (Complete <u>ONLY</u> if the Certificate is to be mailed to an address different from the one listed in Item 4)	

6. MILITARY SERVICE DATA (ATTACH PROOF OF SERVICE - SEE PARAGRAPH "D" ON REVERSE)

A. ITEM	B. PERIODS OF ACTIVE SERVICE		C. NAME (Show your name exactly as it appears on your separation papers or Statement of Service	D. SOCIAL SECURITY NUMBER	E. SERVICE NUMBER (If different from Social Security No.)	F. BRANC SERVI
	DATE FROM	DATE TO				
1.						
2.						
3.						
4.						

7A. WERE YOU DISCHARGED, RETIRED OR SEPARATED FROM SERVICE BECAUSE OF DISABILITY OR DO YOU NOW HAVE ANY SERVICE-CONNECTED DISABILITIES?

□ YES □ NO (If "Yes," complete Item 7B)

7B. VA CLAIM FILE NUMBER

C-

8. PREVIOUS VA LOANS (Must answer N/A if no previous VA home loan. DO NOT LEAVE BLANK)

A. ITEM	B. TYPE (Home, Refinance, Manufactured Home, or Direct)	C. ADDRESS OF PROPERTY	D. DATE OF LOAN	E. DO YOU STILL OWN THE PROPERTY? (YES/NO)	F. DATE PROPERTY WAS SOLD (Submit a copy of HUD-1, Settlement Statement, if available)	G. VA LOAN N (If known
1.						
2.						
3.						
4.						
5.						
6.						

I CERTIFY THAT the statements herein are true to the best of my knowledge and belief.

9. SIGNATURE OF VETERAN (Do NOT print)	10. DATE SIGNED

FEDERAL STATUTES PROVIDE SEVERE PENALTIES FOR FRAUD, INTENTIONAL MISREPRESENTATION, CRIMINAL CONNIVANCE OR CONSPIRACY PURPOSED TO INFLUENCE THE ISSUANCE OF ANY GUARANTY OR INSURANCE BY THE SECRETARY OF VETERANS AFFAI...

FOR VA USE ONLY

11A. DATE CERTIFICATE ISSUED	11B. SIGNATURE OF VA AGENT

VA FORM
MAR 2004 **26-1880**

EXISTING STOCKS OF VA FORM 26-1880, MAY 2002, WILL BE USED.

INSTRUCTIONS FOR VA FORM 26-1880

IVACY ACT INFORMATION: No Certificate of Eligibility may be issued unless VA receives sufficient information to determine that you are eligible (38
.C. 3702). You are not required to furnish the information, including the Social Security Number, but are urged to do so, since it is vital to proper action by
in your case. Specifically, your Social Security Number is requested under authority of 38 U.S.C. 3702 and is requested only if the service department used
r Social Security Number as a service number. Failure to provide a completed application will deprive VA of information needed in reaching decisions
ch could affect you. Responses may be disclosed outside VA only if the disclosure is authorized under the Privacy Act, including the routine uses identified
he VA system of records, 55VA26, Loan Guaranty Home, Condominium and Manufactured Home Loan Applicant Records, Specially Adapted Housing
plicant Records, and Vendee Loan Applicant Records - VA, published in the Federal Register.
SPONDENT BURDEN: VA may not conduct or sponsor, and respondent is not required to respond to this collection of information unless it displays a valid
IB Control Number. Public reporting burden for this collection of information is estimated to average 15 minutes per response, including the time for
iewing instructions, searching existing data sources, gathering and maintaining the data needed, and completing and reviewing the collection of information.
ou have comments regarding this burden estimate or any other aspect of this collection of information, call 1-800-827-1000 for mailing information on where
end your comments.

Mail this completed form, along with proof of service, to the Eligibility Center at P.O. Box 20729, Winston Salem, NC 27120 (for veterans located in the
ern half of the country) or P.O. Box 240097, Los Angeles, CA 90024 (for veterans located in the western half of the country). Veterans stationed overseas
y use either address.

Military Service Requirements for VA Loan Eligibility: (NOTE: Cases involving other than honorable discharges will usually require further development
VA. This is necessary to determine if the service was under other than dishonorable conditions.)
 Wartime Service. If you served anytime during World War II (September 16, 1940 to July 25, 1947), Korean Conflict (June 27, 1950 to January 31.
5), or Vietnam Era (August 5, 1964 to May 7, 1975) you must have served at least 90 days on active duty and been discharged or released under other
a dishonorable conditions. If you served less than 90 days, you may be eligible if discharged because of service-connected disability.
 Peacetime Service. If your service fell entirely within one of the following periods: July 26, 1947 to June 26, 1950, or February 1, 1955 to August 4, 1964.
 must have served at least 181 days of continuous active duty and have been discharged or released under conditions other than dishonorable. If you entered
ice after May 7, 1975 but prior to September 8, 1980 (enlisted) or October 17, 1981 (officer) and completed your service before August 2, 1990, 181 days
ice is also required. If you served less than 181 days, you may be eligible if discharged for a service-connected disability.
 Service after September 7, 1980 (enlisted) or October 16, 1981 (officer) and prior to August 2, 1990. If you were separated from service which began after
e dates, you must have: (a) Completed 24 months of continuous active duty for the full period (at least 181 days) for which you were called or ordered to
ve duty, and been discharged or released under conditions other than dishonorable; or (b) Completed at least 181 days of active duty and been discharged
er the specific authority of 10 U.S.C. 1173 (hardship discharge) or 10 U.S.C. 1171 (early out discharge), or have been determined to have a compensable
ice-connected disability; or (c) Been discharged with less than 181 days of service for a service-connected disability. Individuals may also be eligible if they
e released from active duty due to an involuntary reduction in force, certain medical conditions, or, in some instances for the convenience of the
ernment.
 Gulf War. If you served on active duty during the Gulf War (August 2, 1990 to a date yet to be determined), you must have: (a) Completed 24 months of
tinuous active duty or the full period (at least 90 days) for which you were called or ordered to active duty, and been discharged or released under conditions
er than dishonorable; or (b) Completed at least 90 days of active duty and been discharged under the specific authority of 10 U.S.C. 1173 (hardship
harge), or 10 U.S.C. 1171 (early out discharge), or have been determined to have a compensable service-connected disability; or (c) Been discharged with
than 90 days of service for a service-connected disability. Individuals may also be eligible if they were released from active duty due to an involuntary
action in force, certain medical conditions, or, in some instances, for the convenience of the Government.
 Active Duty Service Personnel. If you are now on active duty, you are eligible after having served on continuous active duty for at least 181 days (90 days
ng the Persian Gulf War) unless discharged or separated from a previous qualifying period of active duty service.
 Selected Reserve Requirements for VA Loan Eligibility. If you are not otherwise eligible and you have completed a total of 6 years in the Selected
erves or National Guard (member of an active unit, attended required weekend drills and 2-week active duty training) and (a) Were discharged with an
orable discharge, or (b) Were placed on the retired list or (c) Were transferred to the Standby Reserve or an element of the Ready Reserve other than the
ected Reserve after service characterized as honorable service; or (d) Continue to serve in the Selected Reserve. Individuals who completed less than 6 years
 be eligible if discharged for a service-connected disability.

Unmarried surviving spouses of eligible veterans seeking determination of basic eligibility for VA Loan Guaranty benefits are NOT required to complete this
n, but are required to complete VA Form 26-1817, Request for Determination of Loan Guaranty Eligibility-Unmarried Surviving Spouse.

Proof of Military Service
 "Regular" Veterans. Attach to this request your most recent discharge or separation papers from active military duty since September 16, 1940, which show
ve duty dates and type of discharge. If you were separated after January 1, 1950, DD Form 214 must be submitted. If you were separated after October 1,
9, and you received DD Form 214, Certificate of Release or Discharge From Active Duty, 1 July edition, VA must be furnished Copy 4 of the form. You
 submit either original papers or legible copies. In addition, if you are now on active duty submit a statement of service signed by, or by direction of, the
tant, personnel officer, or commander of your unit or higher headquarters showing date of entry on your current active duty period and the duration of any
 lost. Any Veterans Services Representative in the nearest Department of Veterans Affairs office or center will assist you in securing necessary proof of
tary service.
 Selected Reserves/National Guard. If you are a discharged member of the Army or Air Force National Guard you may submit a NGB Form 22, Report of
aration and Record of Service, or NGB Form 23, Retirement Points Accounting, or it's equivalent (this is similar to a retirement points summary). If you are
scharged member of the Selected Reserve you may submit a copy of your latest annual point statement and evidence of honorable service. You may submit
er your original papers or legible copies. Since there is no single form used by the Reserves or National Guard similar to the DD Form 214, it is your
onsibility to furnish adequate documentation of at least 6 years of honorable service. In addition, if you are currently serving in the Selected Reserve you
t submit a statement of service signed by, or by the direction of, the adjutant, personnel officer or commander of your unit or higher headquarters showing
ength of time that you have been a member of the unit.

appendix h:
VA Regional Offices

VA Eligibility Centers:

Los Angeles Eligibility Center
If you live in one of the following states:
Alaska, Arizona, Arkansas, California, Colorado, Hawaii, Idaho, Illinois, Iowa, Kansas, Louisiana, Minnesota, Missouri, Montana, Nebraska, Nevada, New Mexico, North Dakota, Oklahoma, Oregon, South Dakota, Texas, Utah, Washington, Wisconsin, or Wyoming

Please send your request for determination of Eligibility (VA Form 26-1880, along with proof of military service) to:
Los Angeles Eligibility Center
P.O. Box 240097
Los Angeles, CA 90024
888-487-1970

Winston-Salem Eligibility Center
If you live in one of the following states:
Alabama, Connecticut, District of Columbia, Delaware, Florida, Georgia, Indiana, Kentucky, Maine, Maryland, Massachusetts, Michigan, Mississippi, New Hampshire, New Jersey, New York, North Carolina, Ohio, Pennsylvania, Puerto Rico, Rhode Island, South Carolina, Tennessee, Vermont, Virginia, or West Virginia

Please send your request for determination of Eligibility (VA Form 26-1880, along with proof of military service) to:
VA Loan Eligibility Center
P.O. Box 20729
Winston-Salem, NC 27120

For overnight delivery:
VA Loan Eligibility Center
251 North Main Street
Winston-Salem, NC 27155
888-244-6711

NOTE: *If you are located outside the U.S., you may use either Eligibility Center.*

The toll-free telephone lines to our Eligibility Centers in North Carolina (888-244-6711) and California (888-487-1970) have been included in our National Automated Response System. Accordingly, callers are now provided a menu of information regarding the guaranteed home loan program, and may exercise options from that menu which allow them to speak to VA Eligibility Personnel. These calls are routed to the appropriate Eligibility Center of jurisdiction based upon the caller's area code. Currently, the most direct route through the menu for those program participants who wish to speak to eligibility personnel includes menu selections in the following order:
  (1)—Touchtone phone
  (1)—Eligibility
  (2)—Status

VA Regional Loan Centers:
For Georgia, North Carolina, South Carolina, Tennessee
Department of Veterans Affairs
Regional Loan Center
1700 Clairmont Road
P.O. Box 100023
Decatur, GA 30031-7023
888-768-2132

For Delaware, Indiana, Michigan, New Jersey, Ohio, Pennsylvania
Department of Veterans Affairs
Cleveland Regional Loan Center
1240 East Ninth Street
Cleveland, OH 44199
800-729-5772

For Alaska, Colorado, Idaho, Montana, New Mexico, Oregon, Utah, Washington, Wyoming
Department of Veterans Affairs
VA Regional Loan Center
Box 25126
Denver, CO 80225
888-349-7541

For Hawaii
Department of Veterans Affairs
Loan Guaranty Division (26)
459 Patterson Road
Honolulu, HI 96819
808-433-0481

For Arkansas, Louisiana, Oklahoma, Texas
Department of Veterans Affairs
VA Regional Loan Center
6900 Almeda Road
Houston, TX 77030
888-232-2571

For Connecticut, Massachusetts, Maine, New Hampshire, New York, Rhode Island, Vermont
Department of Veterans Affairs
VA Regional Loan Center
275 Chestnut Street
Manchester, NH 03101
800-827-6311
800-827-0336

For Arizona, California, Nevada
Department of Veterans Affairs
VA Regional Loan Center
3333 North Central Avenue
Phoenix, AZ 85012-2402
888-869-0194

For District of Columbia, Kentucky, Maryland, Virginia, West Virginia
Department of Veterans Affairs
Roanoke Regional Loan Center
210 Franklin Road SW
Roanoke, VA 24011
800-933-5499

For Puerto Rico
Department of Veterans Affairs
Loan Guaranty Division
150 Avenue Carlos Chardon
Suite 232
San Juan, PR 00918-1703
787-772-7310

For Illinois, Iowa, Kansas, Minnesota, Missouri, Nebraska, North Dakota, South Dakota, Wisconsin
Department of Veterans Affairs
VA Regional Loan Center
1 Federal Drive
Fort Snelling
St. Paul, MN 55111-4050
800-827-0611

For Alabama, Florida, Mississippi
Department of Veterans Affairs
VA Regional Loan Center
P.O. Box 1437
St. Petersburg, FL 33731-1437
888-611-5916 (out of state)
800-827-1000 (in FL)

Index

About the Author

Diana Brodman Summers received her J.D. from DePaul University College of Law and her undergraduate degree from Roosevelt University. She is an arbitrator for both the Cook and DuPage County mandatory arbitration programs and was recently appointed to the Liquor Commission for the City of Downers Grove. Ms. Summers is an active member of the Association of Trial Lawyers of America, the American Bar Association, the DuPage County Bar Association, and the Illinois State Bar Association.

Ms. Summers has taught seminars for lawyers through several bar associations and has written articles on computerizing law offices. She volunteers with other Illinois State Bar Association attorneys in accordance with the local Judge Advocate General's office to provide low-cost legal service for returning members of the military. She currently maintains a law practice in Lisle, Illinois, a suburb of Chicago.